William Shakespeare's
SONNET PHILOSOPHY
Volume 4

William Shakespeare's

SONNET PHILOSOPHY

VOLUME 4

One Letter,
Ten Essays

ROGER PETERS

William Shakespeare's
Sonnet Philosophy
Volume 4

William Shakespeare's Sonnet Philosophy Volume 4
is the companion Volume to Volumes 1, 2, and 3
published as a set by Roger Peters in 2005.
Volume 4 second edition 2019

Letter and Essays
Copyright © 2005 Roger Peters

The Anthony Hartley translations from his 1965 edition of Mallarmé are
reproduced by permission of Penguin Books Ltd

All rights reserved.

This book may not be reproduced, in whole or in part, including illustrations, stored
in a retrieval system, or transmitted in any form or by any means without the prior
permission in writing of Quaternary Imprint or as expressly permitted by law,
or under terms agreed by the appropriate reprographic rights organisations.
The book must not be circulated in any other binding or cover.

ISBN 978-0-473-47373-0 (pbk)
ISBN 978-0-473-47374-7 (hbk)

Page setup by Archetype, Wellington
Second edition revised by M. Horner

Quaternary Imprint
Published for the Quaternary Institute
www.quaternaryinstitute.com

Maree

Other titles by Roger Peters

William Shakespeare's Sonnet Philosophy
(Four volume, slipcase set - 2005)

Volume 1
How Shakespeare structures
his nature-based philosophy into the *Sonnets*
before he publishes them in 1609
(*Volume 1,* second edition - 2019)

Volume 2
A line by line analysis
of the 154 individual sonnets using
the *Sonnet* philosophy
as the basis for their meaning
(*Volume 2,* second edition - 2018)

Volume 3
An analysis of individual plays and poems
to show that the *Sonnet* philosophy
is the basis for their meaning

Volume 4
How the works of
Wittgenstein, Duchamp, and Mallarmé
led to an appreciation
of Shakespeare's philosophy

Shakespeare's Global Philosophy (2017)
exploring Shakespeare's nature-based
philosophy in the sonnets, plays and Globe

Shakespeare & Mature Love (2017)
how to get from nature to love in Shakespeare

Shakespeare's Philosophy Illustrated (2018)
Quaternary teaching aids

QUATERNARY IMPRINT
Published for the Quaternary Institute

www.quaternaryinstitute.com

CONTENTS OF VOLUME 4

Preface	xi
Part 1 **From Duchamp to Shakespeare and Back**	1
A question for Thierry de Duve	2
Introduction	3
A brief meeting	3
Programme	4
Aesthetics and ethics	5
Wittgenstein, Darwin, and Shakespeare	7
Philosophy versus psychology	8
Focusing on the philosophical	11
The consequences of de Duve's approach	15
A systematic philosophy	16
Chapter 1 Marcel Duchamp: aesthetics	17
Subject matter	17
Form and content	18
Beyond taste	22
Limitation of formalism for reading Duchamp	26
Content from the past	27
The aesthetic dynamic out of mythic content	29
Octavio Paz	31
Stéphane Mallarmé	32
The erotic in Duchamp's work	35
The priority of the sexual over the erotic	38
The sexual and the erotic as the 4th and 3rd dimensions	40
The aesthetic	45
The beauty of indifference	49
The mythic logic out of the sexual/erotic dynamic	52
The relation of the *readymades* to the *Large Glass*	53

	The tube of paint as a *readymade*	56
	Kant and the beautiful	57
	Rectifying Kant	59
	Summary	61
Chapter 2	Ludwig Wittgenstein: the logical	63
	The wrong paradigm	63
	Wittgenstein's method	64
	Where the method failed	65
	The trajectory of Wittgenstein's thought	67
	The atomic model does not provide the correct multiplicity	69
	The metaphor of life	70
	Summary	73
Chapter 3	Charles Darwin: the biological	75
	Darwin's consistent method	75
	Misunderstandings	75
	Evolution and the sexual	77
	Mental powers and moral sense	78
	Darwin the philosopher	79
	Priority of the female	80
	Body and mind	81
	Inherent purpose	83
	Summary	85
Chapter 4	William Shakespeare: the Nature template	87
	Review	87
	The *Sonnets*	89
	The uniqueness of the *Sonnets*	90
	The logical dynamic of life	92
	The relation of the *Large Glass* to the *Sonnets*	93
	The basic structure and numbering of the *Large Glass*	94
	The basic structure and numbering of the *Sonnets*	95
	The *Large Glass* and the *Sonnets*	98
	A logical numbering system	99
	The sexual and the erotic in the *Large Glass*	100
	The sexual and the erotic in the *Sonnets*	100
	Sonnets 15 to 19	103

	Eroticism in sonnets 20 to 154	104
	The pattern of 14s	105
	The aesthetic and ethical dynamic of the *Large Glass*	107
	The aesthetic and ethical dynamic of the *Sonnets*	107
	Body and mind: the Nature template	111
	The role of the Poet	113
	The mythic dynamic of the *Large Glass*	114
	The mythic dynamic of the *Sonnets*	116
	Duchamp's limit; Shakespeare's range	118
	Summary	120
Chapter 5	Postscript: from Shakespeare to Duchamp	121
	Darwin's limit, Shakespeare's range	121
	Wittgenstein's limit, Shakespeare's range	122
	The limitation of Thierry de Duve's formalism	124
	Reinstating the complete paradigm	125
	Conclusion: the quaternary dynamic	126
	A comparison of thinkers	127

Part 2	**10 Essays**	**129**
1	Marcel Duchamp	131
2	Stephane Mallarmé	136
3	Sigmund Freud & Carl Jung	156
4	James Joyce & T. S. Eliot	166
5	Germaine Greer	177
6	Stephen Booth & Helen Vendler	194
7	Friedrich Nietzsche & Ludwig Wittgenstein	207
8	George Lakoff & Mark Johnson	221
9	Thomas Jefferson	241
10	Riane Eisler	253

References	268
Index	278

List of Illustrations

Diagrams for Part 1

1	The numbering of the *Large Glass*	95
2	The numbering of the principal elements of the *Sonnets*	97
3	Nature female/male template	100
4	Increase template	102
5	*Sonnet* numbering based on sonnet 14	106
6	Beauty and truth template	110
7	Truth and beauty template	111
8	Body or sexual template	111
9	Mind or erotic template	112
10	Nature template	113
11	Nature template (*Sonnets*)	113
12	The relation of the *Large Glass* and the *readymades*	119
13	The relation of the *Sonnets* and the plays and poems	119
14	The relation of the Poet, the sexual, and ethics	120
15	Nature template	122
16	God template	123

Diagrams for Part 2

The 23 diagrams in the essays of Part 2 are not numbered.
They act as guides to the content of the essays.

Preface

When I began writing up the evidence for a philosophy in *Shake-speares Sonnets*, I decided that more than one volume was required to do justice to its consistency and comprehensiveness. The first decision was to separate the material relating to Shakespeare from that relating to the thinkers whose work enabled me to develop an understanding of the *Sonnet* philosophy.

Of the resulting four volumes, the first three are devoted to Shakespeare. They consider the arrangement of the philosophy of the whole set (Volume 1), the individual sonnets (Volume 2), and the poems and plays (Volume 3). Volume 4, then, presents the relevant material on thinkers such as Marcel Duchamp, Stephane Mallarmé, Ludwig Wittgenstein, and Charles Darwin, and provides a critique of other thinkers who have tried to understand Shakespeare's works.

The role of Duchamp, Mallarmé, Wittgenstein and Darwin in the development of an understanding capable of revealing the *Sonnet* philosophy is considered in Part 1. I studied the four thinkers for twenty-five years before discovering the *Sonnet* philosophy in 1995. A combination of Duchamp's insight into the logic of myth, Mallarmé's profound aesthetics, Wittgenstein's philosophy of language, and Darwin's philosophic approach to the biological enabled me to appreciate Shakespeare's consistent and comprehensive philosophy.

The art of Marcel Duchamp is significant because of the four thinkers he arrived at an understanding of the logic of myth. Because the mythology of any culture embodies the deepest expression of its origins and values, Duchamp's articulation of the logical conditions for any mythology in his major work *The Bride Stripped Bare by Her Bachelors, Even*, commonly referred to as the *Large Glass*, provides the groundwork for relating the contributions of the other three thinkers. There is a direct correspondence between the principal elements of the *Large Glass* and the *Sonnets*.

Since beginning the investigation of the *Sonnets* in 1995, it is evident that without an insight into Duchamp's achievement an understanding of their mythic logic would be nigh impossible. The *Sonnets* have remained impenetrable to traditional scholarly or literary analysis because it lacks the required insight into the logic of myth.

In general terms, Part 1 offers another way to configure the *Sonnet* ideas presented in differing ways in the first 3 volumes. By presenting the relation between Duchamp and Shakespeare as a letter to the Duchampian scholar Thierry de Duve, who makes one of the more philosophical critiques of Duchamp's *readymades*, the gap between current scholarship and the ideas presented in these volumes should become evident.

Part 2 then features ten essays on seminal thinkers who have attempted to understand Shakespeare's works but failed. The essays are intended to provide a variety of entry points into the *Sonnet* philosophy by first articulating a thinker's (or a pair of thinkers) basic contribution to their field, and then showing why they have been unable to understand Shakespeare's natural logic.

The essays on Duchamp and Mallarmé supplement the material in Part 1. The essays on Thomas Jefferson, Riane Eisler, and George Lakoff and Mark Johnson, consider thinkers who moved considerably toward the natural logic of the *Sonnets* without appreciating the precision of Shakespeare's mythic logic. The essays on Sigmund Freud and Carl Jung, James Joyce and T. S. Eliot, Stephen Booth and Helen Vendler, Germaine Greer, and Friedrich Nietzsche and Ludwig Wittgenstein, consider thinkers who have thought deeply about Shakespeare's works but whose adherence to aspects of traditional beliefs have prevented them from understanding the *Sonnet* logic.

Comments on the Second Edition: The text and arrangement of this second edition (2019) of Volume 4 from *WSSP* (2005) remains substantially the same as the original. Twenty typos from the 2005 edition are corrected, N/n for nature is regularised and 'Alien' Poet (as per the 1609 edition) replaces 'Rival' Poet. The names of the Templates throughout the text have been standardised with those in Volume 1. This 2019 edition is the third of the four 2005 Volumes republished using digital printing, with Volume 3 to follow within the next two years.

PART 1

From Duchamp to Shakespeare and Back

A question for Thierry de Duve

I began writing what is now the first part of Volume 4 as a letter to Thierry de Duve, one of Marcel Duchamp's foremost interpreters. I had talked with Thierry de Duve at a conference in Wellington in May 1994 where I asked him about his singular approach to Duchamp's *readymades*. I wondered what he thought of Octavio Paz' more mythic approach to *The Bride Stripped Bare by her Bachelors, Even*, or the *Large Glass*.

Then, not long after beginning the letter, I gained a significant insight into the philosophy of Shakespeare's *Sonnets* based partly on my work on Duchamp. I soon realised that an understanding of the mythic depth of Duchamp's *Large Glass* provides the logical consistency required to begin unraveling the traditional mysteries surrounding the *Sonnets*.

My critique shows how Duchamp's *Large Glass*, which presents the logical conditions for mythic expression, can be used to reveal the more comprehensive philosophic dynamic and numerological structuring of Shakespeare's *Sonnets*. The critique shows how Duchamp's focus on the aesthetic dynamic in the *Large Glass* leads to the minimal expression of the *readymades*, and how the comprehensive and consistent philosophy of the *Sonnets* maximises the mythic expression of Shakespeare's plays. In return the *Sonnets* provide a critique of Duchamp's work.

Thierry de Duve's work is an advance on many of the writings on Duchamp in that it applies a philosophical approach to Duchamp's *readymades*. To understand the achievement of Duchamp's whole oeuvre, though, and consequently to appreciate the complete philosophy of the *Sonnets*, a more acutely philosophic approach is required. Shakespeare's *Sonnets* provide such a philosophy. His nature-based understanding encompasses Duchamp's logical application of aesthetics and adds the logical components required for a complete philosophy.

Introduction

A brief meeting

In the conversation with Thierry de Duve I remember mentioning Duchamp's repeated claim that eroticism was the irreducible feature of his life's work, and that it was principally from Stephane Mallarmé that Duchamp had developed this seemingly singular understanding. Duchamp had said that art should return to the direction Mallarmé traced.

Viewed from the vantage of Duchamp's achievement, Mallarmé's poetic investment of everyday objects, or situations, with a refined eroticism, combined with a critical awareness of the process of writing, had lifted his poetry beyond the expectations of mere Symbolism to an accomplishment of near mythic proportions. In turn, Duchamp's work lifted Mallarmé's profound symbolism to the mythic level by articulating the logical conditions for eroticism out of the sexual.

Thierry de Duve had difficulty grasping what was being suggested. I was surprised as I was putting forward ideas about the mythic dimension in Duchamp's work developed from the mythological critique presented by Octavio Paz in such books as *The Castle of Purity* and *Appearance Stripped Bare*. My suggestions were also based on Duchamp's statements regarding the importance of eroticism for the *Large Glass* and his other works. He had said a number of times that eroticism was the only thing he would always be 'serious' about and that it was the 'platform' for all his works.

As the conversation progressed it was apparent Thierry de Duve had not considered the pivotal role of eroticism in Duchamp's art. Because of the impasse, the conversation turned to his forthcoming book *Kant after Duchamp*. He gave some reasons for a delay in publication and then it was time to return to the conference.

About a year after our meeting in Wellington, in March 1995, I discovered a significant relationship between the work of Duchamp and the philosophy of Shakespeare's *Sonnets*. By chance I had attended a reading of the complete set of 154 *Sonnets*, and immediately intuited a philosophic sensibility corresponding to one I had developed from Mallarmé and Duchamp (as well as from Wittgenstein and Darwin) over the years since the early 1970s.

The *Sonnets* can be shown to be a philosophic presentation of the relationship between the biological processes (nature, female/male and increase) and the dynamic of ethics and aesthetics (truth and beauty) at the level of the mythic that encompasses and completes the more specialised achievements of Duchamp and the above thinkers. The unprecedented insight into Shakespeare's philosophy confirmed the soundness of my earlier intuitions regarding Duchamp. So when Thierry de Duve says, at the end of his *Kant after Duchamp*, that a rationale for Duchamp's achievement still escapes him, my work suggests that a different approach is required from the one he has persisted with.

Programme

In this critique I will be arguing that Duchamp's work expresses the logical conditions for the aesthetic dynamic in art at the mythic level. Duchamp was fully cognizant not only of the *formal* requirements for painting and other forms of artistic expression, (the formal aspect is, as I see it, the principal concern of de Duve's work) but also recognised the determining criteria for *content* in art (the principal concern in Octavio Paz' attempt to understand the mythical dimension in Duchamp's work).

Duchamp demonstrated an exceptional proficiency in the formal aspects of artistic practice. To arrive at a comprehensive understanding of his work, however, more than his mastery of form needs to be considered. His mastery of the philosophic elements that constitute the mythic content of an artwork should also be taken into account. This is particularly the case if, as a development of Paz' work, it can be suggested that Duchamp identified the mythic elements in art from which all content can be logically derived.

I will be demonstrating that Duchamp explored the aesthetic dynamic with a rigour and consistency that enabled him to represent the philosophic basis of the mythic in art. He expressed this both in the complex imagery of his two major works, the *Large Glass* (1912-26) and the tableau *Etant donnés* (1946-68), and in the minimal gesture of the *readymades*.

It is evident from Thierry de Duve's writings on Duchamp that he has responded principally to the formal influence of the *readymades* on the avant-garde of the mid-to-late twentieth century. He seems to see the *readymades* as if down a narrow tunnel of eight decades of formalist art practice.

While acknowledging Duchamp's influence on the avant-garde, the philosophic approach presented here examines the way in which he was able to make substantial works such as the *Large Glass* and *Etant donnes*, with their critical mythic content, as well as works in which such content is reduced to an 'infra-thin' presence, as in the *readymades*. If the *readymades* are an extremely reduced artistic expression based on the same inherent understanding as Duchamp's major works then it should be possible to demonstrate the way in which the *readymades* have their logical basis in the mythic dynamic expressed in the *Large Glass*.

The primarily formal concern of the theoretically sanctioned avant-garde art history of the last few decades (de Duve's concern) can then be contrasted to the way in which form and content are inextricably entwined in the whole of Duchamp's oeuvre. It should be possible to demonstrate why artists and theorists, such as Joseph Kosuth and Clement Greenberg, have ended championing such limited artistic positions when, in response or in reaction to Duchamp's achievement, they have ignored its major premise (the *Large Glass*) and have responded only to an aspect of its minor premise (the *readymades*).

Aesthetics and ethics

Before considering Duchamp's achievement I should stress the logical distinction between the aesthetic and ethical modes of understanding.

The primary meaning of the word aesthetic is 'a sensation or perception unmediated by thought' (OED). This meaning, from the Greek, differs from the eighteenth century, Baumgarten/Kantian, redefinition of aesthetic to refer to the beautiful, to matters of taste, or to the establishment of aesthetics as a science.

I will be demonstrating that Duchamp was aware that the primary meaning of aesthetic ensures philosophic clarity, while the eighteenth century redefinition leads to philosophic confusion. Thierry de Duve does sense such clarity in Duchamp's work. However, because of his narrowed focus on a secondary feature of the *readymades* he is not able to see how a philosopher like Emmanuel Kant was confused about aesthetics.

Furthermore, he is not able to appreciate the way in which Kant misrepresented the logical relationship between aesthetics and ethics. Hence, in

Kant after Duchamp, de Duve has difficulty relating the ethical system of Kant to the aesthetics of Duchamp, a task made more difficult by his use of Kant's illogical phrase 'aesthetic judgment'.

Ethics, in contrast with aesthetics, is the relation of ideas, or the dynamic of thought and expression in language. In keeping with the traditional distinction between ideas and sensations, ideas derive from sensations whether the sensations originate in the external world or in the mind. Logically, as Shakespeare understands it, the aesthetic is any form of sensation and the ethical is any intentional association of ideas. A more complete explanation of the dynamic of the aesthetic/ethical relationship is given below.

Duchamp's insight into the logic of aesthetics and Shakespeare's understanding of the dynamic of aesthetics and ethics derives from their appreciation of the logic of mythic expression. They understand that the relationship between female and male in nature is central to mythic expression because it is the logical basis for the relationship between aesthetics and ethics. The sexual differentiation of male from female in nature (as in the *Sonnets* and the *Large Glass*) is the logical precondition for the differentiation of ideas from sensations in human expression.

Kant's use of the phrase 'aesthetic judgment', for instance, to characterise transcendental expectations is contradictory. He attempted to characterise, through a conjunction of two ideas, or the process of ethics, what is logically an aesthetic event, or a sensation. The phrase 'aesthetic judgment' reduces to the conundrum 'aesthetic ethics', just as Wittgenstein's statement 'ethics and aesthetics are one and the same' reduces to 'aesthetics and aesthetics are one and the same'.

Kant's apologetically driven limitation of the primary meaning of aesthetic (as all sensations) to mean the 'beautiful' minus the 'disgusting' (or a preferred class of sensations) was the consequence of believing literally in mythological expression. Although Kant rejected most mythological imagery in his critique of youthful beliefs, he maintained a belief in the mythology of a male God as 'author'. From the vantage of a consistent philosophy, the contradiction in asserting that aesthetics is a process of judgment and that ethics is conditional on the existence of an exemplary male God, by apologists such as Kant, is readily apparent.

Similarly, to talk of a 'science of aesthetics', if the aesthetic is unmediated sensation, as if it was possible to transcend the effects of sensation, is contradictory. Science is logically a function of ethics or the dynamic of language. Logically the 'science of aesthetics' reduces to the 'ethics of aesthetics'.

Scientific investigation frequently attempts to limit the influence of aesthetics, while artistic expression attempts to limit the role of ethics. But aesthetic effects and ethical determinations are a natural continuum. Pure aesthetic states are imaginary just as ethical determinations are defeasible. Art has at least a little ethics and frequently a large dose of ethics as part of its expression. Similarly science cannot avoid the effect of aesthetics, as is the case in scientific investigations where sensations critically affect the possibility of objective readings.

Duchamp's unvarying procedure for achieving an aesthetic expression in art can be summarised as an attempt to limit the influence of ethics or the logic of language. His catch cry was 'reduce, reduce, reduce'. The mere existence, however, of his many explanatory notes in the *Box of 1914*, the *Green Box*, and the *White Box* tacitly acknowledges the logical impossibility of achieving a complete removal of ethics from art.

Wittgenstein, Darwin, and Shakespeare

To explore the logic of the ethical I will be introducing aspects of the thought of Ludwig Wittgenstein. If Duchamp's work expresses the basic philosophic conditions for art, Wittgenstein's work provides an understanding of the philosophic conditions for language. This is not to say that Wittgenstein's understanding of the nature of aesthetics and ethics is logically sound. He, as with most philosophers, misconstrues the relationship. But, despite Wittgenstein's misunderstanding of the aesthetic/ethical dynamic, his analysis of the logic of language can be used to reveal the nature of the ethical.

The critique will consider Wittgenstein's use of 'true' and 'false' in relation to propositions, his attempt to determine the logical multiplicity between language and the world, his conditions for certainty of knowledge, and his notion of language games where he uses biological metaphors such as 'family resemblances' and the concept 'forms of life'. Even if Wittgenstein's understanding of the relationship of biology and the mind was inconsistent, he went further than most in his attempt to resolve the illogical consequences of the traditional representation of the relationship of language and the world.

To help clarify the logical relation between aesthetics and ethics, I will refer to Charles Darwin's argument from *The Descent of Man and Selection in Relation to Sex* for the relation of biological or sexual processes to 'mental powers' and the 'moral sense'. Darwin understood that the evolutionary biology of the human species was consistent with the development of human understanding. In Part I, 'The Descent or Origin of Man', and Parts II and III, 'Selection through Secondary Sexual Characteristics' he deals with the sexual and the erotic respectively. The logic of the sexual dynamic establishes the possibility of the erotic as the underlying condition for art. I will be showing that Duchamp's notion of 4th dimension is the sexual dynamic, or what he called the 'given'.

It is the philosophy of William Shakespeare, though, that provides a comprehensive overview of Duchamp's accomplishment. In the *Sonnets*, Shakespeare prefigured by 300 years the mythic critique of art apparent in the *Large Glass*. The *Sonnets* present the nature-based logic of the relation between the sexual and the erotic necessary for mythic expression. Shakespeare incorporates into the structure of the *Sonnets* the logical relationship of the ethical to the aesthetic ('truth and beauty') and he bases their logical relationship on the sexual dynamic presented in the increase sonnets. For Shakespeare, the aesthetic is any form of sensation (in the *Sonnets* 'beauty' is archetypically 'seeing') and the ethical is any intentional association of ideas ('truth' is identified with 'saying' in the *Sonnets*).

I will show how the achievements of Duchamp, Wittgenstein, and Darwin, can be combined to arrive at the philosophic clarity of Shakespeare's *Sonnets*.

Philosophy versus psychology

Before considering the consequences of Thierry de Duve's focus on only a few of Duchamp's *readymades*, I want to stress the importance of his decision to consider Duchamp philosophically. Other commentators on Duchamp, such as Arturo Schwarz and John Golding, have relied heavily on psychological analyses and even a critic as perceptive about the 'mythical' content in Duchamp's work as Octavio Paz does not approach Duchamp with the required philosophic acuity.

I acknowledge de Duve's decision, in *Pictorial Nominalism*, to move from a psychological approach to a philosophical one because of the inappropriateness of attempting to understand Duchamp's work from a psychological basis. His decision reminds me of Leo Bersani's caution in *The Death of Mallarmé* where he put aside his psychological hat the better to deal with the philosophic demands of Mallarmé's poetry. And de Duve's decision to relate Kant to Duchamp in *Kant after Duchamp* at least recognises that Duchamp's philosophic accomplishment supersedes the aesthetic philosophy of the 'greatest philosopher of the modern period'.

De Duve's more philosophical approach to Duchamp is evident in the criticism he directs at the excessive psychotherapy and alchemical speculation in Schwarz' account of Duchamp's work.

> The alchemical and cabalistic readings of Duchamp are mystifying, since, quite obviously, their interpretive systems derive from an archaic mode of knowledge, not only one that existed prior to the interpreted system but also one that uses the interpreted system as if it were the blots in an inkblot test. The same is true for certain pseudoclinical psychoanalytic readings of Duchamp such as Schwarz's or Held's. Their problem is not just that they conduct their analyses in the absence of the subject, since Freud himself did that. Above all, what is wrong is that this sort of psychoanalysis is historically anterior – and epistemologically inferior – to the analyzed artwork. Duchamp's acute practice finds itself decoded there through symbolist grids infinitely looser than itself and therefore without any relevance.[1]

De Duve's criticism of the arcane aspects of Schwarz', Golding's, and similar readings, is warranted in that such readings do not and cannot do justice to Duchamp's philosophic accomplishment.

However, the passage also reveals the inadequacy of de Duve's understanding of the role of philosophy. It does not follow that all knowledge 'that existed prior to the interpreted system' is invalid. Besides being logically unsound, his anti-historicist rationale is inconsistent with Duchamp's frequent assertion that he wanted to return art to the 'ideas' of the Renaissance and other periods before the modern era. In this regard, de Duve's writing can be subjected to the same criticism he makes of Schwarz and others. If Schwarz mismatched inadequate and inappropriate systems of symbolism to the work of Duchamp, then de Duve, by focusing principally on a few *readymades* and the formalist art history of Modernism that Duchamp rejected, develops an interpretation of Duchamp's work that is philosophically inferior to the work.

De Duve's assertions, even though they are made within living memory of Duchamp, can be shown to be less sound than logical claims based on a sound philosophy from a previous era. I will show that Shakespeare in the sixteenth century and Darwin in the nineteenth century developed a sound philosophy consistent with the philosophic achievement of Duchamp in the twentieth century. I will be drawing on the logical connections between Duchamp's work and the achievements of Shakespeare and Darwin because they operated with the same degree of philosophic acuity.

By contrast, Kant, albeit as an apologist for the Christian God reduced to a practical necessity, produced a philosophy constrained by the psychology of his beliefs and so fails to meet the logical criteria. Only in the logically acute context of a Shakespearean mind, free of cant, can de Duve's prioritisation of issues as peripheral as 'pictorial nominalism' and 'colour' find their correct logical relation. Their role within Duchamp's overall achievement requires an appropriate level of philosophic insight.

So despite a determination to approach Duchamp philosophically, de Duve's analysis remains affected by psychological traits. In *Pictorial Nominalism*, for instance, he decides to persist with the comparison, albeit a 'parallel one', of Freud's 'Dream of Irma' with aspects of Duchamp's work. While the strategy is not as speculative as that of Schwarz, it still leads to illogical or psychological conclusions. For instance, de Duve modifies Schwarz' suggestion Duchamp had an incestuous relationship with his sister Suzanne into the disingenuous idea he was consciously playing off whatever feelings he experienced towards 'Suzanne' onto the objectivity of an artistic relationship with 'Cezanne'. Even though it seems de Duve is focusing on matters aesthetic more philosophically, the aesthetic possibility is still conditioned by the suggestion Duchamp was influenced by unsublimated personal experiences.

De Duve's attempt to characterise Duchamp's work as meta-psychological presumes he had a psychological problem to overcome and that the problem drove his artistic ambitions. The fallacy is that while the circumstances of life do contribute to insights or realisations, in Duchamp's case his artistic accomplishment is so logically sound it transcends the psychology that may have been part of its genesis. It is pointless then to attempt to understand his philosophic clarity through psychological speculation. Such an approach cannot generate the required philosophic insight.

Duchamp, by all accounts, was psychologically at ease before and after the period of his artistic breakthrough. Because clinical psychology presumes a problem that requires a cure, and because Freud and Jung were not philosophers but sought to cure diseases of the mind through psychoanalysis or psychotherapy, any attempt to explain Duchamp's achievement through psychology must fail. When someone is said to be psychological, a disorder of the mind is implied, but if such issues have been mastered, a person is capable of being philosophical. Whereas psychology deals with conditions of the mind, philosophy deals with the logical relation that persists between the mind and the world.

I will be showing that Duchamp's artistic accomplishment is deeply philosophic. And because Shakespeare accounts for the logical relationship between the biological and the conditions for mythic understanding and expression, his work needs to be understood in the most rigorous philosophic terms.

Focusing on the philosophical

In Thierry de Duve's attempt to avoid the biographical cum psychological analyses that nauseously plague the works of Duchamp (Shakespeare's *Sonnets* have been subjected to a similar litany of inadequate readings) he resorts to both contemporary art history and a selection of items of philosophical interest from Duchamp's *Notes*.

To address the historical significance of the *readymades* de Duve relates Duchamp's work to that of Paul Cezanne, Cubism, the Succession, and the process of avant-garde change. This at least has the virtue of focusing the debate more on the art and less on the person. To address issues that have no obvious psychological connotations he focuses on the more philosophical elements in Duchamp's *Notes*. He selects a few of Duchamp's tersest comments in an attempt to make sense of his work.

The philosophically imbued comment, 'a sort of pictorial nominalism', the 'algebraic comparison a/b', Duchamp's focus on the syntax rather than on the semantics of 'colour', and his determination to make something that both 'was and was not a work of art', all provide at least a glimpse into his appreciation of the logic of aesthetics. Nominalism, particularly, seems readymade for the task. It has a philosophical pedigree and Duchamp mentions it both in his *Notes* and in his interviews.

It seems, however, that Duchamp was not identifying himself solely or even principally as a nominalist, nor was he characterising every aspect of his procedures as nominalistic. He talks of 'a *sort of* pictorial nominalism'. At most, it seems, in his descriptive and qualified use of the term, he wanted to convey something of the difference between art as a retinal activity, where the artist seeks to create a Platonic or ideal 'world', and art as a conceptual or nominal process that acknowledges the futility of such an expectation. Duchamp saw his work offering 'a sort of pictorial nominalism' to challenge the presumptuousness of artists' claims to be expressing or divining a Platonically 'real' category called 'art'. In their logical rigour the philosophic critique in his works is anti-Platonist.

In *Pictorial Nominalism*, by contrast, de Duve characterises Duchamp's whole enterprise under the rubric of the limited philosophical position of nominalism. He seems determined to demonstrate a wholly nominalistic rationale for the *readymades*. He presents the *readymades* as Duchamp's final farewell to painting because he is determined to reduce painterly activity, in terms of readymade tubes of paint, canvas, etc., to the very circumscribed 'nominal' statement 'this is art'. True, in this formal or technical sense of nominalism, 'art' could not then be considered a Platonist state with an existence apart from the reality of the readymade paint and canvas. But such a limited formalist rationale has illogical consequences for de Duve's interpretation of the significance of the other works in Duchamp's oeuvre.

De Duve's pursuit of this rationale led, if not directly, to the extraordinary assertion in *Pictorial Nominalism*, that *The Passage from the Virgin to the Bride* is the pivotal work in Duchamp's oeuvre. This was because it needed to be, for his purposes, the work at the transition point between the history of painting, the 'tube of paint' tradition as practised by those like Cezanne, and an avant-garde 'naming' of the *readymades* as 'art'.

The idea that the *readymades* were similar to named 'tubes of paint' which nominalistically liberated the notion of art from its allegiance to the factured canvas of 'retinal' art to herald unmitigated conceptual intent is no doubt one of the possible implications of Duchamp's use of the phrase 'a sort of pictorial nominalism'. Duchamp's conditional reference to the idea of nominalism, though, would seem to suggest that it was not the philosophic position from out of which he engineered the mythic content of the *Large Glass* and the rest of his oeuvre.

Despite the majority of commentators agreeing with Duchamp's statements, expressed in his *Notes* and interviews, that the *Large Glass* was the central and most important work of his whole oeuvre, de Duve requires the *Passage from the Virgin to the Bride* to be the pivotal work to support his formalist understanding of the *readymades*. Yet the evidence in Duchamp's notes suggests the *Passage* was a 'study' for the *Large Glass*, and the *Large Glass* was the centre-piece in his miniaturised museum *Box in a Valise* around which he intentionally grouped the *readymades* and the *Passage from the Virgin to the Bride* and all his other works.

In *Pictorial Nominalism* de Duve's focus on Duchamp's qualified reference to pictorial nominalism, and his persistence with a psychological analysis of Duchamp's intentions (though less presumptuous than Schwarz'), leads to a conclusion at odds with the pre-eminence of the *Large Glass* in Duchamp's oeuvre. De Duve's reading needs to be weighed against the aspects of Duchamp's work that cannot be explained by a nominalist thesis and against those aspects of his work that he stated a number of times were central to its interpretation.

The formalist rationale in de Duve's critique of Duchamp is similar to that made by Wassily Kandinsky about his own early work in *Concerning the Spiritual in Art*. Ignoring the earthy sensuality of the early works he proposed instead a pseudo-spiritual rationale for artistic expression. Kandinsky's isolation of an aspect of his earlier work from its matrix of artistic creativity led directly to the arid abstraction of his later work. Similarly, de Duve isolates an aspect of Duchamp's work with a rationale that lacks the capacity to account for the mythic depth and persistent complexity of his whole oeuvre.

As the *Large Glass* came after the *Passage from the Virgin to the Bride*, and so had to be retrospectively accounted for in the light of de Duve's claim for nominalist function of the *readymades*, it became for him merely an ironic critique of previous art practice.

> Duchamp made the *Large Glass* in the manner of a conscientious but stupid artisan ... But he also thought of the *Large Glass* as the ironic staging of this craft and its stupidity.[2]
>
> It (the *Large Glass*) works around the bar and accomplishes the mourning of painting, not so much as possible/impossible, but as useless.[3]

For the sake of de Duve's theory, the *Large Glass* had to be reduced to something of an anachronism. There could be no possibility that it was both an ironic critique of previous art practice and an encompassing expression of the mythic dynamic basic to all art. For the sake of his analysis it was not possible for the *Large Glass* to demonstrate both a mastery of the form and articulate the logical conditions for mythic content in art.

I will be suggesting the mythic content of the *Large Glass* is essential to the possibility of appreciating the *readymades* as viable aesthetic resonances. Without an understanding of the complete dynamic of the *Large Glass*, it is impossible to begin to understand fully the role of the *readymades*. It comes as no surprise then that de Duve ends his attempt to relate Kant and Duchamp with the codicil: 'I guess I'm trying to understand why Marcel Duchamp was such a great artist.' How could that be possible when he does not take seriously the philosophic issue of the mythic content or even the erotic content of the *Large Glass* with its pivotal role as the basis for the content in all his work?

The fact that Duchamp sustained his creative impulse to the end of his life cannot be attributed to the one-dimensional realisation that is the basis of a nominalistic rationale. Such an approach ignores, for instance, the exploration of erotic and mythological subject matter in his pre-1912 paintings.

De Duve's rationale radically reduces to a few *readymades* the number of works considered pertinent to an understanding of the substance of Duchamp's achievement. Of those he focuses principally on the *Fountain*. He uses the documentation and recollections of the events surrounding its exhibition, and the algebraic comparison a/b, to make a case that demonstrates nothing if it demonstrates that the *Fountain* and the algebraic comparison were purpose-made devices to absorb the speculative tendencies of art historians.

If Duchamp had reduced the content of the *readymades* to such art historical ciphers, and if the erotic content of the *Passage* was nothing more than an anachronism, then the statement 'This is Art' becomes nothing but the lame judgment of an art historian. But it is more than evident that, despite the apparent stringency of the *readymades*, the eroticism and the mythic critique do not exit from Duchamp's work at the time of the first *readymades*. This is patently obvious in everything from the pseudonymous identity *Rrose Selavy* to the final work *Etant donnes*. In fact *Etant donnes* is the perfect rejoinder to a narrow nominalistic and art historically speculative interpretation of the essence of Duchamp's accomplishment.

Having argued in *Pictorial Nominalism* that Duchamp was a thoroughgoing nominalist, de Duve then introduces Kant, in *Kant after Duchamp*, into the process of elaborating on the philosophical hints that Duchamp gave in his *Notes*, or in his conversations. Having decided, in the name of Duchamp, that the phrase 'This is Art' is central to the possibility of art, de Duve looks for a point of coincidence in the work of Kant.

He finds this, he thinks, in Kant's consideration of the 'beautiful'. He decides that he can substitute the word 'Art' for the word 'beautiful'. I will be demonstrating more fully below how the distinction between the two meanings of the word 'aesthetic' is crucial to understanding what is correct in his intuition and what is terribly awry.

Duchamp, in his desire to avoid 'taste', understood that only the earlier meaning of aesthetic was logically sound. Effectively he critiques Kant's lack of logical discrimination between the two usages. So de Duve's introduction of the phrase 'This is Art' is faulted both because Duchamp never made such a statement of the *readymades*, and because the introduction of such a statement into the midst of Kant's apologetic expectations of a 'beautiful' beyond the 'disgusting' misrepresents the clarity of Duchamp's understanding of the logic of aesthetics. De Duve's, and Kant's, confusion over the phrase 'aesthetic judgment' is symptomatic of de Duve's very limited formalist reading of Duchamp, and of Kant's apologetic agenda of rational Christianity.

The consequences of de Duve's approach

De Duve's thesis applies to one, two or maybe three of Duchamp's twenty or so *readymades*. Not only does he leave all the other *readymades* of various types and other occasional works out of his analysis but he also leaves out the *Large Glass*, *Etant donnes*, and all the pre-1912 work that Duchamp assiduously included in the *Box in a Valise*, and gathered together for the permanent collection in the Philadelphia Museum of Art.

Not only that, de Duve also persists in calling the *Fountain* the 'Urinal' and talks of it as if its title, its reorientation in space (around the physiological hinge point of the groin), the signature 'R Mutt', and the article in *The Blind Man*, were of no consequence in terms of authorial invention.

It seems rather obvious that de Duve's artistic alter ego (who he manipulates to say 'This is Art') in no way replicates Duchamp's achievement of giving a mythic level of content to the found objects he converts to *readymades*. De Duve derives some of his authority to use the incredibly reductive statement 'This is Art' from Duchamp's recognition that the public determined at any one time what was to be called art and what was not. I will demonstrate that it does not follow that this was Duchamp's modus operandi and hence the saying of the phrase 'This is Art' cannot be used as a nominating process in imitation of Duchamp.

The critique demonstrates the consequences of de Duve's decision to severely limit the reading of Duchamp's oeuvre to a few works. It will show that de Duve used the philosophical concerns of Kant more as chapter headings for a simplistic reading of Duchamp rather than as a means to produce a substantial critique of Kant in the light of Duchamp's aesthetic brilliance. Because Duchamp's understanding of aesthetics is logically consistent, even his preference for aesthetics over ethics correctly locates aesthetics in relation to ethics, and the sexual in relation to the erotic, allowing a full critique of Kant's inconsistencies.

A systematic philosophy

The critique shows that Duchamp's appreciation of the philosophic status of aesthetics is central to his accomplishment. This resolves into two crucial realisations.

In the first, Duchamp the aesthete understood implicitly, if not explicitly, that for an artwork to be reduced to the aesthetic dimension of its mythic dynamic it must attempt to divest itself of the ethical. Throughout his life Duchamp consistently avoided propositional language, particularly the verbal critical process. In everything he made he worked to eliminate 'difference'. He expressed a preference for individuals and a disdain for groups. He appreciated that 'indifference' is the hallmark of the aesthetic even if he did not explore the logical consequence that 'difference' is the hallmark of the ethical.

In the second, Duchamp, from the evidence of his *Notes*, understood that there is a logical distinction between the sexual and the erotic. The dynamic is expressed in the *Large Glass*, *Etant donnes*, and is evident in every *readymade* and incidental work he made. The non-consummation of the relationship between the Bride and the Bachelors acknowledges the sexual as a biological process outside the domain of art. The corollary is that erotics, as the function of desire in the mind, cannot, of itself, replace the sexual or the biological potential to produce a child.

The second condition is the more basic and was recognised as such by Duchamp when he stated that the erotic was the only thing about which he would always be serious. The critique shows that the erotic logically conditions both ethics and aesthetics (or ideas and sensations). For this reason Duchamp had to constrain the ethical artificially to allow the logic of the aesthetic to become critically apparent. Hence he used irony and humour to counter the inevitable reassertion of the ethical in most things he wrote. The consequence of Duchamp's concentrated focus on the aesthetic will emerge later.

With these thoughts in mind I will examine in some detail the statements Marcel Duchamp made about his own works. I will then briefly consider Stephane Mallarmé, Ludwig Wittgenstein, and Charles Darwin to reveal an attitude toward life that unites this otherwise unlikely foursome as seminal exponents of natural logic. Then I will show how their contributions can be combined to form the *Nature template*, of which William Shakespeare provides the most consistent and comprehensive expression.

CHAPTER 1

Marcel Duchamp: aesthetics

Subject matter

Marcel Duchamp's paintings from the period 1909 to 1912, before he conceived of the *Large Glass* and the associated *readymades*, differed in significant respects from those of his contemporaries, the Cubists and Futurists. In works such as *Dulcinea*, *Coffee Mill* and *Nude Descending a Staircase* he experimented with serially fragmented movement. Whereas the Cubists and the Futurists literally fragmented the space of an object or its movement in time, Duchamp, with some irony, tracked the cinematic passage of his subjects through pictorial space.

Even more significantly, Duchamp's early works had a distinctive approach to subject matter. Most used the human figure and many explored ideas based on family relationships. Unlike some of his peers Duchamp's increasingly schematic representation of the human figure was not motivated by a desire to create a formally abstract art. On the contrary, as apparent from the *Large Glass* to *Etant donnes*, the human form, or the potential to interact kinesthetically and conceptually with a representation of the human form, is a constant throughout his work.

In his conversations with James Johnson Sweeney and Pierre Cabanne he unequivocally rejected the abstract option. To Sweeney he defended the reduction of a head in movement to a 'bare line'. He reasoned that when a form passed through space it would generate lines rather than anatomy. Because he was looking for ways to express the 'inward' rather than 'externals', the depiction of the human 'skeleton' seemed unnecessary.

> Reduce, reduce, reduce, was my thought; – but at the same time my aim was turning inward, rather than towards externals. And later, following this view, I came to feel an artist might use anything – a dot, a line, the most conventional or unconventional symbol – to say what he wanted to say. The *Nude*, in this way, was a direct step to the large glass, *The Bride*

Stripped Bare by Her Bachelors, Even. And in the *King and Queen* painted shortly after the *Nude* there are no human forms or indications of anatomy. But in it one can see where the forms are placed; and for all this reduction I would never call it an 'abstract' painting.[4]

Asked by Cabanne if he was ever an abstractionist he responded,

> Not in the real sense of the word. A canvas like *The Bride* is abstract, since there isn't any figuration. But it isn't abstract in the narrow sense of the word. It's visceral, so to speak.[5]

If the recognition of the visceral presence of the human body is taken in conjunction with Duchamp's statements that eroticism is a pre-condition for all of his works then any reading of his oeuvre must be able to account for the presence and the persistence of the human dynamic as subject matter throughout his artistic career.

Robert Lebel recounts the importance human-based subject matter had for Duchamp. Having noted Duchamp's use of his family as subject matter he commented that,

> he was frankly advocating an art which, over and beyond aesthetic formulae, was concerned with everyone's fundamental preoccupations (family relationships). There was nothing more elementary, more generalised, more popular if you will, than the complex problems he had set himself to solve. By stubbornly concentrating his efforts on these affective relationships, he had in mind nothing less than a return to the great themes of legend and he strove for the collective dimensions of mythology.[6]

Duchamp's achievement of a mythic level of artistic expression derived from an understanding of the relation of the 'family' dynamic to the logic of mythology precisely mirrors Shakespeare's development of a mythic philosophy in his *Sonnets* and plays.

Form and content

By the time Duchamp conceived of the *Large Glass* and the *readymades* he had not only demonstrated a mastery of the formal conditions necessary for making a work of 'art' he had also developed a mastery of artistic subject matter, or content. The ultimate demonstration of his mastery of content is evident in the *Large Glass*. And true to his intentions of leaving at least a trace of the visceral in his work, the same subject matter, though 'reduced', is present in all the *readymades*. This is apparent both in his choice of object and in the caption usually applied to a *readymade*.

When asked by Richard Hamilton if anyone 'can' make a *readymade* by signing it, Duchamp agreed, but warned that the *readymades* operate under very demanding conditions of choice and taste.

> One can. It should be completely impersonal, because if you introduce the choice, it means that you introduce taste, you go back to the old ideals of taste and bad and good taste and uninteresting taste. And taste is the great enemy of art: A-R-T.[7]

To achieve the required degree of sensitivity it is necessary to understand the logical conditions for artistic content even in seemingly trivial works like the *readymades*. Duchamp warned that though the *readymades* looked trivial, they contain a 'much higher degree of intellectuality'.

The purely formal statement 'This is Art', which *Pictorial Nominalism* suggests transfixes art as a proper name, cannot begin to capture the subtle variety of ways in which the content of the *Large Glass* is present as an 'infra-thin' meaning in all of the *readymades*. The statement 'This is Art' also fails to emulate Duchamp's intent because, while Duchamp was superbly conscious of the role of the spectator in art, in his own works the status of 'art' is perpetually in question.

George Heard Hamilton asked Duchamp if there was any way in which a *readymade* can be thought of as a work of art. Duchamp reckoned the difficulty lay in the attempt to define art. Because every century has a new definition of art, it seemed 'legitimate' not to try defining art.

> So if we accept the idea that not trying to define art is a legitimate conception, then the *readymade* can be seen as a sort of irony, or an attempt at showing the futility of trying to define art, because here it is, a thing that I call art. I didn't even make it by myself; ... I take it *readymade*, even though it was made in a factory. But it is not made by hand, so it is a form of the possibility of denying the possibility of defining art.[8]

The statement from *A l'Infinitif* (the *White Box*) that asks 'Can one make works which are not works of art?' is consistent with Duchamp's aesthetic programme of avoiding the formal claim for any particular object that it could be said of it, 'This is Art'. It is logically impossible to make a wholly conscious judgment that something qualifies as a work of art.

Pictorial Nominalism recounts the conversation Duchamp had with James Johnson Sweeney where Duchamp talked of his attitude to painting in 1913. The passage in *Pictorial Nominalism* correctly reports that in ceasing to paint for 'the public' Duchamp still wants to paint for himself but then it ignores that proviso. Instead it focuses on the moment he says, 'Marcel, no more painting' as if he intentionally abandoned painting altogether.

Duchamp's decision, though, to 'paint for himself' was not a rejection of painting but rather a rejection of the professional sense of pleasing the public, of capitulating to habit or taste. Only through misrepresenting his intentions could Thierry de Duve's claim that Duchamp substituted the statement 'This is Art' for the act of painting be sustained. When Sweeney enquired about Duchamp's break from painting about the time he made the *Chocolate Grinder*, he said it was the moment at which he made the 'big decision'.

> The hardest was when I told myself 'Marcel no more painting, go get a job.' I looked for a job in order to get enough time to paint *for myself*. I got a job as a librarian in Paris in the Bibliotheque St Genevieve. It was a wonderful job because I had so many hours to myself.[9]

Sweeney then asked if he meant painting for himself rather than to please other people.

> Exactly…There are two kinds of artist: the artist that deals with society, is integrated into society; and the other artist, the completely freelance artist, who has no obligations…I didn't want to depend upon my painting for a living.[10]

When questioned about the 'ideal' public he would paint for, he responded that he was positioning himself for that ideal public. He did not want to please the 'immediate public' because of the dangers of success. The only public that interested him was the 'true public' in fifty to a hundred years. Duchamp insisted that he stopped painting for the public to avoid leading himself into a form of taste.

> Repeat the same thing long enough and it becomes taste. If you interrupt your work, I mean after you have done it, then it becomes,

it stays a thing in itself; but if it is repeated a number of times it becomes taste.[11]

And in a conversation with Jerry Tallmer, Duchamp agreed that the idea he gave up painting is a 'myth'.

People get the wrong idea about my not painting. It's true and it's not true at the same time. But I did not take a vow. That's all nonsense... Yes a myth. I'm ready to paint if I have an idea. But it's the idea that counts.[12]

To a question from Cabanne about a decision to stop painting he responded that he 'never made it, it came by itself'.[13] When Denis de Rougemont asked Duchamp if he decided to give up painting forever, he insisted he had not decided anything and was just waiting for ideas. And to Lou Spence of *Time* magazine he said,

I myself haven't given up painting, I'm just not painting now, but if I have an idea tomorrow I will do it.[14]

It is difficult to avoid the suggestion that de Duve's preference for hearing Duchamp say he had given up art altogether is driven by the demands of the formalist avant-garde position to which *Pictorial Nominalism* seeks to give a rationale. How is it possible, though, to appreciate the accomplishment of Duchamp by focusing on other artists, their works and associated art movements, when they have responded in such a limited way to an aspect of Duchamp's oeuvre over the last 70 years and particularly in the last 30 years? Worse than that, how is it possible to appreciate Duchamp's accomplishment through the eyes of the spectator whose function is reduced in *Pictorial Nominalism* to the act of naming, of saying 'This is Art', when it is patent from Duchamp's work and his statements that this was not the way he operated?

The formal statement 'This is Art' certainly does not begin to account for the persistent and consistent content in Duchamp's work. In the interview with Tallmer it is obvious there are other criteria besides simple 'naming' that enable something to become the work of art. When Duchamp says, 'Even a grocer *can* be – *can be* – an artist', the critical word is '*can*'.[15] The possibility that a person 'can' make a work of art from anything is conditional on them 'having an idea'. It is evident from the content of the *Large Glass*, as the basis for the 'operation' that determines the 'ideas' for the *readymades*, what type of ideas Duchamp considers necessary for some thing to be a work of art.

What does it matter if the formalist posturing of a Clement Greenberg or the word games of a Joseph Kosuth are relegated to their deserved art historical cul de sacs? What if it can be shown instead that the 'position' Duchamp wished to develop in his 'painting', in isolation from the insidious effects of taste, influence and success, equates precisely with the content evident in his later work.

Beyond taste

The formalist position argued for in *Pictorial Nominalism* and *Kant after Duchamp* makes the role of the art viewer central to the art process. Thierry de Duve claims the viewer is someone who can imitate Duchamp by saying 'This is Art'. So it is essential to be clear about what role the art viewer has in determining an object's art status.

The role of the art public in the artist's process of conception and fabrication varies from extremely marginal to non-existent. This was certainly the case for the twenty years of complete secrecy that surrounded Duchamp's conception and fabrication of *Etant donnes*, and the revelation of its existence only after his death.

Worse, the formalist position does not heed the fact that Duchamp was looking to create an object that neither was nor was not a work of art. In his *Notes* he asks, 'Can one make works that are not works of art'. The viewer does not even, after Duchamp's supposed offering of it for nomination, say of an object 'This is Art' as if that was the sole function of the potentiality that is art.

Even *Pictorial Nominalism* and *Kant after Duchamp* acknowledge, as have others, that the *readymades* do nothing if they have not, over the last 80 or so years, maintained their enigmatic status as items that hover between the potentiality of being defined as art or not art. Duchamp is explicit when he says he did not call the *Bicycle Wheel* a work of art.

> The wheel serves no purpose, unless it's to rid myself of the conventional appearance of a work of art. It was a fantasy. I didn't call it a work of art. Actually I didn't call it anything. I wanted to finish with the idea with creating works of art.[16]

Because Duchamp was fully committed to an aesthetic expression free of rational constraints, then being an artist or not being an artist was of little moment to him. Similarly, to call a work art or not to call it art was of no interest to him. So if the viewers, at some point after Duchamp has created a *readymade*, decide to incorporate it in the category 'Art', supposedly to do what Duchamp determinedly decided not to do, then they do something outside the immediate influence of Duchamp.

The viewers, if they are acting in the guise of Duchamp, cannot be merely completing what he left in abeyance. If they simply designate a work by Duchamp 'This is Art' then they are not accounting for the whole panoply of meaning fully explored in the *Large Glass* and imbued in the *readymades*.

Why, for instance, is the *Large Glass* not subject to a similar nomination process in *Pictorial Nominalism's* assessment of the public role in determining whether something is a work of art? To suggest the principle function of the *readymades* was to allow for such a public nomination process merely perpetuates a common art historical practice of reinterpreting an oeuvre according to extraneous criteria. It seems evident that *Pictorial Nominalism* and *Kant after Duchamp* do not begin to consider the range, the depth and the logical consistency of the content in his oeuvre.

Thierry de Duve's fascination with the phrase 'a sort of pictorial nominalism' leads to a distortion of the significance of the elements in Duchamp's oeuvre, and has led to a reduction of its multifaceted mythic dynamic to a singular formalist art historical moment in the process of naming. Only for the purpose of art historical categorisation might it make sense to admit the *readymades* into the category of 'Art'. This, however, does not alter one jot the importance of their authorial dependency nor their self-contradictory status.

It seems perverse to claim that the *readymades* are works wrung dry of any possible meaning when a nominalist-based theory can identify only two or three of the *readymades* as candidates. The desire to persist with such claims despite the evidence seems born of a need to demonstrate to theorists like Clement Greenberg that his formalist aesthetic programme cannot escape a Duchampian underpinning. When the significance of the *Passage of the Virgin to the Bride* is displaced, when the significance of the *readymades* is reduced, and when de Duve offers his own challenge to Greenberg's abstract aesthetic with the idea of a 'Blank Canvas' he forces on those works a reading that bears only marginally on Duchamp's whole oeuvre.

De Duve's persistence in referring to the *Fountain* as the 'Urinal' compounds the confusion by not explicitly recognising the authorial interventions that make it ridiculous to consider that a naive viewer has an post- or even co-authorial option to say of a 'urinal', 'This is Art'. In the case of the *Fountain* the viewers do not choose the object, and do not invert it to alter its orientation in space about the 'Hinge Point' of the groin. They do not designate it *Fountain*, nor sign it 'R. Mutt', nor propose it for exhibition, nor resign from the Society of Independent Artists because of its refusal for exhibition by the jurors of the Society.

Neither do the viewers write, or cause to be written, an article in *The Blind Man* defending the *Fountain's* status as an exhibitable object under the rules of the Society. Nor do they have it photographed, or included in the catalogue of works, or make statements to insist the *readymades* take their meaning from their contextualisation within the aesthetic dynamic of the *Large Glass*.

If the viewers had done all of the above then they would identify themselves as a 'anartist' with a disinterest in matters of art or anti-art, religion and anti-religion. In short, they would not be interested in deciding to say 'This is Art'.

Instead, Duchamp was more than interested in moving beyond the exigencies of public 'taste' or judgment. Considering the changes in public response to his work and the likelihood of the vacillations continuing beyond his death, and considering his determination to preserve his works in miniature in the *Box in a Valise*, and in a permanent collection at the Philadelphia Museum of Art, and the likelihood of the arrangement not extending far beyond his death, Duchamp was more acutely conscious than most of the role played by the public in the artistic process.

He does acknowledge that he has no control over the viewers' taste. In an interview with Georges Charbonnier he suggested the artist is not fully conscious of the artistic process.

> I believe that the artist doesn't know what he does. He knows what he does physically and even his gray matter thinks normally, but he is incapable of assessing the aesthetic result. ... I sincerely believe that the picture is made as much by the onlooker as by the artist. Therefore the spectator is as important as the artist in the art phenomenon.[17]

Charbonnier asked if the artist comes to an understanding over time.

> No, because the onlooker, by his interpretation, adds what the artist never even thought of doing. He ...decides what is put into the Louvre.[18]

Duchamp explained further in his talk, *The Creative Act*.

> If we give the attributes of a medium to the artist, we must then deny him the state of consciousness on the aesthetic plane about what he is doing and why he is doing it. All his decisions in the artistic execution of the work rest with pure intuition and cannot be translated into a self-analysis, spoken or written, or even thought out.[19]

The historical distinction between the artist who makes the work of art and the viewers who determines its fortunes is quite clear. But there is no suggestion that the viewers are involved in creating the work before it is open to transference. Nor has the creation of the work involved the artist simply saying 'This is Art'.

If the viewers determine the taste of a period, through their judgment as to whether something is a work of art, then they are acting against what Duchamp considers basic to art. If taste forms the basis of art then art is a 'substantial' mirage.

When Otto Hahn asked what difference there is between art and crazes, Duchamp responded that taste is a temporary fashion that changes over the years and throughout the history of art. He thinks the public 'is the victim of a really staggering plot'. When the critics speak of 'the truth of art' they make it seem like the 'truth of religion' but for Duchamp such truth does not exist. Instead he 'believes in nothing because to believe gives rise to a mirage'. Hahn asked Duchamp if he would rid the world of the mirage.

> No. I only said that art was a mirage. A mirage very pretty to live with, but a mirage all the same. I find that it doesn't exist, but I did not say it was bad.[20]

In response to a question from Charbonnier, Duchamp said art does have meaning when it is free from the dictates of taste.

> Art as I understand it is a much more general thing and much less dependant on each period. The blending of taste with the word 'art' is, for me, a mistake. Art is something much more profound than the taste of the period.[21]

Duchamp's dismissal of period taste is not a complete dismissal of artistic practice nor is his acknowledgement of the influence of the viewer a fatalistic acceptance of the artist's powerlessness. The final comment shows he was aware of a level of artistic practice free of such limitations. The nature of that level of operation inherently critiques a limited nominalistic approach.

The limitation of formalism for reading Duchamp

I do not question the legitimacy of an interest in the more formal aspects of Duchamp's accomplishment. *Pictorial Nominalism* and *Kant after Duchamp* have brought to light neglected areas of Duchamp's approach. And Duchamp's work requires the philosophical attention at the level of a Kant at least.

What I do take issue with are the extrapolations from those philosophical cues to statements about the significance or relevance of his oeuvre as a whole or the position of the *Large Glass* within it. It comes as no surprise that, on the basis of an art historical formalism, Thierry de Duve claims that *The Passage from the Virgin to the Bride* is the crucial work for an appreciation of the accomplishment of the *readymades* and that it is a mistake to think the *Large Glass* is central to all Duchamp did. These claims, though, are completely contrary to Duchamp's own statements, and the acceptance by many others, that the *Large Glass* is the crucial and central work.

Duchamp confirmed to Arturo Schwarz that in his life he had done only one work, the *Large Glass*.[22] He said further that 'the *Large Glass* is the single most important work I ever made'.[23]

In the interview with Jerry Tallmer, in response to the question as to what in his own work did he think had been most worthwhile, Duchamp responded, 'the *Glass*', and affirmed that 'the *Large Glass* for me is the only thing that I think shows no direct influence'.[24] When Rosalind Constable asked Duchamp how he felt about the *Large Glass*, he said 'I like it very much. In my career, if I may call it that, it has been a key painting for me, decidedly'.[25]

Because Thierry de Duve fails to relate the *readymades* to the *Large Glass* in the way Duchamp does, the *readymades* appear as singular instances in his theory of naming. He even attributes a sense of alienation to the 'urinal' that he claims can be read as 'evidence of decadence' or as holding the promise of a 'renewal' through the 'emancipation' of art from its past.

In conclusion, Duchamp's urinal wields the disquieting proof of art's alienation, an alienation that seems definitive to those who read it as evidence of decadence, provisional to those who see it as the premise of renewal, and necessary for those for whom the faculty of negating is what, in the end, promises emancipation.[26]

Neither does it surprise that by the end of *Kant after Duchamp*, after attempting a formalist critique of Kant out of Duchamp's *readymades*, no progress has been made toward understanding what makes Duchamp a 'great artist'. I will be arguing that it is principally through an appreciation of what it means to say Duchamp established a mastery of the possibility of any content that there is a potential for such an insight.

It is inevitable that *Kant after Duchamp*, which falls within the scholarly tradition in its preference for form over content, should wilt so dramatically at the end. An appreciation of Duchamp's achievement capable of connecting the *Large Glass* and the *readymades* in a logically consistent and thematically comprehensive way is required to avoid the privations of formalism and the abysm of spurious speculation over psychological 'content' in the mode of Schwarz and Golding.

Content from the past

Because the formalist programme of modern art has been the basis for Thierry de Duve's interpretation of Duchamp's work, he makes no attempt to account for the content of the *Large Glass* and other works. *Pictorial Nominalism* and *Kant after Duchamp* consistently reduce the content of Duchamp's oeuvre to formalist devices. The significance of *The Passage from the Virgin to the Bride* is reduced to a bare exemplar of the passage from the pictorial to the nominal, which in turn limits the *readymades* to the fact of naming or being named. Then de Duve forges a connection from the *readymades* to Greenbergian abstraction by way of a postulated 'Blank Canvas'. The most that can be said of such an approach is that there is consistency in saying nothing about Duchamp's expressed interest in revisiting the content of traditional art works.

In his conversation with Alain Jouffroy, Duchamp recounted his intention to derive his content from traditional artworks.

> There is a great difference between a painting which goes beyond the retinal impression – a painting which uses the tubes of colour as a

springboard to go further. This was the case with the religious painters of the Renaissance. The tubes of colour didn't interest them. What they were interested in was to express their idea of divinity, in one form or another. With a different intention and for other ends, I took the same concept: pure painting doesn't interest me either in itself or as a goal to pursue. My goal is different, is a combination or, at any rate, an expression which only gray matter can produce...I was interested in ideas – not merely in visual products. I wanted to put painting once again at the service of the mind.[27]

He repeated the claim when talking to James Johnson Sweeney.

In fact until the last hundred years all painting had been literary or religious: it had all been at the service of the mind. This characteristic was lost little by little during the last century. The more sensual appeal a painting provided – the more animal it became – the more highly it was regarded.[28]

And he reiterated his interest in 'other functions' in his dialogue with Pierre Cabanne.

Since Courbet, it's been believed that painting is addressed to the retina. That was everyone's error. The retinal shudder! Before, painting had other functions: it could be religious, philosophical, moral. If I had the chance to take an anti-retinal attitude, it unfortunately hasn't changed much; our whole century is completely retinal, except for the Surrealists who tried to go outside it somewhat. And still, they didn't go so far![29]

When Philippe Collin enquired if the *readymade* is against the 'seduction of the retina', Duchamp affirmed his commitment to traditional 'anecdote'

There is no more anecdote, no more religion; there is nothing else... It's not the visual question of the *readymades* that counts...[30]

This suggests there was more, much more, for Duchamp in the challenge he issued in the *readymades* than a single formal condition for the possibility of an artwork. The comments suggest he was interested in incorporating into his aesthetic dynamic the logical conditions for the full range of content available to the art of ideas in its protean variety throughout the history of art. Arthur Miller noted in 1936 that Duchamp 'hinted he is working out a system to measure the imaginative power in works of art'.³¹

And in a talk given to college students Duchamp is even more explicit about the relevance of the 'para-religious mission' of the artist.

> ...college education, develops the deeper faculties of the individual, the self-analysis and the knowledge of our spiritual heritage. These are the important qualities which the artist acquires in college, and which will allow him to keep alive the great spiritual traditions with which even religion seems to have lost its contact. I believe that today, more than ever before, the artist has this para-religious mission, to keep lit the flame of an inner vision of which the work of art seems to be the closest translation for the layman. It goes without saying that to feel such a mission the highest education is indispensable.³²

The aesthetic dynamic out of mythic content

In the period 1912 to 1913 Duchamp came to appreciate the logical basis for mythic content, and so the logical conditions for art to be able to convey any content at all. This was the period following the rejection of the *Nude descending the Staircase* from the Paris Independents. During his subsequent trip to Munich, Duchamp sketched the first ideas for the *Large Glass*, and formulated the ideas that led to *readymades* such as the *Bicycle Wheel* and *Pharmacy*.

By the time Duchamp had fully elaborated the project for the *Large Glass* he was in complete command of the aesthetic dynamic. His application of the aesthetic dynamic was consistent with the philosophic conditions for mythic expression. He demonstrated this command by the quality, consistency and variety of his artistic output over the next five decades.

Duchamp considered the logical conditions given expression in the *Large Glass* to be a 'group of operations'. The title of the *Large Glass*, *The Bride Stripped Bare by Her Bachelors, Even*, was not intended to evoke any particular myth or mythology. Rather, consistent with his ambition, he wanted to articulate the imaginative conditions for any artwork, traditional or contemporary. He explained to Andre Breton, that the *Large Glass* 'has no more importance for me than a partial and descriptive title and not that of a title with an intentionally mythical theme'.³³

The *Large Glass* incorporates the logical conditions for consistent aesthetic expression. Any form of art takes these conditions as a given whether it acknowledges them or not. In most art works only a proportion of the logical conditions achieve expression. Most art works presume on the mythology prevailing in the culture to provide the balance. It is as if the relationship of the *readymades* to the *Large Glass* in Duchamp's oeuvre mirrors the relationship of the lesser art works in a particular culture or society to its underpinning mythology.

But more than that, the *Large Glass* enunciates the logical conditions for human aesthetic expression. When Duchamp said he based everything he did on the *Large Glass*, he knew his *readymades* also carried within them the consciousness of the logical conditions, or operation, for myth in general. They are the conditions that prevail in the culture but which less complete artistic formulations express largely through their absence.

Duchamp acknowledged the range of possibilities in his talk *The Creative Act*. He introduced the notion of the 'art co-efficient' to take account of the distance between the less and the more complete formulations of content. By his own standards, Duchamp's successful expression of a mythic level of content achieves a relatively high degree of coincidence between 'the unexpressed but intended and the unintentionally expressed'. Apollinaire recognised Duchamp's achievement when he said that Duchamp's work would reconcile 'art and the people'.

(The understanding of the logic of the relationship between art and life is even more comprehensive and complete in the *Sonnets*, poems and plays of Shakespeare. More than Duchamp he expresses what he intends and, unlike Duchamp, he expresses little that is not intentional.)

The received history of recent art, as in the formalist preoccupations of Modernism, has focused almost exclusively on the formal achievement and challenge of the *readymades*. It barely rates by the standard of Duchamp's art co-efficient. As a consequence, the *Large Glass* has been seen down the formalist art historical tunnel. Formalism represents the blind spot to rigorous philosophic art criticism. Neither have readings of the *Large Glass* in psychological or pseudo-scientific (alchemical) terms been any more philosophic. They have been largely speculative.

Only Octavio Paz has attempted to treat the *Large Glass* as a critique of content as subject matter. He, though, was too much of a Platonist to see the connection between the *readymades* and the logical conditions of mythic expression. So the mythic logic presented in the *Large Glass* has remained an enigma which has refused to submit to analysis out of formalist and idealist concerns.

Octavio Paz

Of all the Duchamp's interpreters, Octavio Paz comes closest to revealing the nature of the content in the *Large Glass*. Even though Paz's approach wants dramatically for philosophic rigour, he is at least thematically aware of Duchamp's accomplishment. This is best expressed in his suggestion that the *Large Glass* presents both a 'criticism of myth' and a 'myth of criticism'.

Paz, though, falls back on extant Hindu, Greek, and Christian mythologies because he is unable to determine the logic of the mythic dynamic in the *Large Glass*. He reveals his lack of insight into the role of the *Large Glass* in the complete oeuvre when he says the *readymades* are 'anonymous objects' that Duchamp, through the 'gratuitous gesture' of simply 'choosing', converts into 'works of art'.

Comparing the dynamic in the *Large Glass* to relationships apparent in Hindu mythologies or even in Christian mythology does not explain how the *Large Glass* is so critically mythic. Instead of drawing the appropriate philosophic conclusions in terms of the function of myth and criteria for a mythic possibility, Paz offers comparative mythological examples that do little more than suggest there are common elements between them and the *Large Glass*. Paz, who imagines that the Bride is a 'mechanical incarnation of Kali' or an 'allegory of the Assumption of the Virgin,' writes that,

> Duchamp has said that she is the two-dimensional shadow of a three-dimensional object, which in its turn is the projection of an unknown object of four dimensions: the shadow, the copy of a copy of an Idea. Contiguous to this Platonic vision there is another: Lebel thinks that the fourth dimension is the moment of copulation when the lovers fuse all the realities into one – the erotic dimension.[34]

Paz' conjunction of the Platonic and the erotic and his conjoining of 'copulation' and the 'erotic dimension' ('when the lovers fuse all the realities into one') ignores the logical distinction between the sexual and the erotic. Duchamp leaves the sexual outside the *Large Glass* in the fourth dimension precisely because art is logically erotic.

Despite Paz's imaginative readings from the various mythologies, the iconography of the *Large Glass* is not religious. Duchamp was adamant that he was not interested in the religious or the anti-religious, in theism or atheism. He had no time for the psychological and speculative baggage incorporated in the multitude of mythological expressions worldwide. Rather he isolated the logical elements for any mythological expression.

To his credit, Octavio Paz does recognise that Mallarmé was a major influence on Duchamp. Mallarmé had such a masterly command of the formal and the symbolic dimensions of the aesthetic possibility that his work leads directly to Duchamp's mastery of the aesthetic dimension of the mythic. To understand the nature of the mythic in the work of Duchamp it is necessary to turn to the example of Mallarmé.

Stephane Mallarmé

To appreciate the depth of Mallarmé's influence on Duchamp in the period in which he was developing the imagery of the *Large Glass*, it is important to distinguish between the contributions of Mallarmé and that of Raymond Roussel and others. Duchamp did acknowledge that 'it was fundamentally Roussel who was responsible for my Glass ... (he) helped me greatly on one side of my expression'.[35] The unique form and technological imagery of the *Large Glass*, its arrangement of hilarious mechanisms, would not have been possible without the influence of Roussel.

The substantive subject matter or content of the *Large Glass*, however, derives not from Roussel but from Mallarmé. Mallarmé's *Herodiade*, *The Afternoon of the Faun*, and most of his sonnets, prefigure the erotic dynamic of the *Large Glass*. Mallarmé had perfected the theme of sexual non-consummation allied seamlessly to the inception of the poetic tract developed around a simple image.

Mallarmé's erotic verse recognises that the traditional association of substantive meaning with the 'absolute', or its counterpart 'despair', is not prior to the sexual/erotic dynamic. Ironically, of course, in traditional mythologies the erotic always contextualises the absolute. The everlasting male God, the formation of Adam from clay, and the virgin birth of Christ are a few of the erotic elements in Judeo/Christian mythology without which the notion of the absolute is inexpressible.

The way Mallarmé applied erotic logic to his poetry is the key to understanding Duchamp's work. The resolution Mallarmé affected in his mature work is the direct precursor to the 'content' in Duchamp's *Large Glass* and later works. It is of sufficient philosophic depth for the appreciation of the content of the *Large Glass*. Duchamp acknowledged the significance of

Mallarmé both as a crucial influence and as a poet to whose work the trajectory of art should return.

> A great figure. Modern art must return to the direction traced by Mallarmé: It must be an intellectual and not merely an animal expression.[36]

Though Duchamp was influenced by Lafourge, Jarry, Roussel and others, and even by Seurat, Cezanne, Matisse, and Picasso, only Mallarmé's work shows a philosophic appreciation of the basis of substantive content. It was not by chance that Mallarmé was a close friend of Edouard Manet whose paintings show a similar awareness of significant content, particularly his *Olympia* and *Luncheon on the Grass*.

Mallarmé's appreciation of the erotic logic of poetry gives his work a greater depth than that of other Symbolists such as Ghil, Symons, de l'Isle-Adam, Huysmans, Valery, Redon, or Moreau. His pre-eminence as the arch Symbolist, as the only one of the Symbolist group of poets to transcend the vicissitudes of style, is due to the philosophic acuity of his vision, and his awareness of the deep symbolism in the work of others (including Shakespeare).

More than any other influence, Mallarmé's profound symbolism leads to an appreciation of Duchamp's philosophic precision. Duchamp's attraction to Mallarmé's deep symbolism was enhanced by Mallarmé's tendency towards a pure aestheticism. Similarly, Duchamp's lifelong ambition was to avoid the ethical or propositional language in favour of the aesthetic or singular expressions. The absence of an ethical dynamic in their work leads logically to its esoteric nature. The philosophical limitations of their aestheticism can be compared to the philosophic range of Shakespeare's *Sonnets* and plays.

Partly because of its esotericism, but principally because of the erotic logic of its content, Mallarmé's work has suffered a similar reception to Duchamp's. His last major work, *Un coup de dés*, has been treated principally as a typographic masterpiece in the same way that the *Large Glass* and the *readymades* have been treated as formalist moments by the academic avant-garde as it rewrites history.

To overcome this narrowed perspective and so be better able to understand Duchamp's accomplishment it is necessary to grasp the significance of Mallarmé's formative years. In his early twenties Mallarmé confronted the 'abyss' that arose from the denial of the absolute, itself an abstraction of the denial of the existence of the Christian God of his youth. Mallarmé forged a philosophic and poetic resolution to the debilitating sensation of the abyss. If the abyss could be characterised as the whiteness of the unmarked page, then the first mark on the page that began the process of expressing his aesthetic insights amounted to a liberation. Because Mallarmé's resolution was philosophic he avoided both the crisis that led Rimbaud to forgo poetry and the psychological darkness that affected the writing of Baudalaire, Lafourge, Poe, and others.

As Leo Bersani acknowledges in his book, *The Death of Stephane Mallarmé*, Mallarmé resolved the quandary in a unique way. Bersani, having rejected a psychoanalytic approach to Mallarmé's accomplishment, found himself having instead,

> to recognise the identity in Mallarmé between a sexualised mental text and a culturally viable art. What is truly radical about Mallarmé is perhaps this demonstration that the most refined cultural product need not exercise any repressive authority over human desire. Nothing is stranger than the textual difficulty which results from this harmonious relation between civilised discourse and desiring impulses...disappearance in Mallarmé is frequently a procreative act. If his writing makes manifest the negativising moves of consciousness, it also makes negativity itself an object of irony. Non-negativising moves of consciousness can cover, and abolish, the differential – and permanently unreadable – moves of an eroticised mental text. Mallarmé's work never stops producing a sense which is nowhere, and this means that Mallarmé is at once impossible to read and extremely easy to read.[37]

Mallarmé succeeded in elevating his concerns beyond the subjective and beyond the psychology of desire by recognising the correlation between the writing process and the sublimation of desire. His poetry acknowledges the primacy of the erotic mind for any expression in language.

Gordan Millan in his recent biography of Mallarmé makes a similar point about Mallarmé's identification of the body/mind relationship as the true source for beauty in poetry. Mallarmé went through a metaphysical crisis where he confronted the Abyss. He was not inclined to use traditional idealised representation to allay the sensation. Neither did he turn to a mere abstract formulation. Instead he realised that poetry or the poem itself provided certainty once committed to the page. But that was not all, as he said:

> I have descended deep enough into the void to be able to speak with certainty. Beauty alone exists and it has only one perfect expression, Poetry. Everything else is a lie – except in the case of those who live the life of the body – love and, for that love of the mind, friendship.[38]

For Mallarmé there is no such thing as a thought so abstract that it is not in some way delicately erotic. This is because the life of the human being, even in its most exquisite poetic moments or in its communion with what it takes to be the absolute, is logically conditioned by its status in the world as a body. So living the life of the body as love and expressing beauty as poetry provide insights compared to which the disembodied absolute is a 'lie'.

The erotic in Duchamp's work

The erotic tension so evident in the longer works of Mallarmé, such as *Herodiade* and *The Afternoon of the Faun*, and present as a constant theme in his sonnets and verse is given definitive expression in Duchamp's *Large Glass*. There the mutual desire of the Bride and the Bachelors cannot be consummated because that possibility would transgress the boundary that delimits the artistic possibility. In his *Notes* for the *Large Glass* Duchamp commented,

> No obstinacy, ad absurdum: of hiding the coition through a glass pane with one or many objects of the shop window the penalty consists in cutting the pane and feeling regret as soon as possession is consummated. Q.E.D.[39]

Duchamp recognises implicitly that art is made of 'pictorial' images logically separate from the contingency and the necessity of the sexual as a feature of the ongoing life of human beings. Art's reality is an artifice logically dependent on the dynamics of a human mind, which is logically dependent on the body. By recognising the logical divide between the sexual and the erotic Duchamp knowingly creates 'a sort of pictorial nominalism'.

In his *Notes* Duchamp provocatively calls the sexual the 4th dimension precisely because sexual consummation cannot logically be figured into an artwork. Eroticism, as the logical condition of the mind and hence of art, is the 3rd dimension because it is the 'shadow' of the 4th dimension. It is but a shadow of the sexual as the biological dynamic. The logical derivation of the erotic from the sexual led Duchamp to say a number of times that eroticism is the one inescapable element in his work. All other elements such as puns, humour, irony, the technical and the mechanical are secondary and hence dispensable.

> Seriousness is a very dangerous thing. To avoid it, one must call for the intervention of humour. The only serious thing which I might consider is Eroticism – because that is serious! – And I have tried to use it as a platform – in the Bride for instance.[40]

Duchamp is clear about the logical connection between eroticism and life. Not only does the logic of the erotic forge a link to the 'animal' or sexual, it also exposes the underlying 'fantasy' behind mythologies like the Christian.

> Eroticism is a subject very dear to me, and I certainly applied this liking, this love, to my Glass. In fact I thought the only excuse for doing anything is to introduce eroticism into life. Eroticism is close to life, closer than philosophy or anything like it, it's an animal thing that has many facets as is pleasing to use, as you would use a tube of paint, to inject into your production so to speak. It's there stripped bare. It's a form of fantasy. It has a little to do also… the stripped bare probably had even a naughty connotation with Christ. You know that Christ was stripped bare and it was a naughty form of introducing eroticism and religion…'[41]

In his interview with Pierre Cabanne, Duchamp emphasises that eroticism is the basis of 'everything' despite the attempt by religions such as the Catholic to hide the erotic by dogmatically proscribing the eroticism within its mythology. After Shakespeare, Duchamp presents the most penetrating critique of the unwillingness of traditional philosophy to investigate the implications of the erotic status of mythologies. When Cabanne asked what place eroticism has his work, Duchamp replied that it was 'enormous', both 'visible and conspicuous' and 'underlying'. Cabanne asked if the eroticism is evident in 'The Bride'.

> It's there too, but it was a closed-in eroticism, if you like, an eroticism that wasn't overt. It wasn't implied either. It's a sort of erotic climate. Everything can be based on an erotic climate without too much trouble. I believe in eroticism a lot, because it's truly a rather widespread thing throughout the world, a thing that everyone understands. It replaces, if you wish, what other literary schools call Symbolism, Romanticism. It could be another 'ism' so to speak. You are going to tell me there can be eroticism in Romanticism, also. But if eroticism is used as the principal basis, a principal end, then it takes the form of an 'ism' in the form of a school.[42]

When asked what personal definition of eroticism he would give, Duchamp said,

> I don't give a personal definition, but basically it's really a way to bring out in the daylight things that are constantly hidden – and that aren't necessarily erotic – because of the Catholic religion, because of social rules. To be able to reveal them, and to place them at everyone's disposal – I think this is important because it's the basis of everything, and no one talks about it. Eroticism was a theme, even an 'ism' which was the basis of everything I was doing at the time of the *Large Glass*. It kept me from being obligated to return to existing theories, aesthetic or otherwise.[43]

Cabanne seemed unprepared for the idea that eroticism has been an abiding element in Duchamp's work. He wondered if the eroticism 'has remained disguised for a rather long time'. Duchamp responded by saying 'disguised, more or less, but not disguised out of shame'.

In the *Dialogues* with Cabanne, Duchamp is explicit in identifying the erotic as central, not only to his practice but also to the multitude of mythologies that have provided the underlying ethos for cultures since the invention of language. Duchamp's repeated mention of eroticism and its pervasive presence throughout his works far outweighs his interest in 'nominalism', which rises little above being a 'sort of' way to appreciate his procedures.

The priority of the sexual over the erotic

In the various literatures that mention the sexual or the erotic, the terms are frequently confused. Arturo Schwarz and even Robert Lebel make no clear or consistent distinction between the sexual and the erotic. Schwarz talks of 'sexual intercourse' being displaced to the 'mental level, as if to compensate for this loss of erotic tension'.[44] Lebel thinks he sees in the *Large Glass* evidence that 'love' is a pessimistic 'mechanism' neither 'spiritual' or 'physical'.

> Should Duchamp have revealed the basic pessimism of his scheme so publicly? He would seem to see in love only a simultaneous mechanism which in no way implies a spiritual or even physical union, man and woman acting on each other *from a distance* and on separate planes, she, the victim of her illusions, always keeping herself above the point of contact, while he, the prisoner of his instincts, is resigned never to reach it.[45]

Schwarz does not clearly distinguish the 'physical' aspect of sexual intercourse from the mental dynamic of eroticism. And Lebel does not distinguish the erotics of the *Large Glass* from the sexual elements in physical union. Their confusion is telling because the common dictionary definitions of 'sexual' and 'erotic' provide the required clarity.

Paz seems to have a clearer appreciation of the relation of the sexual to the biological and the erotic to the conceptual.

> Eroticism lives on the frontiers between the sacred and the blasphemous. The body is erotic because it is sacred. The two categories are inseparable: if the body is mere sex and animal impulse, eroticism is transformed into a monotonous process of reproduction; if religion is separated from eroticism, it tends to become a system of arid moral precepts… The body is immortal because it is mortal; this is the secret of its permanent fascination – the secret of sexuality as much as of eroticism.[46]

Missing from their conceptualisations of the sexual and the erotic is an appreciation that the sexual is the prior condition for the erotic. The combination of insight and confusion in the use of words like 'pessimism', 'prisoner', 'mere sex', 'monotonous process' and 'secret' overlooks

Duchamp's precise demarcation of the sexual from the erotic in the creation of a work of art.

Duchamp's work does not deny the significance of sex nor is it pessimistic toward sex. It carries an affirmation, an ironic affirmation, in as much as art is logically erotic and sex is the reproductive process that is the logical precondition for art. The sexual dynamic of the body provides the logical precondition for the erotic logic of the mind. And, in turn, the capacity to think about the sexual or bodily functions is guaranteed by the logic of the relationship between the sexual and the erotic.

Idealistic paradigms, such as the Platonic and the Cartesian, which claim there is a logical disjunction between the mind and body, do not allow of such a possibility. The persistent influence on modern thinking of apologetic idealism, with its justification of the inconsistencies in beliefs based on biblical mythology, is the principal reason Duchamp's work has proved so difficult to understand.

Even a sympathetic reader like Octavio Paz is sufficiently confused to read a Platonism into Duchamp's understanding of the 4th dimension. Like Schwarz' reliance on the psychology of alchemy, Paz' attempt to understand the mythic depth in Duchamp's work is awry because he does not appreciate the distinction between the sexual and the erotic for the mythic possibility. The natural logic common to Mallarmé, Duchamp, Shakespeare, and evident in Darwin's writings on evolutionary biology, acknowledges the priority of the body over the mind and the sexual over the erotic.

In *Kant after Duchamp*, for instance, Thierry de Duve makes no attempt to address the logic of the sexual and the erotic. The focus remains stolidly on the formal issue of 'naming' with the consequence that only a few of Duchamp's works are granted significance. Consequently, de Duve's speculative assertions bear little resemblance to the facts. There is a persistent failure to take note of Duchamp's reiterated claims as to the centrality of eroticism in his life's work.

And the relevance of sexual generation was never far from Duchamp's mind. When writing to Michel Carrouges he uses a genealogical metaphor to say that 'it is likely that my ancestors made me speak, as they did, about what my grandchildren will also say too',[47] and to Katherine Kuh he identified the sexual precondition for the *readymades*.

> man can never expect to start from scratch; he must start from ready made things like even his own mother and father.[48]

Although Duchamp fathered a love-child when young and was briefly married in 1928, he remained a bachelor for most of his life. Consistent with his avowal not to be encumbered with children and housekeeping, he settled into a marriage only when the possibility of having children was past. Yet he sustained a strong sense of family. He portrayed members of his family in many of his early paintings and maintained relations with his brothers and sisters throughout his life. Duchamp acknowledges the significance of both the family connections and the early exploration of the erotic in the formative period that leads up to the *Large Glass* and the *readymades* when he included many of his early paintings in his *Box in a Valise* and ensured they were represented in the permanent collection of his work at Philadelphia.

Duchamp's appreciation of the difference between the sexual and the erotic is consistent with his aim to return art to the mythic level of conceptualisation typical of the past. He was repulsed by the retinal fascinations of the early twentieth century. So it should not surprise that Duchamp's 'greatness' allies him with other great artists who sought to give expression to the prevailing mythology of their culture. Unlike them, though, Duchamp went further and expressed the logical conditions for any mythology.

Any attempt to determine Duchamp's 'greatness' by his contribution to the avant-garde movements of the early to mid-twentieth century, that is by looking back to the *readymades* down the narrow tunnel of art historical influence based on formalist criteria, is extremely prejudicial to a full understanding of his achievement.

The sexual and the erotic as the 4th and the 3rd dimensions

Duchamp's work demands a fundamental reorientation in traditional expectations. His references to the 4th dimension in the *Notes* for the *Large Glass* are not to abstract concepts such as time, or the Platonic ideal. Rather he identifies the 4th dimension as the sexual act.

As a function of the physical body or the biological, the 4th dimension is the logical source of the 3rd dimension or the possibility of the erotic as the underlying 'dimension' for a work of art. An appreciation of the logical relation between the sexual and the erotic is essential for an understanding of Duchamp's idea of the 4th dimension. As Lebel relates, Duchamp 'considers the sexual act as the pre-eminent fourth-dimensional situation...'[49] And Steefel records that for Duchamp,

The 4th Dimension should, logically, be the dimension behind the painting since 3D forms are the 'shadows cast by 4D forms'. For Duchamp the 4th D is the plane of consummation, analogous to or exemplified by the sexual act.[50]

The sexual 'act' is clearly identified as the 4th dimension. It is the 'plane of consummation' that cannot be represented in an artwork because an artwork can only represent the erotic, or the unconsummated three-dimensional shadow of the 4th dimension.

In a written response to Serge Stauffer in 1961 Duchamp confirmed the 'act of love' as the 4th dimension. Even though he uses the word erotic rather than the word sexual, by specifying the 'erotic act' he distinguishes it from the erotic as desire. This is confirmed when he identified the 4th dimension with touch rather than with the other senses such as seeing and hearing, which are more readily associated with the dynamic of desire.

> –l'acte erotique, situation quadridimensionelle par excellence' – although I use other words, this is an old idea of mine, a hobby-horse explained by the fact that a tactile sensation which envelopes an object on all four sides approximates a tactile sensation of four dimensions. Naturally, none of our senses finds such a quadrimensional capability except maybe that of touch, and therefore the act of love as a tactile sublimation might enable one to visualise, or better, tactualise a physical interpretation of the 4th dimension.[51]

And again, in response to Michel Carrouges' *Les Machines Celibataires*.

> In the Bachelor Machine an erotic desire in action is 'brought' to its 'projection' of appearance and mechanised character. In the same way the Bride of the pendu femelle is a 'projection' comparable to the projection of an 'imaginary entity' in 4 dimensions on our world of 3 dimensions (and even in the case of flat glass to a re-projection of these three dimensions on a surface of 2 dimensions).[52]

This is a substantially different claim from that proposed by other commentators who are confused about the logical status of the sexual and the erotic. Schwarz, in a note to the *Complete Works*, states his objection to the statements of Lebel and Steefel.

> Both Robert Lebel and Lawrence Steefel claim that Duchamp's fourth dimension can be identified with the erotic. Although this idea may be attractive, it seems to be left unconfirmed by what has just been outlined. Duchamp's interest in getting away from the metaphysical would hardly have permitted its reintroduction through eroticism.[53]

It is evident that Schwarz is confusing the 'erotic' as the process of desire characteristic of the mind, with the physical 'act' of sex. In his text Schwarz has just suggested that Duchamp was involved in 'cold cerebral speculations in reaction to Romantic sensualism'. To add to the inconsistency Schwarz confuses concepts such as eroticism, metaphysics, cerebral speculations, and Romantic sensualism.

Schwarz' note continues with the claim Duchamp confirmed his understanding.

> Duchamp has, in conversation, confirmed my viewpoint in categorical terms: 'I would not say that sex is the fourth dimension; far from it, I would never say that. Sex is three dimensional as well as four-dimensional. There is however an expression beyond sex which can be transferred into a fourth dimension. But the fourth dimension is not sex as such. Sex is only an attribute, which can be transferred into a fourth dimension, but it is not a definition or the status of the fourth dimension. Sex is sex.'[54]

But as Craig Adcock puts it,

> Duchamp's interest in four-dimensional geometry has been connected with his interest in eroticism... Duchamp partially affirmed and denied this interpretation.[55]

Schwarz's memory of the conversation cannot be trusted. He has already transposed 'erotic' for 'sex' in discussing the written statement of Lebel and Steefel. And neither is his claim that this statement categorically confirms his viewpoint at all evident from the drift of Duchamp's *Notes*. It would be interesting to know Schwarz's precise question and the circumstances that led Duchamp to be so 'categorical' in a private conversation with him.

In Schwarz Duchamp is dealing with an interpreter who has persistently ignored his disclaimers that he was influenced by alchemy. Given Schwarz's fanciful alchemical interpretation of Duchamp's work, caution is necessary. Serge Stauffer reports that Duchamp mentioned the 'inadequacy' of attempts to 'do alchemy'.

> While stating that he has never read a single treatise on alchemy, which he believes 'must be quite inadequate', Duchamp argues that one cannot 'do alchemy' as one can, with an appropriate language, 'do law or medicine'. 'But one cannot,' he declares 'do alchemy throwing words around or in full consciousness superficially.'[56]

Duchamp also humorously cold shouldered Schwarz' Freudian claim that he had had an incestuous relationship with his sister Suzanne. Duchamp's method of dealing with the ludicrousness of unbridled theory is captured in his response to a talk delivered by Schwarz. John Russell recounts that Duchamp listened for two and a half hours with 'total composure to Mr. Schwarz's high-pressure hypothesising'. He says Duchamp 'gazed into the middle distance' while Schwarz credited him 'with all manner of vagrant fancies and subterranean implications' such as 'was the violin a symbol of onanism rather than a valuable component in family chamber music?'

Russell, later at supper, heard Duchamp exclaim to Schwarz, 'Capital! I couldn't hear a word, but I enjoyed it very much.' However, he records that 'Teeny Duchamp and close friends were deeply shocked by Schwarz's analysis of the *Large Glass*, which is based on the hypothesis of Duchamp's incest with his sister Suzanne'.[57]

It seems that Duchamp would have been sceptical of Schwarz's ability to move beyond his preconceptions to understand the logic of the *Large Glass*. In another reference to the 'sexual' and the 'erotic', Schwarz identifies a number of the logical elements of the *Large Glass* such as the displacement of the sexual to the mental and the Bachelor's 'voyeurism'. But his psychological interpretation misses the logical distinction between 'sexual intercourse' and 'erotic tension'. His confusion is captured in his use of the non-Duchampian word, 'modesty'.

> Thus, sexual intercourse is again displaced from the physical to the mental level, and, as if to compensate for this loss of erotic tension, the pleasure derived from voyeurism is enhanced by the Bride's modesty.[58]

Should we be surprised that Schwarz seems to be regarding the physical as both the sexual and the erotic. If sexual intercourse is 'displaced from the physical to the mental' does it become an anodyne quality associated with 'modesty'?

In the logic of the *Large Glass*, the sexual is the physical act of consummation and the erotic is the activity or output of the mind. Duchamp characterised all his artwork as erotic. When he uses the words 'sex' or 'sexual' in his *Notes* it is with specific reference to the physical organs or their functions.

> ...elements of the **sexual life** *imagined* by her the Bride-desiring.

> ...the love gasoline, as secretion of the Bride's **sexual glands**...

> This pulse needle will thus promenade in balance the **sex cylinder** which *spits at the drum the dew* which is to nourish the vessels...

> C = artery channeling the nourishment of the filament substance, coming from the **sex wasp** (?) while passing by the desire regulator...

> Each of the 8 malic forms is cut by an imaginary horizontal plane at a pnt. called the **pnt of sex**.[59]

When Duchamp says 'sex is only an attribute, which can be transferred into a fourth dimension, but is not the definition or the status of the fourth dimension. Sex is sex', then it is a limited sense of the sex that is being considered. He characterises all his work as erotic and goes as far as to say in response to Cabanne's question, 'How do you see the evolution of art?'

> I don't see it, because I don't see its value deep down. All of man's creations aren't valuable. Art has no biological source. It is addressed to taste...its a little like masturbation.[60]

Considering Schwarz' misunderstanding of the relation between Romantic 'sensual' painting and the function of the erotic in art, and that his reported conversation with Duchamp is not unequivocal but quite equivocal, it would seem Duchamp intended the sexual and the erotic to characterise the 4th and the 3rd dimensions respectively. Because the artistic dimension is not 'biological', he characterises it as the 3rd dimension and the erotic is logically the 3rd dimension.

Duchamp understands art as having a logically different function from the biological function of human increase. If the biological is not part of art then sex as procreation is not part of art. The sexual, as an inherent characteristic of the body in evolutionary terms can be characterised as the 4th dimension. The 4th dimension for Duchamp is not the artistic dimension.

The primary insight Duchamp derived from Mallarmé was the distinction between the sexual and the erotic. Effectively, biological processes are sexual and art is erotic. To understand the difference is to understand the generative distinction between life and art. The semiotic, the symbolic, the mythic in any culture is founded on the distinction. Duchamp's work articulates the logical conditions for mythic expression in any culture because he understands the logic of the erotic.

The sexual is the biological, the relation between the male and the female, the reproductive process. The erotic as desire is any activity or thought whose immediate objective is not purely sexual. The erotic arises out of the sexual. The sexual is prior to the erotic.

Again, Shakespeare expresses the relationship precisely. Shakespeare is explicit when he draws the distinction between the sexual and the erotic in the *Sonnets*, whereas it is more implicit in the work of Mallarmé and Duchamp, being hinted at primarily in their statements and notes.

The aesthetic

Throughout his career Duchamp had a singular focus. He was determined to explore the logical status of the aesthetic. His preoccupation is summarised in the phrase 'aesthetic validity'.

> My intentions as a painter…were directed towards problems of an 'aesthetic validity' principally achieved through abandoning visual phenomenon from the point of view of retinal relationships as from the anecdotal point of view.[61]

Duchamp was aware of the two meanings of the word aesthetic. The older and possibly root meaning derives from the Greek. It refers to 'sensations and perceptions unmediated by thought'. Baumgarten and others introduced the second meaning in the eighteenth century. As faith in the ideal of divine beauty attributed to a male God diminished, a substitute was found in the sublimity evoked by some natural phenomena. In this second sense it became and is still used as a synonym for good taste. Duchamp sought to 'discourage' the 'aesthetic' of taste.

> When I discovered the *readymades* I intended to discourage the aesthetics hullabaloo. But in Neo-Dada they are using the *readymades* to discover their 'aesthetic value'! I threw the bottle rack and the urinal in their faces as a challenge and now they admire them as something aesthetically beautiful.[62]

In an interview with Philippe Collin, Duchamp stated clearly that the aesthetic does not involve taste.

> Instead of choosing something which you like, or something which you dislike, you choose something that has no visual interest for the artist. In other words to arrive at a state of indifference towards this object; at that moment, it becomes a *readymade*…If it is something you like, its like roots on the beach. Then its aesthetic, it's pretty, it's beautiful; you put it in the drawing room. That's not the intention at all of the *readymade*…[63]

The confusion between the two meanings of aesthetic leads to the contradiction in making an 'aesthetic judgment', a trap Kant falls into and which de Duve perpetuates in *Kant after Duchamp*. If there was any sense in having a title *Kant after Duchamp* it would have to consider the fact that Duchamp does not make 'aesthetic judgments'. He makes this clear in an interview with Alain Jouffroy. When Duchamp talked of abolishing judgment, Jouffroy asked whether he means moral or aesthetic judgment. Jouffroy wanted to know how choice, without judgment, can be made between works of art and men.

> I think the mistake is that one believes to be judging when one is simply following a sub-conscious which is the strongest of all and makes you decide and not judge. Judgment is something on the surface. If you like, it is a superficial expression of the subconscious. It is called judgment because you live in a society where there are judgments, the judged and the judgers.[64]

When Jouffroy questions the consequence of making a choice without discrimination, Duchamp expresses his understanding that the aesthetic does not involve 'the true and the false'. With the aesthetic there is no 'judgment'.

> Because the subconscious attends to the choice… In reality everything has happened before your decision. But this has no more sense than

the true and the false. Moreover, from the moment you start to speak you talk nonsense, in this order of ideas – and me too. So to speak of judgment is senseless.[65]

Duchamp's appreciation of the logic of aesthetics is exact. Ironically, as an out and out aesthete, he had little interest in the logic of language or ethics, hence his dismissal of speaking as nonsense. Shakespeare shows in the *Sonnets* how to operate consistently with both aesthetics and ethics.

Duchamp's comments reveal the difference between aesthetics as sensation and aesthetics as taste. The first points to a profound philosophic understanding, the second, if applied logically, leads to nonsense. Hence the confusion that abounds in Kant's discourse on aesthetic judgment and the consequent difficulties *Kant after Duchamp* has in attempting to make sense of Duchamp's aesthetic awareness when de Duve resorts to Kantian apologetics. Kant's predisposition toward aesthetic judgments, driven by his belief in a moral God, is contrary to Duchamp's eschewal of good and bad taste and his dismissal of religion and anti-religion.

It is important to remember that Kant philosophised under prejudice. He was a rational Christian committed to the apologetic process of attempting to reconcile the Protestant faith of his youth with the logic of pure reason. In his *Critique of Pure Reason* he accepts that there is no rational basis for the existence of the Christian God. In the *Critique of Practical Reason*, though, he thought he had found a way for the re-entry of 'God' and 'Immortality' along with 'Freedom'. His concept of 'aesthetic judgment' attempted to transcend the limits of reason using reason.

Duchamp was determined to avoid rational processes. He realised that confounding rational processes provided the basis for any aesthetic effect. For 70 years he adhered to an unqualified understanding of the aesthetic. His understanding of the aesthetic is logically exact (not 'pure' in the disingenuous sense employed by Kant), and he adhered to it consistently in his life's work.

When Duchamp objects to the tradition of taste he is objecting to the inappropriate use of the word aesthetic as it was redefined by the Romantics or Neo-classicists of the seventeenth century. He wanted to return art to a state where the aesthetic meant simply 'sensations or perceptions unmediated by thought'. He identifies the aesthetic as that aspect of a work of art that is equivalent to sensory experiences.

> Art can never be adequately defined because the translation of an aesthetic emotion into a verbal description is as inaccurate as your description of fear when you have actually been scared.[66]

Duchamp makes a sharp distinction between 'taste' and what he terms the 'aesthetic echo'.

> art cannot be understood through the intellect, but is felt through an emotion presenting some analogy with religious faith or a sexual attraction – an aesthetic echo…Taste gives a sensuous feeling, not an aesthetic emotion. Taste presupposes a domineering onlooker who dictates what he likes and dislikes, and translates it into beautiful and ugly – Quite differently, the 'victim' of an aesthetic echo is in a position comparable to that of a man in love or a believer who dismisses automatically his demanding ego and, helpless submits to a pleasurable and mysterious constraint. While exercising his taste, he adopts a commanding attitude; when touched by an aesthetic revelation, the same man in an almost ecstatic mood, becomes receptive and humble.[67]

In *The Creative Act*, Duchamp affirmed his understanding of aesthetic as any form of sensation.

> What I have in mind is that art may be bad, good, or indifferent but whatever adjective is used, we must call it art, and bad art is still art in the same way a bad emotion is still an emotion…The creative act…is a series of efforts, pains, satisfactions, refusals decisions which also cannot and must not be fully conscious on the aesthetic plane.[68]

The above statements suggest Duchamp understood that the 'aesthetic echo' of the most refined work of art is of the same family of experiences as the sensation of 'fear' or the emotion of 'love'. It is as if the aesthetic echo, which may derive from the most refined reaches of the mind, and the sensation of fear, which derives from the more primitive aspects of the mind, have a commonality because logically they are appreciated through the agency of the same mental process. Duchamp's logical understanding of the aesthetic allowed him to operate at will in the zone of unmediated thought.

Many philosophers have maintained there are two modes of understanding, that of 'ideas' and 'sensations'. Duchamp is consistent in identifying 'sensations' with the aesthetic. More by omission, however, he identifies the dynamic of 'ideas' with ethics. The basic distinction is crucial for understanding exactly what Duchamp was attempting to do and why he pushed ethics aside in his desire to pursue the aesthetic possibility to its logical conclusion.

The beauty of indifference

The one word that best characterises the manner in which Duchamp set about his task is 'indifference'. 'Difference', as the linguist Ferdinand de Saussure demonstrated, is at the heart of the human capacity to differentiate and so logically to distinguish one thing from another. The very possibility of language, of rational, discursive, propositional language is based in differentiation. Duchamp is very clear that this possibility did not interest him. In a letter to Jehan Mayoux he responded to a commentary by Michel Carrouges in his *Les Machines Celibataires*.

> I am a great enemy of written criticism, because I see these interpretations and these comparisons as an occasion to open a faucet of words.[69]

He refuses to think about philosophical clichés, and considers himself a 'simplified form' of nominalist.

> I do not believe in language, which instead of expressing subconscious phenomena in reality creates thought by and after the word. (I willingly declare myself a 'nominalist', at least in that simplified form.)[70]

He dismisses all forms of 'twaddle', while conscious of the irony of using words to do so.

> All this twaddle, the existence of God, atheism, determinism, liberation, societies, death, etc., are pieces of a chess game called language, and they are amusing only if one does not pre-occupy oneself with 'winning or losing this game of chess'. As a good nominalist, I propose the word 'patatautology', which, after frequent repetition, will create the concept of what I am trying to explain in this letter by these execrable means: subject, verb, object, etc.'[71]

In an interview in *L'Express* Otto Hahn suggested Duchamp likes games with language, drawing the inevitable response.

> Language is an error of humanity. Between two beings in love, language is not which is the most profound. The word is a very worn pebble which applies to thirty-six nuances of affectivity... Language is useful to simplify, but it is a method of locomotion that I detest. That's why I like painting: an affectivity which is addressed to another. The exchange is made with the eyes.[72]

When pressed by Hahn about his use of language in the pseudonym *Rrose Selavy*, Duchamp claimed he did so to amuse himself. And in an interview with William Seitz he vehemently reiterated his position on language. He said that words such as 'truth, art, veracity', are stupid and that language is a 'great enemy'.[73]

In Duchamp's third interview with George Charbonnier he said that 'our language no longer provides us with precise enough symbols...we can no longer rely on language'. He continued,

> I don't believe at all, that language or words can translate in an exact or precise way everything that really happens in the world, that is to say what happens within the individual and not outside the individual. The translation by words of these phenomena is very approximate, more than approximate and often untrue.[74]

Duchamp's consistent strategy, then, is to counter the 'difference' basic to language. Instead of difference he offers 'indifference' or non-difference. So his phrase 'beauty of indifference' says no more and no less than that beauty is logically synonymous with the aesthetic, with sensations, with the lack of difference. In Duchamp's philosophic world there is no place for a psychological interpretation of the sensation of 'indifference'.

Throughout his life's work and throughout his *Notes* Duchamp uses and lists numerous ways to counter difference and so create the appropriate sensation or aesthetic effect. He uses humour, puns, sequences of meaningless words, chance, technological devices, mass-produced items, visual phenomena, crazy science, etc. In the *Notes* he muses on what it means,

> to lose the possibility of recognising (identifying)
> > 2 similar objects
> > 2 colours, 2 laces,

> 2 hats, 2 forms whatsoever,
> to reach the impossibility of
> sufficient (visual) memory
> to transfer
> from one
> like object to another.[75]

And Duchamp mentions other operations designed to upset 'difference'.

> The 'phenomenon of stretching the unit of length'.
> The 'labyrinth of the 3 directions'.
> The 'spangles lighter than air'.
> The 'removal of the sense of guilt'.
> The Dust breeding 'a reversed image of porosity'.[76]

He applies the various methods for disorientation in the Bachelor apparatus of the *Large Glass* to bring the Bachelors to the appropriate state of indifference to be artists within the work that sets out the logical conditions for art. As Schwarz reported,

> This state of dizziness contributes to relieving the Bachelor of any conscious responsibility in this love affair.[77]

Rather the dizziness is the 'indifference' necessary for 'beauty'.

Even Duchamp's interest in chess is not exempt. His book on endgame moves is aptly titled *Opposition and Sister Squares Reconciled*.

Duchamp's desire to avoid or reject the discursive, the propositional, the rational in favour of the aesthetic was not and could not be logically followed through to a practical conclusion. A significant proportion of his *Notes* and writings explaining his ideas and the operations of the *Large Glass* are in the language of normal discourse. Duchamp was determined to reduce the artistic to the aesthetic but, as the article on the *Fountain* in the broadsheet *The Blind Man* demonstrates, an item of such reduced visual cues requires a complementary text.

Duchamp identifies the aesthetic as the hallmark of the artistic but he also has to accept that the artistic is not wholly determined by the aesthetic. The ethical as language has a significant role in artistic production. In his *Sonnets* Shakespeare shows how to relate the ethical and the aesthetic without prejudice.

With his aphorism 'beauty of indifference' Duchamp expressed a sound appreciation of the logic of aesthetics, and he applied the understanding consistently throughout his works. His phrase 'ironism of affirmation' conveys the same philosophic awareness.

If difference makes propositional language possible, and if difference is founded on an act of distinction that negates the original undistinguished thing by replicating it with a singular sign, then an act that in turn eliminates difference returns it to its previous undifferentiated state. Hence, ironically, the double negation returns 'difference' to an aesthetic state. The double negation is logically an affirmation. So Duchamp called the process the 'ironism of affirmation'.

Because much of the imagery of the *Large Glass* derives both from the early paintings, and from the aesthetic devices or *readymades* Duchamp made at the time, the content of the *readymades* and the *Large Glass* are inextricably intertwined. But an understanding of Duchamp's drive for an unmediated aesthetic expression as distant as possible from ordinary language, and an appreciation of the intelligent and fastidious devotion with which he constructed the artworks, only begins to explain the mythic content of the *Large Glass* and by implication that of the *readymades*.

The mythic logic out of the sexual/erotic dynamic

In the *Castle of Purity* Octavio Paz discusses Duchamp's appreciation of the mythic in terms of criticism. He detects in the *Large Glass* a criticism of the traditional mythologies and an expression of a modern form of myth that is self-critical. He recognises the Bride and the Bachelors as characters involved in an erotic ballet whose configuration expresses the essence of the mythic. In what sense then does the erotic, and its basis in the sexual, relate to the appreciation of the aesthetic as the mode of sensation, or the 'beauty of indifference?'

Duchamp's awareness of the sexual as the biological dynamic has already been discussed. In general terms the sexual process is one in which difference between male and the female is continually reconciled in the formation of a singular other, a child. The child at the moment of conception is the undifferentiated, the sensate, the unworded. The sexual process then, is the 4th dimension that, in turn, gives rise to the possibility of the 3rd dimension or the erotic.

The erotic albeit mechanical ballet of the *Large Glass*, involving male and female elements in a process of mutual and auto excitation, is the 'reduced' cultural equivalent of the biological moment of conception. At the moment of mutual erotic epiphany, the Bride and the Bachelors lose, as much as it is possible, their sense of individuality. Both parties contribute to the arousal process and so both lose themselves in the welter of sensation. They experience a sense of non-difference or achieve a state of ironic affirmation.

In this way they echo, or in fact are, what it means to accomplish the necessary aesthetic status to be a work of art. Art is masturbation not because art is meaningless. It is masturbation because it never can, it logically cannot, replicate the biological process. Art is meaningful because it imitates the biological moment. It artificially mirrors and extends the human potential erotically or non-sexually.

So the *Large Glass* not only incorporates a multitude of devices for accomplishing the aesthetic experience, it transfigures the generative process in the form of its shadow, eroticism (in the name of the human condition), as the fundamental aesthetic dynamic for any artistic accomplishment for any human being. In this sense the *Large Glass* expresses the logical precondition at the heart of the mythic possibility. It goes beyond the achievement of Mallarmé's symbolist poetry.

In the *Afternoon of the Faun*, where Mallarmé most obviously has male and female characters in a mutual interrelationship of erotic abandon, there is not the erotic exactness, the philosophic rigour, the mythic numbering, or the irony of achievement evident in the *Large Glass*. And, in the context of this critique, the 'precision' Duchamp worked toward, and the mythic connection between the 1 Bride and 9 Bachelors, is more evident in the structure of the *Sonnets*.

The relation of the *readymades* to the *Large Glass*

When the logic of the mythic possibility dawned on Duchamp in 1913 and he began in a short space of time to formulate the imagery and the mechanics of the *Large Glass*, he also became conscious of the possibility of encapsulating the same dynamic in an object or project of incredibly reduced facture and seeming insignificance. He remembers that his catch cry of the time was 'reduce, reduce, reduce'.

The *readymades*, then, are a reduced form of the dynamic of the *Large Glass*. All that was required to create such an object was a hint of the erotic dynamic of the *Large Glass*. Duchamp the consummate artist could elicit from the viewer the unconscious and kinaesthetic predisposition all human beings have as a biological given. By a process of studied indifference Duchamp was able to reduplicate the level of content laid out on the *Large Glass* and glossed in the *Notes* in an extremely reduced device that confounded rational expectations.

According to Duchamp's statements and practice an appreciation of the *readymades* can only be achieved through an understanding of the logical operations of the *Large Glass*. It seems that the first *readymades* were made with no artistic intent or at least with an intent not to make an art object. In this they differ completely from the *Large Glass*. By the time Duchamp gave the growing number of objects the status of *readymades* it was obvious that even the earlier ones were influenced by the concerns explored in the *Large Glass*. At the very least they shared the aesthetic focus of the *Large Glass*' indifference to taste.

When Otto Hahn asked if the *readymades* were the 'fruit of a lengthy development' like the *Large Glass*, Duchamp replied that they had a 'completely different' genesis from the *Large Glass* in that they were made with no intention other than 'unloading ideas'.[78] If the function of the *readymades* was to unload ideas, Duchamp also acknowledged the importance of 'ideas' for the *Large Glass* when talking to George Heard Hamilton.

> In other words the ideas in the *Large Glass* are more important than the actual realisation.[79]

A note in the *Green Box* stipulates that *The Bride Stripped Bare by Her Bachelors, Even*, 'operates' to create a distinction between the *readymades* and 'found objects'.

> The Bride Stripped Bare by her Bachelors, Even –
> to separate the mass produced readymade from the readyfound, 'object trouve' – the separation is an operation.[80]

The *Large Glass* contextualises the *readymades* within a mythic level of artistic expression. The mythic dynamic of the *Large Glass* enables Duchamp to create the *readymades* as 'infra-thin' expressions of mythic logic. When Walter Hopps asked Duchamp about the relationship between the *Large Glass* and the *readymades* he responded that they are 'kind of ready made talk of what goes on in the *Glass*'.[81]

In the chapter 'Art was a Proper Name', in *Kant after Duchamp*, de Duve focuses on the unaltered, or the minimally altered *readymades*, the ones that most resemble 'found objects'. These at least seem to be the only ones of which a credulous art viewer is able to say, with the sort of conviction that resembles the action of the artist in simply choosing such an object, 'This is Art'. Such a claim seems primarily based on Duchamp's suggestion that the art viewer plays a significant part in the art process.

But if the content of Duchamp's *Large Glass* and *readymades* are logically the same, it is contrary to the logic of the *readymades* for anyone to suggest they simply express in a formally concise way that 'Art' was a 'Proper Name'. Besides the logical difficulty of determining the meaningfulness or lack of meaningfulness of a proper name, the reduction of the art moment or the art possibility to such simplistic terms contradicts Duchamp's philosophic determination that what constitutes the aesthetic of an art work is the impossibility of saying any such thing.

The process of naming is not one of 'indifference'. Rather it is decidedly one of using words to acknowledge difference pure and simple as a logical precursor to their use in language. Hence many of Duchamp's titles were formulated as puns to reduce the literalness of the name, or as in the case of *The Bride Stripped Bare by Her Bachelors, Even* he added an effectively meaningless adverb.

Duchamp's advocacy for the 'public' to decide or 'judge' which art works should at any particular time be accorded the status of a work of art, acknowledges the art connoisseur's influence on contemporary taste. But his frequent advocacy for the role of the public, because it does not affect the inherent worth of a particular artwork, could also be a consequence of his life-long attitude that gave little or no value to anything other than the 'individual'. His views on the contribution of the art public might have been an 'aesthetic' compensation for his dismissal of the role of the group in his personal life.

Duchamp stated categorically that his interest has always been in the individual and not in the group, and his life-long friend Pierre Roche described Duchamp as a perfect individualist who did not care for the collective interest and was happy to pursue his own concerns.

But Duchamp's apparent generosity in allowing the viewer a part in the art process compensates, if only in a reflexive way, for his aesthetically determined individualism. It is true that the viewer does contribute to the art process but it is also true that even in the conferring of the status of an artwork on an object the authorial intervention is both prior and substantive. (Shakespeare shows how to develop a comprehensive mythic level of expression without the extreme individualism of a Duchamp.)

The tube of paint as a *readymade*

From the vantage of the mythic dynamic of the *Large Glass*, the *readymades* are inextricably entwined in its mythic aesthetic. The statement 'This is Art' is of interest only to an art historian who wishes to plot the dictates of taste.

So, for Thierry de Duve to propose, on the basis of a theory of nomination, that an unaltered tube of paint could be a *readymade* ignores two facts. One is that Duchamp never did confer the status of a *readymade* on a ready made item from the artist's technical kit. The fact that nobody ever has is simply because such a gesture ignores the logic of art practice where the bare conditions for the possibility of painting cannot, by themselves, represent anything.

In Wittgensteinian terms, the logic of the language, or the conditions for the possibility of a language, can only be shown. Of themselves they do not say anything. So the ready-made or unfactured aspect of any artwork is a constant whether the work is a painting or a *readymade*.

When Duchamp mentions a tube of paint in his *Notes* he was observing that, in the case of painting, a tube of paint is equivalent to the status of the *readymade* prior to his choosing it and inscribing it with meaning, albeit in a most reduced but still discernible way. Even the minimally altered *Bottle Rack*, whose original inscription was lost, whose normal function is disrupted with the absence of the bottles (an absence reinforced by the title) and whose interdependence with the erotic suggestiveness of the rest of Duchamp's oeuvre is patently obvious, can no longer be regarded simply as a drying rack for bottles.

De Duve's other suggestion or postulation of a 'Blank Canvas' as a *readymade* to fill the gap between the Duchampian aesthetic dynamic and Greenbergian formalism depends first on an unwarranted reduction in the meaningfulness of the *readymades* to a mere cipher of formalist intent. Second, it begs the question about the credibility of the formalist train of art historical theorising that led by the 1940s to a form of art of monumental self-contradiction in that its spiritualist claim out of Kandinsky and Malevich came face to face with the resolute objecthood of the canvas.

Duchamp's position in relation to these high-flown claims was constant. When asked by Cabanne where his anti-retinal attitude derives from, Duchamp replied,

> From far too great an importance given to the retinal.... If I had the chance to take an anti-retinal attitude, it unfortunately hasn't changed much; our whole century is completely retinal, except for the Surrealists, who tried to go outside of it somewhat....[82]

De Duve's proposal of a tube of paint and a blank canvas as *readymades* arises from an attempt to demonstrate a formalist connection between the activities of Duchamp and the abstractionists as an antidote to Greenberg's excessive formalism and rejection of Duchamp's work. In the process, though, the significance of the *readymades* is so undervalued as to render them mute nominal ciphers divorced from all the artistic 'ideas' Duchamp claimed to be resurrecting from the content of the art of the past.

Kant and the beautiful

In *Kant after Duchamp*, Thierry de Duve applies his theory that Duchamp reduced art to the possibility of calling an object 'art' to Kant's understanding of the aesthetic. He considers the role of taste in the relationship between Kant's understanding of the 'beautiful' and Duchamp's rejection of the 'beautiful'. He proposes that the word 'beautiful' can now be replaced with the word 'art'.

Kant's preferred sense of the 'beautiful', though, was allied to Baumgarten's redefinition of the aesthetic to mean the ideal as the goal of art. Instead of appreciating the aesthetic as any form of sensation, Kant related the aesthetic to the absolute as the sublime, and to good taste. Although Kant was aware of the meaning of aesthetics as sensation unmediated by thought, he refused to accept that in the realm of sensations the 'disgusting' was logically the same as the 'beautiful'.

Instead he based his 'aesthetics' on the idea of 'aesthetic judgment'. But because an 'aesthetic judgment' is logically a combination of aesthetic and ethical processes it cannot be the unmediated reception of a sensation.

Since in Kant's philosophy the aesthetic includes the possibility of an 'aesthetic judgment', then it is not possible to substitute it for a nominalistic moment derived from the Duchampian aesthetic dynamic. Duchamp refused to entertain the ethical logic of taste or judgment as part of his aesthetic dynamic, and so he tacitly rejected Kant's idealised acceptance of the dynamic of taste.

In talking of the *readymades* with Don Morrison of the Minneapolis Star, Duchamp clearly stated his understanding that 'beauty' must incorporate the 'ugly'.

> I don't choose them for their beauty. Beauty is terrible because we accept it and it becomes commonplace and comfortable. Ugly doesn't mean anything either, because it's just beauty with a minus sign.[83]

If Kant said 'this is beautiful' and distinguished it from the sense of 'disgust' then he is simply making an ethical statement or an 'aesthetic judgment'. Whether he is evaluating nature, art, or his dog, he is making a statement of taste, or value. He is deciding consciously what he prefers in a particular circumstance.

If Kant was caught unawares and exclaimed, 'this is beautiful', and on reflection said, 'I just said that without thinking, but it accords with how I feel', then he has experienced an aesthetic effect. He may in fact exclaim 'this is beautiful' of something he had up to that time considered disgusting or at least not beautiful. Then he would reflect 'I just said that. I am surprised. It is contrary to what I have thought in the past, but it does accord with my current feelings'. Then that too is an aesthetic effect. A judgment by contrast is made consciously, it is logically an exercise of the will, it is a relation of ideas, and so is ethical.

The problem arises when the logic of ethics, of rational ideas, of discursive processes, of propositional language, is confused with the logic of sensations and perceptions unmediated by thought. A person may sense the appropriateness or inappropriateness of a possible course of action from a feeling or intuition, and feel inclined along a certain path. That is the aesthetic effect. But by itself, or if it was added without pause to one hundred other aesthetic effects, there would reign a set of countermanding impulses that would not amount to an ethical act.

The use of the capacity to reason, through the learnt development of a basic trait in conjunction with the aesthetic faculty, is what is required for reasoning and so for human conscience. But accepting human nature as an inalienable part of the logic of human understanding is foreign to the transcendental psychology of Kant, making his beliefs vulnerable to contradiction and nonsense. The logic of Duchamp's aesthetics and Shakespeare's aesthetics and ethics provides the antidote that renders the illogical logical.

If Kant transferred the determination of a judgment to the realm of aesthetics and that judgment is prejudiced in the sense that 'this is beautiful' refers to a particular standard of taste determined in advance, then Kant is not isolating aesthetics at all. He is making an ethical claim. The confusion arises because Kant, as do most thinkers, omitted a vital part of the ethic/aesthetic dynamic, the logics of the sexual/erotic priority that, ironically, is given expression in their traditional Christian mythology. The consequence of ignoring the logical basis of understanding in the sexual/erotic dynamic is the distortion of the aesthetic/ethic dynamic to compensate for the absence of sexual logic.

So to substitute 'this is art' for 'this is beautiful' merely perpetuates the illogicality that Kant generates about ethics and aesthetics. This is the unfortunate legacy of both *Pictorial Nominalism* and in *Kant after Duchamp*. They not only misrepresent Duchamp's intentions by claiming he wanted to reduce art to the possibility of saying 'This is Art', they also totally disregard his clarity about the logic of aesthetics. While Duchamp avoids the ethical he does so consistently because he accepts as a given the sexual/erotic dynamic in nature, which ensures the correct philosophic appreciation of aesthetics at a mythic level.

Rectifying Kant

Duchamp's work allows a critic to rectify Kant's confusion of the aesthetic and the ethical. Duchamp's consistent logic should have pre-empted the decision in *Kant after Duchamp* to replace Kant's patent contradiction with a glib formalist device.

The problem arises because Kant's rational idealism imparts aesthetic attributes to the ethical. His sense of transcendental ethics was no more than a sophisticated sense of aesthetics, just as his sense of aesthetic judgment was no more than ethics as thought or expression in action. Kant's confusion of the logic of ethics with the logic of aesthetics, while psychologically useful in compensating for the illogicalities of the male-based mythologies of the last 300 years, contributes nothing to the logical understanding of the dynamic of reason and sensations. Unless the two modes of awareness are kept clear and distinct contradiction and nonsense abound.

The difficulty arises because in practice the dynamic of ideas and sensations does not admit of discreet and extended moments in time in which one or the other is in operation. They operate continuously and in unison all the time, every moment, across the full range of possibilities from the sublime to the instinctive and from the clichéd to the philosophic. A thought can just as well result in the expression of an idea as result in a sensation, just as a sensation can lead immediately to the realisation of a rational distinction.

So an analytic process such as Kant's that decides to isolate one or the other for examination and definition confuses its own contribution to that process. An intense aesthetic response, to a sophisticated art work for instance, conditioned as it must be by rational considerations, can seem to have the characteristics of reason, but is no more than an immediate sensation or perception unmediated by thought. That such a sensation is surrounded, in effect, by thought, by deliberation, by criticism, does not alter the fact that it is a genuine sensation. Similarly the most deliberate of rational thought processes are subject to a 'eureka' or an 'uncertainty principle' where sensation or perception assert themselves regardless of conscious control.

Critically absent from the whole of Kant's writings is the issue of eroticism as a logical component of body/mind relation. When Kant talked of 'things in themselves' he imagined he was referring to a state beyond immediate perception. Darwin rectified Kant's confusion by demonstrating that 'things in themselves' are nothing more than our unthinking bodies and the unlanguaged world. Darwin argued that 'mental powers' and 'moral sense' are derived through the evolutionary process from more primitive versions of those faculties.

Other thinkers have developed Darwin's idea of the mind as a faculty derived logically from the body. George Lakoff and Mark Johnson, and Antonio Damasio, for instance, though they do not consider the erotic, present cases for the natural and logical relationships of body to mind. It is only another step to appreciate that the sexual is logically prior to the erotic. (See the essay on Lakoff and Johnson in Part 2.)

The absence of such considerations from Kant's philosophy leads to the telescoping of the logical consequences of their omission within the discussion of reason. His *Pure Reason* and to a greater degree *Practical Reason* are founded on a misconception as to the source of the reasoning function.

If for instance, Kant was determined to discover a logic that holds for any reasoning process regardless of the being in whom it is installed, then it is not logic he is investigating. Rather he is indulging in apologetics. Kant's determination to discover a moral maxim that holds despite all circumstances is equally illogical. Not only did he formulate various versions of his universal maxim to cater for the various applications, in some applications the maxim leads to contrary outcomes.

Kant's desire to establish reason as the superior faculty is consistent with his apologetic programme of establishing the priority and moral necessity of the male God. Darwin subsequently argued, on the basis of the evidence for evolution, that the faculty of reason is the outcome of the latest development in a process in which the body, the aesthetic, and the ethical have arisen over time.

So the order of priority is body, aesthetic, and then 'reason'. And, importantly, natural priority establishes precedence and not superiority. Darwin's apt title *The Descent of Man* has often been given the apologetic form 'The Ascent of Man' in popular programmes on evolution. The body can only be understood with nature as a given, the aesthetic can only be understood with nature and the body as a given, and the ethical can only be understood with nature, the body, and the aesthetic as givens. Duchamp is acutely conscious of the correct order of priority. In his final work *Etant donnes* he acknowledges the erotic as the basis of the aesthetic possibility.

Duchamp deliberately avoids the ethical and so avoids including the dynamic of reason in his work. He limits his work to the exploration of only one of the two modes of understanding. But the Kantian claim that reason is the most distinguishing human characteristic does not warrant the presumption that a consistent statement about the logic of being can be formulated without reference to the sexual/erotic dynamic of the body.

So Thierry de Duve's theory that interpolates mistaken understandings of Duchamp's philosophic insights into the illogical representations of Kant, and which uses the external form of Kant's deliberations as chapter headings for art historical musings, doubly misrepresents Duchamp's accomplishment.

Summary

In summary, I suggest that a refusal to account for the sexual in relation to the erotic in Duchamp's work leads to inevitable illogicalities in Thierry de Duve's understanding of the aesthetic and the ethical in *Pictorial Nominalism* and in *Kant after Duchamp*. And by focusing on a limited aspect of Duchamp's achievement he creates a distortion in the relationship between the *Large Glass* and the *readymades*.

Instead of recognising in Duchamp's work an expression of the philosophic conditions for the mythic possibility, de Duve reduces Duchamp's accomplishment to a formalist moment of simple naming. Not only does that position barely account for the influence of the *readymades* on the avant-garde of the mid to late twentieth century, it has absolutely no explanatory power for the mythic logic of the *Large Glass* or for the mythological works of previous centuries.

Before considering the comprehensive philosophy of Shakespeare's *Sonnets*, a brief examination of the contributions of Wittgenstein and Darwin is warranted. It should then be possible to appreciate better what the *Sonnets* offer as a rejoinder to the academic reduction of Duchamp's achievement to a mere formalist cipher.

CHAPTER 2

Ludwig Wittgenstein: the logical

The wrong paradigm

The inclusion of Ludwig Wittgenstein in this selection is not meant to suggest that his way of thinking, his understanding of the world, is in complete agreement with that of Mallarmé, Duchamp, Darwin or Shakespeare. On the contrary, Wittgenstein found himself unable to appreciate the greatness attributed by others to Shakespeare and did not believe the evolutionary process was capable of generating the qualities he valued in the human mind (see quotes below). The logic of eroticism, which is at the basis of the works of Mallarmé, Duchamp, Shakespeare, and even Darwin, had no apparent influence on his writings.

Because Wittgenstein operated within the proscriptions of traditional apologetic philosophy he took no account of the relation of the sexual to the erotic in his appreciation of the logic of language. Similarly, he excluded physiological sensations from his metaphysical sense of 'aesthetics'. He did entertain the idea, though, that language derived its capacity to represent the world from an inherent logical relation between the world and the mind. And he maintained that everyday language did not need logical reform because it already adequately represented the world.

But it is principally in Wittgenstein's later work, where he uses biological metaphors to account for the logic of language, that there is a suggestion of a logical connection between functions of the body and the operations of the mind. His later investigations move closer to the understanding of Mallarmé, Duchamp, and Darwin and Shakespeare.

While Wittgenstein takes no account of the logical implications of the sexual/erotic dynamic for the operations of the mind, neither can it be said that Mallarmé or Duchamp explicitly elaborated a position on the sexual. Both, though, did produce artworks that recognise the logical status of the aesthetic in terms of sensations, and an art conscious of its logical status as erotic. But unlike Wittgenstein, they did not purposefully engage with the ethical. Duchamp had an attitude of determined indifference towards anything that was not 'aesthetic' or reducible to sensation.

Darwin, though, did have a consistent and comprehensive appreciation of the relationship between the sexual dynamic and the dynamic of understanding in the human mind. In *The Descent of Man and Selection in Relation to Sex* he argues for the logical development of the human mind from evolutionary predecessors. He gives greater consideration, though, to the ethical or 'moral sense' than he does to the aesthetic. This is in keeping with his comment that his scientific researches allowed little time for artistic pursuits.

Because Darwin had little or no time to consider the aesthetic in depth he deferred to Kant, the most noted philosopher of his day. Darwin's clarity of insight belies the fact that Kant, as an apologist, was quite confused about both ethics and aesthetics. Kant took no account of the philosophic implications of sexual dynamic, so he misrepresents the priority of the body over the mind, and hence confounds the logical relation of aesthetics and ethics.

Kant, like anyone with an apologetic programme, was unable to present a consistent understanding of the operations of the mind. Kant cannot be understood, nor can Descartes, except as apologists. Both attempted to reconcile the processes of reason to their transcendental faiths. Along with Spinoza, Kierkegaard, Schopenhauer, and many others, they were apologists for their beliefs. Historically, philosophical apology or its complement scepticism were, like theology, no more than psychology disguised as philosophy.

Wittgenstein is the first professional philosopher to attempt systematically to present a philosophy free of the psychology of apologetics. Yet his work was still conditioned by residual elements of the traditional psychological programme. Wittgenstein's achievement was to establish a logical bridgehead beyond the psychology of apologetics while avoiding the indeterminacy of scepticism.

Wittgenstein's method

The philosophic method Wittgenstein introduces into Western thought stands in marked contrast to the methods of apologetic thinkers. It avoids Kant's disembodied transcendentalism as much as it avoids Hume's scepticism. His method treats philosophy not as a process of justification in which the formal methods of philosophy are used to give the appearance of rationality to a set of beliefs, nor as a means to counter those justifications. Rather it considers the philosophic as the pre-existing basis or dynamic for thought and language that enables effective expression in terms of the processes of life. Wittgenstein attempted to apply the method to the relationship between the world and language throughout his life.

Wittgenstein's method offers a philosophic approach capable of distinguishing between the philosophic basis of life and the psychological ramifications of apologia or ideology and their logical counterpart, scepticism. For apologists, the possibility of forming thoughts and ideas independent of other human beings is a prime condition for the possibility of an intelligent relationship with a transcendental entity such as God. Wittgenstein's arguments avoid the illogicality of such apologetic expectations.

When Descartes attempted to isolate the certainty of the subjective act of knowing, he hoped to demonstrate the independence of reason. Kant similarly isolated reason because he wanted to validate his belief in God. Likewise attempts to reshuffle the pack of reason, without addressing its logical basis in nature, failed for Schopenhauer as much as it does, in the final analysis, for Wittgenstein.

Wittgenstein's argument against the possibility of a private language in the *Philosophical Investigations* demonstrates the logical relation between language, as a human faculty, and life. In the private language argument he demonstrated, against the premises of his earlier work, that the only way to account consistently for human reason was from an understanding whose criteria were determined by the social function of language within the dynamic of life. In general terms Wittgenstein was moving away from the illogical belief in the priority of the ideal, toward a philosophic understanding that prioritised the processes of life, or, as he called the cultural manifestations of life, 'forms of life'.

Where the method failed

Wittgenstein's gradual development toward a sound philosophic method in his later period did not mean he applied the method consistently to all aspects of philosophy. He retained practices from the idealist philosophy of the *Tractatus*. Because he developed his new method from a critique of his earlier idealism, the method was not fully grounded in the logic of the dynamic of the body and mind. It was only in his last writings, in the collection of thoughts that constitute the book *On Certainty*, that he came close to such a possibility. Even though he worked toward a consistent application of his new method he did not correctly identify the basis of the certainty it engendered.

The residual idealism of his later work ensured he remained something of a Kantian, particularly in his confusion over the status and relationship of ethics and aesthetics. Wittgenstein's earlier position that 'aesthetics and ethics are one and the same' depended on just such a transcendental understanding of ethics as beyond the contingency of propositional discourse. In terms of the logic of aesthetic and ethics derived from Duchamp and Shakespeare this amounts to saying 'aesthetics and aesthetics are one and the same'. Wittgenstein never overcame the early influence of Schopenhauer's modification of Christian apologetics. Schopenhauer's elevation of the Will, following on the abstract tendency in thought epitomised by Hegel, to the transcendental throne merely perpetuated the reduction of ethical processes to the aesthetic.

Yet at the same time as Wittgenstein denied the possibility of the ethical to propositional language in his early work, he developed a complex theory of language to account for seemingly ethical concerns as the truth and falsity of propositions. These, he claimed, referred to contingent facts that supposedly had no ethical or moral status. Nor did his arguments acknowledge the logical status of aesthetics. His idealism prevented him from appreciating that aesthetics includes all possible sensations from the immediacy of pain to the apprehension of sublime unity. Nor did he explore the logic of understanding where a sensation, once named in the language dynamic, enters the domain of ethics.

Wittgenstein's dismissal, in the *Tractatus*, of Darwin's evolutionary ideas is symptomatic of his difficulties. He did not appreciate that Darwin was presenting verifiable facts in a way more logically sound than did the *Tractatus*. Darwin at least based his understanding on the human dynamic and not on speculations about atomic and molecular physics. To have both an awareness of profound sensations and a capacity to express sensations profoundly as language is what it means to be human in the Darwinian sense. (Shakespeare details the dynamic in the logical structure of his *Sonnets* and explores its ramifications in his poems and plays.)

Neither was it possible for Wittgenstein, out of his later theory of 'language games', to see the logical relationship between the language games of ethics and the language games of aesthetics. His philosophical position admitted of no unified reading that would show the logical connection between different games. He did not consider the possibility that the idea of language games carried a logical connection that accounted for the relation of 'language games' to the bodily dynamic.

Wittgenstein, however, did make some effort to modify his understanding of the transcendental. Rather than being a mystical realm beyond language, in his later work it became embodied in the limit of the actual, at the boundary of language. 'Value', both ethical and aesthetic, was at the limit of language and so still not expressible in language.

Darwin and Shakespeare avoid Wittgenstein's self-inflicted impasse by locating the source of logic, and so the possibility of language, in the sexual or bodily dynamic that ensures the continuation of human being. Not surprisingly Wittgenstein confessed in his notes and conversations an inability to comprehend the basis of Shakespeare's greatness. He also had great difficulty accepting that the evolutionary understanding of Darwin had sufficient 'multiplicity' to account for the complexity and depth of human understanding.

In his later work Wittgenstein was unable to overcome his acquired resistance to natural logic. His attempts to correct and supersede the flawed crystalline structure of the *Tractatus* failed because he was caught between the comfort of the old beliefs and an appreciation that logic is based in nature not God. Consequently, the *Philosophical Investigations* (like many of his posthumously published writings) was published as an 'album of notes'.

While Shakespeare, Darwin and Duchamp were able to produce structured philosophic works of great logical consistency, Wittgenstein failed miserably in his first attempt in the *Tractatus*, and gave up trying in his second attempt. Behind his failure is the shadow of Kant's overt apologetics in the *Critique of Practical Reason* following on the covert apologetics in the *Critique of Pure Reason*.

The trajectory of Wittgenstein's thought

Despite these considerations or difficulties, there is a trajectory followed by Wittgenstein's intense philosophic questioning from the early to the later periods that is relevant to the thoughts presented here.

A trajectory toward a greater consistency in the logic of language is absent from the writings of Hume or Kant. Hume, whose radical scepticism provoked the transcendental philosophy of Kant, was not able to relate his philosophical scepticism to the events of everyday life. And Kant's later thought is retrogressive rather than progressive as he moved to connect his early arguments with his beliefs.

The direction of Kant's thinking after the *Critique of Pure Reason*, with its prima facie case for the independence of reason, was compromised by the apologetic requirement of reintroducing the concepts of 'God, Immortality, and Freedom' into the area of practical reason. This was not an option favoured by Wittgenstein. He grounded his philosophy firmly in the facts of language, in the logic of everyday discourse. He was able to prevent everything but his most private reflections turning to such possibilities as a 'Last Judgment'.

If Duchamp offers an expression of the logic of aesthetics, or sensation, then Wittgenstein offers a persistent analysis of propositional language, which was anathema to Duchamp. At the same time Wittgenstein was attempting to detail the logic of language in the *Tractatus* (1914-8) Duchamp had successfully expressed the logic of aesthetics in the early schematic for the *Large Glass* (1912-5). Duchamp appreciated that the inexpressible was the aesthetic, while Wittgenstein thought it was both the aesthetic and the ethical. Both sought to proscribe language in favour of the inexpressible. That both thinkers were independently considering the relation of the two modes of understanding is an irony Duchamp may possibly have enjoyed, but one that was beyond the reach of Wittgenstein's crystalline world.

Consequently it is not surprising that Wittgenstein determined 'it is impossible for there to be propositions of ethics'. Yet he persisted in claiming in the *Tractatus* that propositions present the 'existence and non-existence of states of affairs', that they can be analyzed into the relationship between the 'true or the false', that they have 'truth-grounds', 'truth-functions', 'truth-operations', and that there can be the 'good and bad exercise of the will'.

Critics point out that Wittgenstein appears to want it both ways. On the one hand he claims that, because ethics is beyond discourse and can only be 'shown', all the propositions of the *Tractatus* are nonsensical, to be transcended so that one 'will see the world aright'[1] Yet he also said that only the propositions of natural science merit 'saying' because it is only in the scientific process that determinations are made between the true and the false.

Wittgenstein's conflation of aesthetics with ethics and his dismissal of ethical processes as non-ethical is a consequence of his adherence to the remnants of apologetics. Wittgenstein's distinction between the aesthetic/ethical as 'showing' and 'saying' as non-ethical confounds the natural division of understanding into sensations and ideas, or aesthetics and ethics. Some scientists such as Einstein, affected by the same corrupt paradigm, believed the scientific programme of discovery and verification of facts was a-moral.

Wittgenstein was unable to accept that the aesthetic is the dynamic of sensations and the ethical is the dynamic of ideas. It is not surprising then that he struggled to understand Shakespeare's achievement. Wittgenstein's Romantic flight from the ethics of discourse is an option Shakespeare rejects. Its direst consequence is the distortion of the logical relation between the aesthetic and the ethical.

The atomic model does not provide the correct multiplicity

Wittgenstein's basic intuition was that for language to be meaningful it must have the same logical multiplicity as the world it represents. In his early work the model he used to demonstrate the relationship was pre-determined by that used by his contemporaries in philosophy, Bertrand Russell and Alfred North Whitehead, which was in turn derived from the atomic physics of scientists such as Heinrich Hertz, Ludwig Boltzman and Ernst Mach. By analyzing language into atomic and molecular propositions in the *Tractatus* Wittgenstein thought he could show the one-to-one relationship between the micro-world of atomic physics and the logic of language.

Under the influence of scientific determinism and religious idealism, some atomic physicists did not doubt their capacity to locate the ultimate constituents of matter. Albert Einstein's unwillingness to accommodate the uncertainty inherent in quantum mechanics was a consequence of his faith in the capacity of language and reality to be, at some point, reconciled with the discoveries of atomic physics. He brought a religious fervour to his scientific investigations. His idealist philosophy of science was a form of apologetics. The logical consequence of the idealist attitude to science was that both Einstein and Russell considered science a-moral. In reporting the 'facts' of the world both idealists ignored the logic of language.

The young Wittgenstein was influenced heavily by their scientific idealism. It led to his denial of an ethical consequence to propositions, and the location of the ethical in the 'mystical'. Consequently the seemingly 'a-moral' microscopic world of atoms and molecules was the level of 'reality', or the 'describable' world, on which Wittgenstein based his logical structure of language. The expectation that elementary particles of physics could be equated with the constituents of language implied that human logic was derived from the atomic, or microscopic, dimension.

Ironically, the inability of science to isolate individual colours of the visible spectrum without implicitly referring to the rest of the spectrum led to the collapse of Wittgenstein's faith in discrete atomic objects as the logical basis for language. The basic units of meaning in the *Tractatus* could not represent the conventional names for colours in the spectrum. Although Wittgenstein's later work addressed the inadequacy of comparing human beings and their language to a model derived from atomic physics he never satisfactorily resolved the dilemma.

Once Wittgenstein realised the inadequacy of the atomic model for demonstrating philosophic consistency between the world and language, he began to move toward a model that more adequately accounted for the human dynamic in language. He shifted his focus from discrete atomic objects to the 'subjective' aspects of human observation, basic to the sense of indeterminacy in perception (which influenced Niels Bohr and others to formulate the uncertainty principle). Not surprisingly the reforming idealist in Russell did not understand the significance of Wittgenstein's abandonment of the theories of the *Tractatus* in favour of a deeper investigation into the living logic of language.

Wittgenstein's move from an idealised scientific model to one based in human propensities was still not rigorous enough to account for correct logical multiplicity between the world and language. He was not able to give his later thoughts, which took account of the vagueness in meaning, the logical structure of the early work. Only Shakespeare's *Sonnets* show how to combine the structural expectations of the *Tractatus* logically with the *Philosophical Investigation's* unstructured 'album of notes'.

The metaphor of life

Not only did Wittgenstein's later work look to language as human beings use it in everyday life, he began to use everyday 'life' as a metaphor for the description of the range of possibilities manifest in what he now called 'language games'. Phrases such as 'family resemblances' and 'forms of life' came to represent the type of multiplicity that language games exhibit in the language of everyday life.

Even Wittgenstein's sense of 'certainty' was founded on such givens as 'family' or 'parents'. In place of the abstractions based in atomic physics of his earlier work there was the gradual intrusion of biological metaphor into his descriptions of the function and limitations of language.

> What a Copernicus or a Darwin really achieved was not the discovery of a true theory but of a fertile point of view...I think there is some truth in my idea that I think only reproductively.[2]
>
> I can think of no better expression to characterise these similarities (between various forms of games as a model for the nature of Language Games) than 'family resemblances'; for the various resemblances between members of a family: build, features, colour of eyes, gait, temperament, etc. etc. overlap and criss-cross in the same way. – And I shall say: 'games' form a family.[3]
>
> Now it gives our way of looking at things, and our researches, their form. Perhaps it was once disputed. But perhaps for unthinking ages, it has belonged to the unthinking *scaffolding* of our thoughts. (Every human being has parents.) [4]
>
> I cannot say that I have good grounds for the opinion that cats do not grow on trees or that I had a father and a mother.
>
> If someone has doubts about it – how is that supposed to have come about? By his never, from the beginning, having believed that he had parents? But then, is that conceivable, unless he had been taught it?[5]
>
> The procedure in a court of law rests on the fact that circumstances give statements a certain probability. The statement that, for example, someone came into the world without parents wouldn't even be taken into consideration there. [6]
>
> Now I would like to regard this certainty, not as something akin to hastiness or superficiality, but as forms of life.[7]
>
> But that means I want to conceive it as something that lies beyond being justified or unjustified; as it were, as something animal.[8]

Wittgenstein's later work is transitional between the logical atomism of a Russell, and the acceptance of the biological level for philosophic structuring in the recent work of cognitive scientists such as Lakoff and Johnson in *Woman, Fire, and Dangerous Things*, *Metaphors We Live By*, *The Body in the Mind*, and *Philosophy in the Flesh*. (See essay 8.)

So instead of the microscopic modeling of the religion of science or the macroscopic modeling of the science of religion, Wittgenstein begins to use the intermediate or basic level imagery of the human form (basic level in the sense of a cognitive category). This is the level at which the human being operates for its evolutionary persistence through the sexual dynamic.

Symptomatic of the residual apologetic reluctance to accept the biological as the basic level of cognition was the above-mentioned difficulty Wittgenstein expressed about understanding Shakespeare.

> It is remarkable how hard we find it to believe something that we do not see the truth of for ourselves. When, for instance, I hear the expression of admiration for Shakespeare by distinguished men in the course of several centuries, I can never rid myself of the suspicion that praising him has been the conventional thing to do; though I have to tell myself that this is not how it is. It takes the authority of a Milton really to convince me. I take it for granted that he was incorruptible. – But of course I don't mean by this that I don't believe an enormous amount of praise to have been, and still to be lavished on Shakespeare without understanding and for the wrong reasons by a thousand professors of literature.[9]
>
> My failure to understand him could (then) be explained by my inability to read him easily. That is, as one views a splendid piece of scenery.[10]
>
> I do not believe that Shakespeare can be set alongside any other poet. Was he perhaps the creator of language rather than a poet.
>
> I could only stare in wonder at Shakespeare; never do anything with him.[11]
>
> The reason why I cannot understand Shakespeare is that I want to find symmetry in all this asymmetry.[12]

And in a conversation with Maurice Drury, Wittgenstein revealed the difficulty he had with the implications of Darwin's arguments.

> I have always thought that Darwin was wrong: his theory doesn't account for all this variety of species (in the Zoological Gardens, Dublin). It hasn't the necessary multiplicity. Nowadays some people are fond of saying that at last evolution has produced a species that is able to understand the whole process which gave it birth. Now that you can't say![13]

Wittgenstein's mistaken suggestion that Darwin presumed to 'understand the 'process' that gave birth to species is amplified by Drury's empathetic response,

You could say that now there has evolved a strange animal that collects other animals and puts them in gardens. But you can't bring the concepts of knowledge and understanding into this series. They are different categories entirely![14]

To which Wittgenstein replied, 'yes , you could put it that way'.

Summary

In his early work Wittgenstein failed to find an appropriate model for rendering the correct multiplicity between the world and language. His attempt to represent the logic of language was foiled by the scientific idealism in the *Tractatus*. The logical multiplicity he sought for the *Tractatus*, using the model of atomic physics, could not provide the appropriate relationship between language and the world. Wittgenstein's idealism led him to confuse the meaning of aesthetics and ethics by considering them 'one and the same'. And he designated propositions as true and false without attributing any sense of ethics to the rational processes of thought.

Wittgenstein acknowledged most of these failures and spent the second half of his life attempting to rectify them. He went beyond his contemporaries but was still conditioned in significant respects by residual aspects of his old way of thinking.

In Wittgenstein's later work the idealism of the *Tractatus* is replaced by his notion of 'language games' which conformed more closely with language as it is used by human beings in everyday life. He turned to biological metaphors to evoke the appropriate degree of multiplicity that language games involved. While his attitude to ethics did not change, he no longer held to the claim that the aesthetic and ethics are the same. The variety of uses of each word gives rise to the sense of interrelating language games. Their commonality is reduced to the idea that ethics and aesthetics are something inherent in 'forms of life', the boundary conditions without which any language has no community of usage, no community of purpose.

Wittgenstein does not, or was unwilling to, draw the obvious conclusion that language derives directly from the natural world. He does not accept that, for the human being, the mind is conditional on the body. In this regard he remained decidedly an apologist. His natural logic had not distilled itself sufficiently to appreciate the clear and simple logic of

Darwin's unconditional acceptance of life. A quote from Kant reveals the similarity of their struggle to counteract the consequences of their illogical programmes.

> The schematisation by which our understanding deals with the phenomenal world ... is a skill so deeply hidden in the human soul that we shall hardly guess the secret trick that nature here employs.[15]

I can take Wittgenstein no further. He is significant because he has enabled me to see more clearly the logical moves needed to correct the consequences in his work of an illogical agenda and in Duchamp's work of the effects of a logical but limited agenda and in Darwin's work of a logical but empirically focused enterprise. He points in the direction that helps make sense of Duchamp's narrowed focus on aesthetics to the exclusion of ethics. He points in the direction of Darwin's more comprehensive philosophic position. And they all point toward Shakespeare's complete and consistent philosophic system.

CHAPTER 3

Charles Darwin: the biological

Darwin's consistent method

It is helpful to look to Charles Darwin's philosophic method to appreciate better Marcel Duchamp's accomplishment, and then to relate their philosophic achievements to the even greater one of Shakespeare. Since Darwin's time, much has been discovered or revealed about the body/mind relationship through advances in science. No scientist, though, has presented empirical findings with the logical consistency of Darwin. No contributor to the understanding of the biological processes, and their relevance for an understanding of the mind, has exhibited a similar philosophic consistency and adherence to the evidence.

Darwin's evolutionary understanding establishes the logical relationship between the body and the mind or, in Wittgensteinian terms, between the world and language. Darwin's mind was free enough from personal and public prejudices and agendas to represent the relationship between the body and the mind with consistency.

Despite the completely different nature of their achievements, Darwin and Duchamp had similar temperaments. Duchamp's freedom from traditional prejudices ensured an appreciation of aesthetics that was logically sound. Their common ability to work without apologetic psychology can be combined with Wittgenstein's desire to understand the logic of human language to provide an insight into Shakespeare's achievement.

Misunderstandings

Since Darwin's day most contributors to the evolutionary literature have had difficulty disentangling their psychological expectations from the requirements of a consistent philosophic agenda based in nature. For instance, the atheist philosopher Anthony Flew wrongly criticised Darwin for championing an 'evolutionary ethics', in which the need for a species to evolve is seen as the highest 'good'. In his *Evolutionary Ethics*, Flew seems determined to discredit the influence of evolution on both physiological and psychological dispositions (including ethics) by demonstrating the inadequacy of evolution as the highest good. Yet Darwin never argued for a preferential course for evolution. Significantly, Flew resorted to the writings of others such as T. H. Huxley to make his case against Darwin. He ignores the clear evidence in Darwin's work for the logical relation between the body and the mind developed over evolutionary time.

Stephen Jay Gould, in his writings on evolutionary cycles, revived the nineteenth century debate over uniformitarianism and catastrophism. In his determined advocacy of catastrophism, based on such events as comet strikes, he seems to ignore the gradual process of re-speciation required to recover from such catastrophes. Instead Gould moves without demur from advocating the punctuated evolution of the catastrophic model to characterise the development of organic life from over billions of years as the perpetual age of bacteria.[16]

Gould's idealist agenda, which prioritises catastrophic events over the step-by-step process of gradual development, leads to inconsistent claims. His penchant for adversarial advocacy is in contrast to Darwin's philosophic exactness, adherence to the evidence, and, at worst, cautious speculation.

Daniel Dennett, in *Darwin's Dangerous Idea*, characterises evolution as algorithmic. He attributes to Darwin his own expectation that all designs in the biosphere could be products of such an algorithmic process.[17] Because the algorithmic process can seem 'automatic' or 'mindless' Dennett suggests the origin of life arose from just such a 'mindless' state. He reasons that,

> Artificial Intelligence says you are composed of automata because Darwinism says you are descended from automata.[18]

If automata preceded 'life', then according to Dennett,

> Whereas animals are rigidly controlled by their biology, human behaviour is largely determined by culture, a largely autonomous system of symbols and values, growing from a biological base, but growing indefinitely away from it. Able to overpower or escape biological constraints....[19]

Hence, he argues, a completely independent artificially intelligent being is feasible. Dennett as a supposed defender of Darwin uses a formal process based on algorithms to characterise the emergence of organic life as a sudden transformation from a mechanistic universe. He needs to postulate a mechanistic universe to reconcile the evolution of human understanding with his personal disposition toward the ultimate autonomy of artificial intelligence. Such counterintuitive and demonstrably illogical claims are typical of the distortions to which Darwin's philosophic rigour and reliance on evidence have been subjected.

It is not the purpose here to present the many misreadings of Darwin's work. Robert J. Richards examines the various agendas and argues forcefully that the clear and simple presentation of the basic issues by Darwin in the *Origin of Species* and *The Descent of Man* has been patently ignored.[20]

Evolution and the sexual

In the *Origin of Species* Darwin presents a compelling case for the natural process of evolution. He argues that all organic beings are descended from progenitors dating back millions rather than thousands of years and that they have varied significantly from those progenitors through a gradual process of biological change. One of the mechanisms that enables such changes to occur is the process of natural selection.

Though more has been revealed about the mechanisms of evolution since Darwin's time, the one fact that was evident then, and is a constant for sexual organisms, is the requirement for increase through the sexual dynamic. Every genetically unique individual is the consequence of the sexual dynamic. Every such individual is at the head of an unbroken line of cell division that necessarily extends back millions or billions of years. While food or other sustenance is essential for the life-span survival of an individual or social group it is the sexual dynamic that ensures the survival of the species into the next generation. Logically no amount of food or other sustenance can substitute for the sexual connection (see sonnet 11).

For the human being, evolution and the sexual dynamic are inseparable. The dynamic cannot be circumvented through technological advance. Because organic and inorganic life is a continuum, for a living human being to be artificially reproduced the whole of the universe would have to be recreated. It is not possible to isolate an individual from its connection to the universe without, as in the *Merchant of Venice*, spilling a 'jot' of genealogical blood in the process.

The arguments and evidence of Darwin's *Descent of Man and Selection in Relation to Sex* demonstrate the priority of the sexual as the crucial condition for human continuation. This is borne out in the organisation of the *Descent of Man* where Parts 2 and 3, or two thirds of its volume, are devoted to 'Sexual Selection'. Sexual selection is the mechanism for evolution allied to natural selection. Darwin examines the sexual and the erotic (what he calls secondary sexual characteristics) in various sexual species and considers their implications for human life. It is instructive that Darwin should devote a significant portion of his *Descent of Man* to sexual selection rather than some other requirement for human survival such as food or shelter.

Mental powers and moral sense

Part 1 of the *Descent of Man* was written in response to challenges made after the publication of the *Origin of Species*. Critics doubted that the process of evolution could account for the intellectual and moral faculties in humankind. In the *Descent of Man* Darwin argues that, just as physical characteristics are derived from progenitors, the attributes of the human mind can be accounted for by examining their rudimentary or less sophisticated form in other species. In the chapters on the 'mental powers' and the 'moral sense' he argues for the continuity of development of those faculties over evolutionary time.

In Part 1, Darwin was not arguing for what has become known as 'evolutionary ethics'. 'Evolutionary ethics' has been defined as 'a general theory that we value things and persons in accordance with their capacity to sustain and maintain survival in evolutionary terms'.[21] The definition suggests there is an inherent or necessary good in acting for the survival of the species above all else or that there is something in our genetic makeup that unequivocally conditions such a possibility.

But Darwin's text reveals no more than the clarification of the correct relationship between the physical attributes and the mental attributes of being. The requirement to survive is not an imperative as a species may well decide to become extinct voluntarily, or may do so accidentally. If an individual or a group wishes to survive beyond the current generation, then the sexual dynamic is the gateway for that possibility.

A mythology that proscribes sexual persistence cannot be taken literally. This is the case with idealistic belief systems such as Christianity. The Christian eschatological promise offers freedom from the natural processes of birth and death. Yet, inconsistently, Christianity is dogmatic in promoting the values of family life based in the sexual dynamic. The belief in the eschatological promise of a sexless life in heaven would have negative consequences for the continuity of human life on the planet if it were practised universally.

Darwin the philosopher

Darwin's analysis of the relation of the body and the mind is deeply philosophic. It is not prejudiced by traditional psychological expectations. His philosophic sensibility is evident in the logical organisation of *The Descent of Man and Selection in Relation to Sex*. After examining the derivation of mental powers and moral sense in Part 1, he examines the descent of 'man' as a sexual species and the function of secondary sexual characteristics (or the erotic) in Part 2.

Because Darwin remained relatively untutored in the philosophical sophistications of ethics and aesthetics, some of his comments lack the consistency of his insights into the evolutionary process. He expressed his deference toward Kant in some matters of philosophy. He used the word aesthetic in the reformulated sense discussed above, and bowed to Kant's thoughts on duty.[22]

Contrary to Kant, though, he had no doubt that the mind is logically derived through evolutionary processes from less developed species. In his discussion of mental powers and moral sense he uses evolutionary processes as a necessary given to present a logical picture of the mind. His criticisms of John Stuart Mill,[23] for instance, though not elaborate, are telling in their identification of the essence of the error addressed.

Darwin's philosophic method gives his work its enduring appeal. Not only did he treat the various points of argument with a philosophic rigour, the whole of his argument, beginning with the *Origin of Species*, was organised in a philosophic pattern to ensure its logical impact.

He based his argument on the principles of *vera causa* in which he presented evidence from known instances that were then generalised to explain events where direct evidence was not available. His rigorous approach to evidence gives the *Origin* a feeling of inevitability lacking in previous tomes that called on divine or other inexplicable causes. It should not surprise, then, that the structure of *The Descent of Man* replicates the relationship of the body to the mind.

Darwin argues that the processes of life and their evolution over time have the necessary multiplicity to account for the full range of mental and moral faculties of humankind. Darwin's logical clarity contrasts with Wittgenstein's denial that mental and moral dispositions had a natural explanation. The inability of Wittgenstein to appreciate the influence of physiological factors on the philosophic, yet his readiness to use biological metaphors to suggest multiplicity, show that his philosophical difficulties arose from the residual psychological expectations of the traditional paradigm.

The priority of the female

Another consequence of the reorientation of understanding along evolutionary principles is the recovery of the biological priority of the human female over the human male. Although the possibility of sexual differentiation implies a synchronised origin of female and male, the female retains the greater number of the characteristics from an asexual progenitor. The relation of x-x chromosomes in the human female to x-y chromosomes in the male, the inheritable elements in the larger cytoplasm of the female gametes, the requirement that the male return to the female for reproductive purposes, the child-bearing function of the female, all suggest the female is the basic unit out of which and back toward whom the male component travels.

Darwin reverses the philosophic priorities of biblical mythologies. By founding his system on the biological processes in which the female has priority over the male and in which the body is prior to the mind he corrects the root cause of inconsistencies in traditional apologetics. In Platonic, Augustinian, Thomist, Cartesian, and Kantian apologetics the male usurps priority over the female and the mind is given priority over the body. The psychology of apologetics attempts to demonstrate the autonomy of the mind to guarantee the non-biological status of the male God and the invincibility of the soul.

The failure of the apologetic project, particularly after the arguments of Hume, created a hiatus into which philosophers such as Kant, Hegel, Schopenhauer, and even Wittgenstein, further collapsed the understanding of ethics and aesthetics. As long as the illogical relationship of the mind to the body prevailed, metaphysics alone had to be the origin and repository of moral intent and artistic expression. The absolute, the ideal, the sublime, the moral good, were all seen to be inherent and inalienable characteristics of the incorporeal mind.

Kant, for instance, claimed that things in themselves (in one interpretation) were not knowable as they embodied the inaccessible state of pure being. And the early Wittgenstein argued that things 'showed' themselves in a way that language could only inadequately 'say' anything about. The function of philosophy was to determine the limit of sensible propositions and then consign the desire to know more to a mystical silence.

The characterisation of what is beyond knowledge or language as an unknowable or inexpressible lacuna created a metaphysical hiatus of an indeterminate nature. This is the abyss into which Kant was to reintroduce the concept of God, Hegel the concept of the Ideal, Schopenhauer the concept of the Will, and Nietzsche the concept of the Superhuman. The faculty of reason, logically the repository of ethical determinations, is reduced to a mere appendage that struggles futilely to reconcile itself with the unknown.

Out of the disarray of apologetic inconsistencies Duchamp organised his *Large Glass* on the logical principles consistent with those established by Darwin. He first acknowledged the priority of the female in nature. Duchamp's female or 'Bride' not only characterised the top half of the *Large Glass*, she also represented the whole of the *Large Glass*, making the *Large Glass* pre-eminently feminine. Appropriately then, Duchamp characterises the lower half of the *Large Glass* or the 'Domain of the Bachelors' as completely dependent on the priority of the feminine dimension for their existence. The same logical structure occurs with the priority of the female over the male in Shakespeare's *Sonnets*.

Body and mind

For Darwin, the scientific evidence confirmed that all the dispositions of the human mind could be accounted for through evolutionary processes. By giving priority to the physical over the mental in the evolution of the human species Darwin provides a logical basis for the discussion of mental powers and moral sense. Because evolution involves both body and mind, to leave the body out of philosophy commits a fundamental error in logic. The only way to present the logical relationship between the mind and the universe is by considering the logic of the development of the mind from bodily processes.

The human being (as with other organic beings) is dependent on cellular processes. For every human being the dependence is epitomised by its growth from a single cell at conception into a multi-cellular organism. The propagation of the species through the pairing of sexual cells to form a single cell is a perpetual reminder of the cellular logic of organic life. As cells are the basic unit of organic life from which the body and mind develop it is logical to expect that the developing body has a profound influence on the development of the mind.

Evolutionary arguments establish the priority of the body over the mind. Only when the priority of the body is acknowledged can progress be made in accounting for the nature of the mind. The 'mind/body' problem in traditional philosophy is a direct consequence of the apologetic belief that the mind is prior to the body.

As language developed in concert with bodily development over evolutionary time, the logic of the human body determines the logic of human cognition. Human language is a natural development of the more primitive languages of human forebears. The genealogical tree of evolution is a branching structure of successes and failures based on the structural unit of the dynamic that is the parent/child relationship. The same dynamic and multiplicity is exhibited in the relationship of sensations and ideas. The sexual dynamic of female and male uniting to form a child is directly analogous to the process of the interchange of ideas and sensations.

The possibility that ideas are based on 'difference' and sensations on 'indifference' is a consequence of the logical relation of the sexual dynamic and the conscious mind. That cognitive processes are logically related to the bodily dynamic is evident in structure of syllogisms and symbolic representations of mental structures, such as the Christian trinity. Consistent with natural logic is the mythological use of the tree in Genesis as a symbol for the relation of the dynamic of the mind to life processes.

Even without taking the sexual dynamic into account, Lakoff and Johnson and others have demonstrated an extraordinary conjunction between bodily dispositions and cognitive structures. Antonio Damasio[24] uses recent discoveries in brain functions to argue that there is a direct correspondence between the mind's capacity for thought and language and the structures and activities of the brain.

A philosophical system that discounts such facts reveals it dependence on psychological rather than philosophic criteria. Such expectations are apologia that compensate for the short-circuiting of the relationship between the mind and the world at large. When the 'body' is removed from the philosophic dynamic, its inherent sense of certainty needs to be accounted for within the mind alone. Certainty then becomes associated with the transcendental. While it is possible to entertain such thoughts it is useless to use them to account logically for human reason.

Inherent purpose

Darwin's recovery of the logical relationship between the body and mind also recovers the sense of purpose inherent in the processes of life. The sexual dynamic (female/male, child) has its logical counterpart in the dynamic of understanding (the ethical and the aesthetic). When the logical relation of body and mind is acknowledged there is no need to imagine a trans-ethical state beyond the knowable world.

Kant's transcendental ethic, Hegel's Ideal, and Schopenhauer's Will, are illogical consequences of the attempt to compensate for prioritising the mind over the body. Because the logic of body and mind is not respected, the apologetic need to verbalise such transcendental experiences of universal purpose or value fails to respect the logic of sensations or aesthetics.

The 'naturalistic fallacy' proposed by G. E. Moore in his *Principia Ethica* is also a consequence of an illogical conception of the ethical. While he criticised others for making the sensation of pleasure or other natural sensations the focus of ethics, he could not see that his inability to define 'good' arose from a confusion of ethics and aesthetics. Moore's singular 'good' is logically an aesthetic effect in the mind that is disengaged from the 'endless jar' of right and wrong in the ethical dynamic of language.

If Moore had begun his analysis of the ethical by acknowledging its derivation from nature and the sexual dynamic instead of beginning with the singular sensation of 'good' he would not have invented such a prejudicially named fallacy. Significantly, he considered 'evil' as an afterthought only in the last pages of his book instead of as an integral part of the logic of ethics.

A similar disjunction is created between 'is and ought' by Hume in *A Treatise of Human Nature*, and by others between 'fact and value'. They do not distinguish between immediate aesthetic of 'facts' as objects perceived through sensation, and the ethical determination of 'fact' or 'value' through the dynamic of ideas in the mind. A 'fact' can be knowledge arrived at through the process of deliberate judgment, as when a previously unknown planet is discovered through calculation or a hypothesised continent such as

Antarctica is discovered. In the dynamic of ethics, new facts are continuously being discovered and old facts re-evaluated according to new circumstances.

When apologists give the mind priority over the body, then both the ethical and the aesthetic are presumed to have originated beyond the mind, creating the illogicalities of idealist psychology. Logically, the effect of the traditional attempt to find moral purpose solely in the ideal as an absolute, and Moore's attempt to isolate the singular sense of good beyond the influence of facts, is the same. When the body/mind dynamic is represented illogically it is inevitable that 'values' will seem at odds with 'facts'.

If the body/mind priority is restored as the logical basis for understanding then the ethical is any consideration, determination, valuation, judgment, investigation that uses the process of 'difference' in language. Science as the pre-eminent discipline for understanding is not an 'a-moral' activity because it deals with facts, but is an inherently ethical activity because it determines true and false through language-based procedures. Because science is logically an ethical activity based in language, it follows that the phrase, 'science of ethics' is effectively a tautology.

The aesthetic, by contrast, is the realm of unmediated sensation or undifferentiated ideas. Any appeal to an absolute is logically an appeal to the aesthetic. Because there is no conscious knowledge of the absolute except as a sensation, the phrase 'science of aesthetics' is effectively a contradiction. The double capacity of the mind to simultaneously coordinate ideas and sensation is a logical consequence of the sexual dynamic of the body. The dynamic of the body relates the logic of ideal and sensations to the processes of life.

For Darwin, the moral impulse is inherent in life. Through the evolutionary process the human mind derives the dynamic of ideas and sensations from bodily relationships. The decision to withdraw value from the processes of science in the determination of 'facts' or 'natural laws' is a purely arbitrary one motivated by the desire to ignore the logical relation of the body to cognition. Similarly the decision to attribute moral value solely to what is the realm of aesthetics confers on the aesthetic impulse characteristics that are logically ethical.

It is possible for a sensation to determine a course of action. But the human being, by upbringing, by education, is so inured to immediately evaluate a sensation by rational processes that the tendency is to attribute to the sensation the characteristics of thought. It is the combination of the sensation with the conscious determinations of the will that characterise the activities of the human mind.

To name and describe a sensation after experiencing the sensation cannot substitute for the experience of the sensation. Likewise the sudden interjection of a word such as 'hell' or 'Christ' into the consciousness to signal an instantaneous intuition from the subconscious mind is as much a sensation as the sensation of pain. Usually the moment of intuition is surrounded quickly by conscious thoughts as the aesthetic and ethical dynamics interact.

Like Duchamp, and Shakespeare, Darwin recognises that nature is synonymous with the dynamic of life. A consistent understanding of the aesthetic and the ethical emerges only when the priorities in nature of the female over the male and the body over the mind is respected.

Summary

The little Darwin did write about the ethical and aesthetic is more consistent than the volumes written by Plato, Descartes or Kant. In Wittgensteinian terms the apologetic expectation can be characterised as the difference between believing in the reality of a set of imagined states of affairs in preference to a set of existing states of affairs.

Imaginative exercises within the mind become illogical if they are believed to be existing states of affairs. Humankind has survived, it may be argued, by bringing to fruition certain possibilities that were once only imagined. The problem arises when imagined states of affairs based in the deep sensations of the mind assume a certainty that is logically attributable only to existing states of affairs. A consistent philosophy cannot logically take account of such over-determined states of affairs without first recognising their illogical status.

Hume showed the inconsistency that arises in apologetic claims when states of affairs are over-determined. Hume, however, had little or no sense of the full dynamic of natural logic. His trademark scepticism was a logical consequence of his inability to see beyond his critique of the God of faith. He found, though, that he could not sustain his philosophical scepticism in real life. His confusion about 'is and ought' was a consequence of the irresolution between his scepticism and the existence of everyday things and events.

Darwin's evolutionary understanding of the body and mind consistently accounts for current states of affairs and allows for the potential existence of any possible states of affairs over time. It has the appropriate logical multiplicity to enable an understanding of both nature and of the dynamic of the human mind.

Darwin managed to arrive at a consistent understanding of the dynamic of the human mind even though he was not a professional philosopher. It is ironical that in forty years of philosophising Wittgenstein was only able to go part way toward Darwin's clarity about human existence and purpose. Instead, an artist with little love for the logic of language provides the fullest expression to the natural logic of life since Darwin. In his *Large Glass*, Duchamp presents an understanding of aesthetics that is consistent with the sexual dynamic from which Darwin derives his understanding of human thought and expression.

After reviewing some of the literature on Duchamp and considering the work of Wittgenstein and Darwin, it is apparent that Thierry de Duve's attempt in *Pictorial Nominalism* and *Kant after Duchamp* to account for Duchamp's work from the vantage of recent art history seriously misrepresents his accomplishment. The attempt to understand Duchamp's philosophy out of the phrase 'a sort of pictorial nominalism' and out of Kant's notion of 'aesthetic judgment' overlooks the natural logic of the *Large Glass*. Because neither nominalism as a philosophical style nor Kant as an apologist would accept the logical relation between the body and mind available in Darwin's *Descent of Man*, the analysis of Duchamp's work in *Pictorial Nominalism* and *Kant after Duchamp* does not begin to fathom its profundity.

Darwin's recovery of the body/mind relation provides a logical basis for incorporating the contributions of Duchamp and Wittgenstein into a consistent and comprehensive philosophy. It explains why Duchamp's seemingly offhand works have such an unlikely hold on the imagination and how they challenge psychological prejudices. Darwin's contribution to the understanding of natural logic presented in these volumes has been essential for a clear and complete understanding of the logical relationship between the works of Duchamp and the *Sonnets* of Shakespeare. And it is in Shakespeare's precise philosophic system that these issues are most consistently and comprehensively resolved.

CHAPTER 4

William Shakespeare: the Nature template

Review

In the previous chapters I considered the mythic dynamic in Duchamp's work, the use of biological metaphors by Wittgenstein, and the natural logic of Darwin's approach to his evidence for evolution.

An appreciation of the mythic logic behind Duchamp's understanding of aesthetics is essential for an appreciation of both his major works and the *readymades*. When evaluating the significance of his achievement it is necessary to take seriously his intent to revisit the level of artistic content that was a priority for artists before the formalist preoccupations of early twentieth century art. As this was his frequently stated intention, and as the analysis in *Pictorial Nominalism* and *Kant after Duchamp* merely furthers the formalist intrigues he wished to negate it is not surprising that Thierry de Duve was unable to fathom what makes Duchamp 'great'.

I have shown how Duchamp single-mindedly explored aesthetics to the exclusion of the other side of the human sensibility, ethics. Duchamp was presciently aware that the aesthetic involved the full range of sensations from the simple sensation of 'fear' to the sensation associated with the profound experience of a work of art. He called the aesthetic experience of a work of art the 'aesthetic echo'. His ambition to return art to the non-retinal impression of ideas was associated with the 'aesthetic echo'. He wanted to evoke the conceptual sensation of an idea rather than the 'retinal' sensation of a sensation. He considered that art, under the Realists, the Impressionists, the Cubists, the Expressionists and the Abstractionists had deteriorated to the lower end of the aesthetic spectrum of unthinking sensory excitation.

I have also noted that the pervasive eroticism in Duchamp's work is founded on the sexual dynamic. The sexual 'dimension', from the evidence of Duchamp's *Notes* and comments, is the unexpressed pre-condition for the *Large Glass*. The sexual dynamic, characterised as the 4th dimension, is prior to the erotic as the 3rd dimension. Duchamp was 'always serious' about eroticism because of its logical relation to the sexual as the a priori basis for human persistence. The sexual is the biological as physical consummation, and the erotic is the conceptual or the un-consummate product of the mind. Any form of human activity not directly biological is erotic, making artistic activity logically erotic. Hence Duchamp's characterisation of all his artistic activity as invariably 'erotic'.

In both his attitude towards the aesthetic and the erotic Duchamp was influenced by Mallarmé. Mallarmé wrote of evoking the effect produced by a 'thing' in the mind rather than describing the external aspects of the thing itself. And his deeply symbolic poetry shows he was fully aware of the sexual/erotic dynamic.

The work of Wittgenstein was used to introduce the role of language to complement the understanding of art or aesthetics developed by Duchamp. Language as a mode of understanding was ignored or even denigrated by Duchamp, and for his part Wittgenstein was never clear about the nature of aesthetics. Just as all sensation is logically the dynamic of aesthetics, propositional rational language is logically the domain of ethics. As a consequence of Wittgenstein's failure to find a logical system that provides the correct multiplicity between the 'world' and 'language' in terms of atoms and molecules, he moved toward a philosophy that used biological metaphors. Ironically, this was despite his lifelong prejudice against Darwin's evolutionary ideas.

Darwin investigated the logical role of sexuality in human evolution and understanding. He argued that 'mental powers' and the 'moral sense' could be derived through the evolutionary process. On the basis of the evidence he showed there is a logical relationship between the sexual and human understanding, between the body and the mind.

It is now possible to align these contributions with the comprehensive philosophy articulated in *Shake-speares Sonnets* of 1609. The *Sonnets* present the natural logic of the human mind in relation to the world about. The logic of the *Sonnet* dynamic can be evaluated by its self-consistency and by its success in accounting for the consistencies and inconsistencies in the works and statements of Duchamp, Wittgenstein, and Darwin.

In the mid-to-late 1980s, well before I encountered the *Sonnets* of Shakespeare, I derived from my investigations of the above thinkers a rudimentary form of the philosophic understanding basic to an appreciation of the *Sonnets*. The rudimentary understanding has provided a critical reference point around which the logical connections between the philosophic insights of Duchamp, Wittgenstein, Darwin and Shakespeare have become clearer over the last few years.

The *Sonnets*

The material presented here has been derived since 1995 from a study of *Shake-speares Sonnets* of 1609. I will be focusing on the *Sonnets* because Shakespeare specifically presented and gave mythic expression to his comprehensive philosophic understanding in the set of 154 sonnets. As Shakespeare uses it, the sonnet form is the most effective way to express a profound philosophy that incorporates the logic of myth. Shakespeare's philosophy rejects the psychologically based philosophy of the last few millennia that seeks to rationalise biblical beliefs. (See the essay on Stephen Booth and Helen Vendler.)

The philosophy of the *Sonnets* articulates the philosophic basis for all Shakespeare's plays and other poems. Because the plays have a specialised role as theatrical narrative, the philosophy is the given behind the facade of the interface with the audience. The *Sonnets* by contrast are designed principally for contemplation. As anyone who has read them for the first time will attest, their intricate ideation and patterning can give rise to the simultaneous experience of immense attraction and utter bewilderment.

A reading of the *Sonnet* literature reveals, virtually without exception, that the apologetic paradigm has been applied inappropriately to the *Sonnets* of Shakespeare for the last 400 years. The result is that the *Sonnets* have been considered mysterious, arcane, esoteric, nonsensical, badly edited to the point of requiring emendations, embarrassing, having no philosophy, with an endless litany of other complaints that do no more than conceal that the *Sonnet* commentators are philosophically at odds with the *Sonnet* philosophy.

The classic comment must be that of William Hazlitt who would have otherwise considered himself an expert on the plays.

> (The *Sonnets*)... I think overcharged and monotonous and as to their ultimate drift... I can make neither head nor tail of it.[25]

The *Sonnets* have been reduced to little more than a biographical battleground regardless that such a reading of a great piece of literature is the lowest possible level of interpretation. A. L. Rowse must be the champion of the diversionary art of solving the biographical mysteries of the *Sonnets* by the naming of lords and ladies. Only a bare handful of commentators are prepared to question the mindset that has given rise to such beleaguered bewilderment.

The uniqueness of the *Sonnets*

Duchamp is unique in presenting a critical understanding of the aesthetic dimension of myth that corrects the illogicalities of apologetics in art. No other artist, or recognised philosopher, has accomplished such a rigorous pictorial presentation of the mythic dynamic. No other artist has created a tour de force as consistent as Duchamp's *Large Glass* and neither has anyone isolated *readymade* objects from everyday life with such critical mythic depth. No visual artist of the last 2000 years has developed such a consistent understanding of aesthetics as Duchamp. And no one yet has presented a consistent understanding of Duchamp's achievement.

It is symptomatic of the pervasiveness of the influence of the apologetic syndrome of the last few millennia that the more comprehensive and consistent philosophy of William Shakespeare has not been recognised in 400 years. Shakespeare does not rate a mention in the philosophical dictionaries whereas the apologetic psychology of Augustine, Aquinas, and Dante, and others is represented without question.

Even those indisposed to acknowledge the *Sonnets* philosophic worth acknowledge that *Shake-speares Sonnets* are unique. While T. S. Eliot accuses Shakespeare of making, 'great poetry out of an inferior and muddled philosophy of life',[26] and that the pattern in his work was, 'the poorer by a rag-bag philosophy',[27] he acknowledges that Shakespeare's pattern was 'more complex and his problem more difficult than Dante's'.[28]

Because Eliot regarded Dante's 'Christian philosophy' highly, he cannot believe that Shakespeare,

> who has no 'philosophy' and apparently no design upon our behaviour, sets forth his experience and reading of life, he is forthwith saddled with a 'philosophy' of his own and some esoteric hints towards conduct.[29]

Both in the popular mind and in academic commentaries, however, the uniqueness of the *Sonnets* has been persistently associated with the perceived harshness or judgmental relationship that the author is reckoned to have had with a youth and a woman. For instance, Wordsworth, from his Romantic perspective, remarks,

> These sonnets beginning at 127 to his mistress are worse than a puzzle-peg. They are abominably harsh, obscure and worthless. The others are for the most part much better, have many fine lines and passages. They are also in many places warm with passion. Their chief faults – and heavy ones they are – are sameness, tediousness, quaintness, and elaborate obscurity.[30]

Eliot and Auden's introductions reveal such conceitedness as to the superiority of the apologetic/romantic paradigm that history will principally record their inability even to begin to appreciate the comprehensive philosophy Shakespeare embodied in his *Sonnets*.

Ted Hughes, who attempted to understand the mythic depth of Shakespeare's plays in his *Shakespeare and the Goddess of Complete Being*, also adhered to the limited apologetic paradigm. His analysis of the mythical dimension in the plays is flawed by his expectation that Shakespeare was committed to a Neo-Platonist or Gnostic perspective. His dismissal of the increase sonnets as 'persuasions of hired labour'[36] and his assertion, based on Christian morality, that sonnets 116 and 129 were the key to understanding of the *Sonnets* leaves the majority of the sonnets unaccounted for and pivotal sonnets overlooked or denigrated.

Only a few commentators sense a profoundly logical sequence even though they are unable to determine its philosophic rationale. Benedetto Croce wrote that,

> Shakespeare does not cease to be Poet, because he is never altogether able to separate himself from himself, everywhere he infuses his own thought and modes of feeling, those harmonies peculiar to himself, those movements of the soul, so delicate and profound. This has endowed the *Sonnets* with the aspect of biographical mystery, of a poem containing some hidden moral and philosophical sense.[31]

Coleridge also had an intimation of a greater purpose and design with his reference to the 'condensation of thought' in the *Sonnets*.

Garry O'Connor, in his factional account of the life of Shakespeare, makes some interesting speculations about the genesis and final form of the *Sonnets*.

> We are led, then, inexorably to this conclusion: the original ordering of the *Sonnets* is highly professional. Only one person was capable of such professionalism: i.e., the author himself. Shakespeare definitely wanted the *Sonnets* published and he delayed this until 1609 because he, too, was seeking an imaginative unity in the poems through his subtle and careful ordering..... He wanted the mystery: he orchestrated the obscurity.....[32]

Despite this expectation, O'Connor had no answers.

> Even so, a final coherence eluded him. And this is not surprising. The *Sonnets* describe so many disparate aspects of vanity and sexual experience, yet in many of them the very distillation of the thought expressed deprives it of continuity. To try to arrive at the perfect sequence was the final experiment he could conduct with this form: no doubt he found it highly enjoyable.[33]

In Thierry de Duve's reading of Duchamp's work, he advances no ideas as to how the *Large Glass* and the *readymades* are interdependent and advances no ideas regarding the structural dynamics of the *Large Glass*. Shakespeares Sonnets have suffered from a similarly low level of expectation. Those, such as Paz or Hughes, who do have an apprehension of something more significant, have not produced readings consonant with their expectations.

The logical dynamic of life

The understanding outlined here is unique in the *Sonnet* literature. It was made possible by the study of thinkers who have challenged the traditional paradigm with philosophic precision. Of those, Marcel Duchamp has contributed most to the possibility of understanding the mythic depth of the *Sonnets*. His is the only work to express the mythic dynamic at the heart of the *Sonnets* comprehensive philosophy.

It is somewhat ironic that Thierry de Duve's attempts to isolate and interpret the *readymades* should be based on a misunderstanding of the nature of the 'mythological'. While it is true that mythologies become dated, at issue here is the philosophic conditions for the mythic level of expression, the logical conditions for the philosophic possibility of the mythological.

Attempts to understand Duchamp's achievement in mythological terms, such as those of Schwarz and Paz, commit the alternate error of looking hopefully to the Classical, Medieval, Eastern, or Renaissance world of pseudo-science and pseudo-religion in an effort to do justice to Duchamp. In neither case is the mindset of apologetics circumvented. In none of the cases is the logical dynamic of life appreciated. Duchamp expressed a sense of being at ease with life: 'To live is to believe; that's my belief, at any rate'.[34]

He was happy with his lot in life and was bemused by the way good fortune aided his work. For most of his life he was a confirmed bachelor but surprised himself by enjoying his marriage in 1954 to Teeny Slater. The inscription on his gravestone leaves no doubt that he felt life needed no apology.

...AND BESIDES / IT'S ONLY THE OTHERS THAT DIE

By all accounts Shakespeare was similarly a man at ease with life. He did not share the expectation of transcendental immortality that was common amongst his contemporaries and has been wrongly attributed to him by many commentators. In the plays, he suggests human beings are like actors on a stage, who should make the most of their 'brief' lives. He had a sound philosophy based in nature that led to a consistent understanding of the persistence of human life through 'increase', the process without which there would be no human beings and hence no human understanding.

The relation of the *Large Glass* to the *Sonnets*

The next few sections will examine the direct correspondence between the mythic content of Duchamp's *Large Glass* and the aesthetic component of the complete mythic dynamic of *Shake-speares Sonnets*. It will become apparent why Duchamp was led to conceive the minimal statement of the *readymades* in conjunction with the *Large Glass* while Shakespeare was able to maximise, in his 36 1623 *Folio* plays and four longer poems, the philosophy expressed in the *Sonnets*. To appreciate the correspondences between the *Large Glass* and the *Sonnets* their principal features will be compared.

It is worth noting in passing that Duchamp's final work, *Etant donnes*, and the allegorical poem that occurs after the *Sonnets*, *A Lover's Complaint*, both give a more allegorical expression to the philosophy of their parent works, the *Large Glass* and the *Sonnets*. The increase in realism gives the secondary works a tantalising sense of immediacy.

The basic structure and numbering of the *Large Glass*

The whole of the *Large Glass* represents the all-encompassing priority of the female in nature. Duchamp stated that he considered the whole work to be the Bride. Steefel reports that 'Duchamp stressed the fact that not only the female image (the Bride of the top half) but the *Large Glass* as a whole was the Bride'.[35]

The whole work is unified under the aegis of the Bride or female dimension. It logically represents the state of being prior to the division in nature of the male from the female. The masculine element, the 'Bachelor Machine', derives its energy, its life, from the 'Desire Motor' of the Bride. The whole work as a major unity can be represented as 1.

$$\text{The whole of the } Large\ Glass = \mathbf{1}$$

The *Large Glass* is divided into two parts. The top half is the Domain of the Bride and the bottom half is the Domain of the Bachelors. The Bride is positioned above the 9 Bachelors to indicate the priority of the female over the male. It is clear from Duchamp's notes that the 9 Bachelors, as the male element, are dependent on the Bride for their existence. The Bride in the top half of the *Large Glass* represents the priority of the human female within nature.

The top half as a minor unity can also be represented as 1.

$$\text{The top half of the } Large\ Glass = \mathbf{1}$$

The lower half of the *Large Glass* is the 'Bachelor Machine'. The Bachelors' existence is conditional on the potentiality of the Bride. They are the 'brick base' on which she flourishes. Initially there were to be 8 Bachelors but Duchamp revised this number to 9. He explained that 3 is the number for generality and this corresponds to his use of 3 in other works such as the *Standard Stoppages*.

The bottom half of the *Large Glass* can be represented as 9 (Diag 1).

$$\text{The bottom half of the } Large\ Glass = \mathbf{9}$$

Because the Bachelors are wholly dependant on the Bride it is interesting to note that the change from 8 Bachelors to 9 allows the Bachelors to be summed with the 1 of the Bride to reconstitute the major unity of

WILLIAM SHAKESPEARE: THE NATURE TEMPLATE

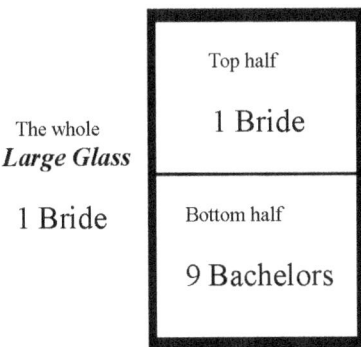

DIAG 1: *The numerology of the* Large Glass

the all-determining female dimension. The *Large Glass* can be represented by the equation (by the process of mystic addition).

9 (Bachelors) + **1** (Bride) = 10 = 1+0 = **1** (Bride)

The significance of the numbering will become obvious when the *Sonnets* are considered.

Despite his acute intuition of the required numerical relationship between the Bride and the Bachelors, Duchamp did not appreciate the logical significance of the numbering and had no idea of its role in the *Sonnets*. By the standards of his own 'art co-efficient' there is much in his work that was unintentionally present. His focus on aesthetics to the exclusion of ethics and the non-inclusion in the *Large Glass* of the sexual or the role of the artist also indicates there is much in his work that was intentionally absent.

The basic structure and numbering of the *Sonnets*

Before summarising the principle features of the *Sonnets* it should be noted that the understanding presented here derives from *Shake-speare's Sonnets* exactly as Shakespeare published them in 1609. It accepts that Shakespeare began writing the *Sonnets* in the 1590s and in the period leading up to their publication in 1609 compiled and revised them in a way consistent with his philosophic understanding. All the reordering, emendations, biographical conjecture, and speculation about their authenticity that has occurred over the last 400 years is symptomatic of the application to the *Sonnets* of the inappropriate apologetic or other paradigms.

Shakespeare was influenced by his predecessors and contemporaries in a number of ways. The *Sonnets* have a numerological structure that could have been a response to the numerology employed by Dante in the *Divine Comedy* and more directly to that of his contemporary Sir Phillip Sidney in *Astrophel and Stella* and in the sonnet sequences of Samuel Daniel and Michael Drayton. Whereas the numerology of Dante supports a classic work of apology, which divides equally into three parts and has '100' cantos that represent the theological divine, and Sidney's is a literary pattern based on an aspect of Homer's *Odyssey*, Shakespeare's system has a whole and parts that relate directly to an all-encompassing mythic structure of philosophic precision.

The numerological values are derived through the process of mystic addition. In the case of Dante's 100 cantos, the divine unity is determined by adding the individual numerals of the 100 together to give $100 = 1+0+0 = 1$. Other significant numbers such as 145 ($145 = 1+4+5 = 10 = 1+0 = 1$) add to a unity. To my knowledge this process has not been applied to Shakespeare's *Sonnets*.

There are a total of 154 sonnets. The whole set of 154 sonnets represents 'Nature' or the sovereign mistress. This is made explicit in sonnet 126.

> Nature (sovereign mistress over wrack)
> (Sonnet 126.5)

The 154 sonnets add to a unity giving nature a value of 1.

$$154 = 1+5+4 = 10 = 1+0 = \mathbf{1}$$

The *Sonnets* are divided into two parts of 126 and 28 sonnets. The break at sonnet 126 separates the 126 sonnets to the 'Master Mistress' or youth from the 28 sonnets to the 'Mistress' (misleadingly called the dark lady in the literature). The 28 sonnets to the Mistress are addressed to a female. The Mistress' value of 1 indicates the human female's logical relation to nature.

$$28 = 2+8 = 10 = 1+0 = \mathbf{1}$$

The 126 sonnets to the Master Mistress or youth are to a male. Their numbering identifies the youth's logical relation to the Mistress. His numerological value of 9 acknowledges her priority.

$$126 = 1+2+6 = \mathbf{9}$$

The principal elements can be represented in a diagram (Diag 2).

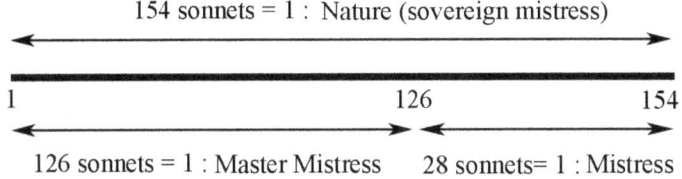

DIAG 2: **The numbering of the principal elements of the** Sonnets

Giving the numerological values,

    sovereign mistress (Nature) $154 = \mathbf{1}$

    Mistress $28 = \mathbf{1}$

    Master Mistress $126 = \mathbf{9}$

Unique to the *Sonnets* and not appreciated in the *Sonnet* literature is that the 'Poet' of the *Sonnets* has a crucial structural role in the numerology. The Poet, as the person who appreciates the relation between the Mistress and the Master Mistress, and acknowledges his logical place in nature, is associated with the number 145. The 145 reflects the Poet's more elemental human nature compared with the more complex 154 of nature at large. The Poet appreciates, but does not fully comprehend, nature.

    Poet $145 = \mathbf{1}$

The only other personality or persona in the *Sonnets* is the Alien Poet. He has no structural part to play because he is merely the unaccomplished form of the Poet, an inferior poet who focuses on form ('rhyme' and 'style') rather than content ('love'). He represents the prospect for the Master Mistress if he does not heed the advice of the Poet. The sequence of 9 Alien Poet sonnets, from sonnet 78 to 86, links him logically with the number 9 of the Master Mistress.

The *Large Glass* and the *Sonnets*

The basic structure of the *Large Glass* and the structure of the *Sonnets* can now be compared.

Large Glass		*Sonnets*
Bride (the whole *Glass*)	= **1** =	Nature, sovereign mistress
Bride (the top half)	= **1** =	Mistress
Bachelors	= **9** =	Master Mistress

The Bride, as the whole *Glass*, corresponds to nature, the sovereign mistress. The Bride, the representative of womankind, corresponds to the Mistress. The Bachelors, the male element, correspond to the Master Mistress or youth. In both cases the male dimension is characterised as 1 short of unity. The male requires the 1 from the female dimension to restore him to unity.

$$9+1 = 10 = 1+0 = 1$$

The logical requirement for the male to return to the female reinforces the inherent unity of the female and accords with the unity derived from the larger unity that is nature. The male needs to return to the female to restore the unity lost when he differentiated from the female in the biology of evolution. The male cannot be represented by the number 8, for instance, as 8 + 1 = 9 would still leave him 1 short of attaining the required unity.

Duchamp does not incorporate a persona for himself as artist into the *Large Glass*. As the artist does not feature in the work there is no role comparable to the Poet of the *Sonnets*. The feminine persona *Rrose Selavy* that Duchamp created for himself has an aesthetic role more in keeping with the reduced function of the *readymades*. It does not encapsulate or critique the artist's role in conceptualising the *Large Glass*.

The absence of Duchamp as artist from within the *Large Glass* can be explained by considering his attitude toward the individual. Duchamp's extreme sense of individuality precluded the possibility of representing the artist's generic function within of the erotic dynamic of the *Large Glass*. Duchamp's singular focus on the aesthetic drew the singularity of the individual into the zone of indifference or non-difference. The imbalance led to his willingness to emphasise the role of the 'public' in determining what was 'art' for any particular period.

For our purposes it is sufficient to recognise something of the numerological consistency between the *Large Glass* and the *Sonnets*. It would seem Duchamp arrived at the basic mythic numbering purely through the acuteness of his intuition. Because both Duchamp and Shakespeare were considering the logical conditions for the expression of the mythic possibility, it is no coincidence that the three logical elements of the *Glass* and the *Sonnets* are the same.

A logical numbering system

The numerological system within the *Large Glass* and the *Sonnets* is philosophic. It does not represent an arcane, esoteric, or alchemical system of symbolism. Duchamp was indifferent to attempts to understand his work using such practices. If alchemical references were apparent in his work, then the associations were fortuitous. Similarly in sonnet 14, a crucial sonnet in the logic of the whole set, Shakespeare dissociates the logic of truth and beauty from astrology, alchemy, heaven, or the whim of Princes.

> Not from the stars do I my judgment pluck,
> And yet methinks I have Astronomy,
> But not to tell of good, or evil luck,
> Of plagues, of dearths, or seasons quality,
> Nor can I fortune to brief minutes tell;
> Pointing to each his thunder, rain and wind,
> Or say with Princes if it shall go well
> By oft predict that I in heaven find.
> **But from thine eyes my knowledge I derive,**
> **And constant stars in them I read such art**
> **As truth and beauty shall together thrive**
> (Sonnet 14.1-12)

The precise numerology common to Duchamp and Shakespeare elegantly configures the logic of life. The relation of the sexual and the erotic in nature and the relation of ethics and aesthetics (or truth and beauty) are given form through a basic mythic numbering.

The sexual and the erotic in the *Large Glass*

The sexual, which is the 'given' or the logical precondition for the erotic, is not accounted for in the *Large Glass*. Only by omission does Duchamp distinguish between the sexual as the biological dimension and the erotic as the artistic dimension. The relation of the sexual to the erotic is implicit in the *Large Glass*' mythic logic. The elements in the *Large Glass* are characterised wholly in the erotic.

In his *Notes* Duchamp calls the sexual and the erotic the 4th and the 3rd dimensions respectively. The 4th dimension as the sexual does not, or logically cannot, appear in the 3-dimensional *Large Glass*. The *Large Glass* is orientated toward one mode of understanding, the aesthetic.

The sexual and the erotic in the *Sonnets*

In the *Sonnets*, the inclusion of the sexual in the increase sequence enables a representation of both modes of understanding, the aesthetic and the ethical. The *Sonnets* are organised to delineate the logical relation between the sexual and the erotic.

The sovereign mistress, or Nature, is represented by the whole set of 154 sonnets. The sexual differentiation into female and male is represented by the division of the 154 sonnets into the 28 Mistress (female) and 126 Master Mistress (male) sonnets. The priority of the female over the male is indicated both by the logical characterisation of Nature as 'sovereign mistress' and by the respective numbers assigned to the Mistress (1) and Master Mistress (9). The *Sonnets*, as does the *Large Glass*, corrects millennia of contradictions generated by the illogical prioritising of the male (God) over the female.

The simple structural arrangement of the *Sonnets* presents the logical status of human nature as a sexual species derived from nature (Diag 3).

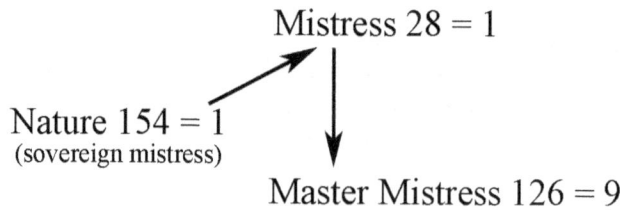

DIAG 3: *Nature female/male template (Sonnets)*

The configuration forms the primary template for a consistent philosophy. It establishes the logical basis for deriving the erotic dynamic of the mind from the sexual dynamic of the body.

The first 14 sonnets of the Master Mistress or youth sequence then give expression to the second part of the sexual dynamic. Shakespeare structures into the beginning of his set of sonnets the logical consequence of the sexual division into female and male. He presents the increase argument in sonnets 1 to 14, and argues for the logic of increase as the natural dynamic for human persistence.

The deliberate inclusion of the sexual dynamic in the set of the *Sonnets* embodies an element not represented in the *Large Glass*. It seems that no other set of sonnets or work of art incorporates such a decided and organised statement of the priority of the body over the mind. If only in this respect the *Sonnets* of Shakespeare are unique in the literatures of the world.

It is worth remembering that the increase sonnets are the most denigrated sequence in the *Sonnets*. They have been variously dismissed as 'juvenilia', 'marriage sonnets', and 'the labour of hired persuasion' by Ted Hughes,[36] or as having a literary tautological relationship with copying by John Kerrigan.[37] Another claim made frequently is that the subject matter of the increase sonnets is unrelated to that of the remaining sonnets. Against these prejudices it is inescapable that, in the 1609 edition, they do begin the whole set of 154 and they read as a consistent sequence devoted entirely to the topic of increase. And there are many references and allusions throughout the rest of the *Sonnets* to the pivotal ideas first introduced in the increase sonnets.

In the *Sonnet* logic the increase sonnets are a group that logically precedes the remaining sonnets. The remaining sonnets present the truth and beauty dynamic in full awareness of the mind's erotic status in relation to the sexual dynamic of the body. For the human being increase is logically prior to truth and beauty. Not only is increase prior to truth and beauty but the mind derives its dynamic from the increase potential.

Shakespeare would have purposefully chosen the word increase to convey the sense of genealogical persistence. Increase is the single most determining factor in human survival and individuality. The increase sonnets emphasise that all human beings are born.

> Thou art thy **mother**'s glass and she in thee
> (Sonnet 3.9)

You had a **Father**, let your Son say so.
(Sonnet 13.14)

The contention is not that procreation is a necessary activity for every human being, but rather that logically if all human beings, in imitation of the youth, decided not to increase humankind would cease to exist.

Herein lives wisdom, beauty, and increase,
Without this folly, age, and cold decay,
If all were minded so, the times should cease,
And threescore year would make the year away:
(Sonnet 11.5-8)

Shakespeare ties the possibility of 'love' to this logical realisation.

Is it for fear to wet a widow's eye,
That thou consum'st thyself in single life?
...
No love towards others in that bosom sits
That on himself such murd'rous shame commits.
(Sonnet 9.1-14).

The first 14 youth sonnets specifically argue for the logic of increase because the youth, as a male, is required to return to the female for the continuation of humankind. Each increase sonnet makes a literal case for persistence through sexual means. The Poet exhorts the youth to appreciate the increase argument in a series of propositions that remind him he was born of a mother and a father (sonnets 3 and 13) and that without increase no humans would persist into the next generation. The division formed when the female and male were derived from nature is sexually resolved in the birth of a child. The dynamic has the same logical form as the primary template out of nature (Diag 4).

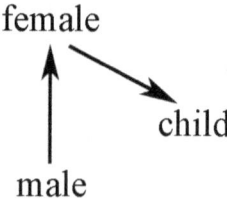

DIAG 4: *Increase template*

Sonnets 15 to 19

Traditionally it has been claimed there are either 17 or 19 increase sonnets. The claim that sonnet 17 is the final one is made because to apologetic ears sonnet 18 is rated the first poetically accomplished sonnet in the set.

> Shall I compare thee to a Summer's day?
> Thou art more lovely and more temperate:
> (Sonnet 18, lines 1-2)

Commentators praise sonnet 18's intense lyricism without realising that the intensity is generated through the combination of poetic effect and seamless logic. In line 12 the double image of 'lines' of descent and 'lines' of poetry convey the logical relationship that exists between the logic of increase and poetry.

> But thy eternal Summer shall not fade,
> Nor lose possession of that fair thou ow'st,
> Nor shall death brag thou wand'rest in his shade,
> **When in eternal lines to time thou grow'st,**
> So long as men can breathe or eyes can see,
> So long lives this, and this gives life to thee.
> (Sonnet 18.9-14)

But the combination of tightly structured philosophic themes with exquisite verse is anathema to commentators who prefer their art to provide a singular aesthetic experience. The problem is exacerbated by an apprehension the philosophy Shakespeare presents is contrary to the apologetics of their schooling.

A further claim that sonnet 19 is the last of the increase sonnets is based on the persistence in sonnets 18 and 19 of issues relating to increase. The equivocation as to whether 17 or 19 is the last increase sonnet at least recognises that sonnet 20 makes a significant break in theme.

In keeping with the logical distinction between the sexual and the erotic, sonnets 15 to 19 provide an interlude that takes account of the role of the Poet and process of writing. Sonnet 16 eases the transition from the sexual dynamic to the erotic with a literary pun on the word 'pen' as penis.

> ....(Time's **pencil** and my pupil **pen**)
> (Sonnet 16.10)

And appropriately sonnet 17, the central sonnet of the poetry and increase group, introduces the word Poet into the set.

Eroticism in sonnets 20 to 154

Sonnet 20 is the first sonnet in which sexual allusions take on a decidedly erotic tone with a pun on 'prick'.

> By adding one thing to my purpose nothing.
> **But since she pricked thee out for women's pleasure,**
> **Mine be thy love and thy love's use their treasure.**
> (Sonnet 20.12-14)

From then on, erotic puns and allusions and suggestions abound until sonnets 153 and 154 present an unbridled erotic romp.

> I grant (sweet love) thy lovely argument
> Deserves the **travail of a worthier pen,**
> Yet what of thee thy Poet doth invent,
> He robs thee of, and pays it thee again,
> He lends thee virtue, and he stole that word,
> From thy behaviour, beauty doth he give
> **And found it in thy cheek:**
> (Sonnet 79.5 - 11)

> Love's not time's fool, **though rosy lips and cheeks**
> **Within his bending sickle's compass come,**
> (Sonnet 116. 9-10)

> **Cupid laid by his brand** and fell asleep,
> A maid of Dian's this advantage found,
> **And his love-kindling fire did quickly steep**
> **In a cold valley-fountain of that ground:**
> (Sonnet 153.1-4)

By characterising the aesthetic, or beauty, as the *Rose* in both the Master Mistress and Mistress sequences, the Poet avails himself of the anagrammatic form of Eros. He acknowledges that all writing is logically erotic because it is logically non-sexual. All the sonnets are logically erotic, including the increase sonnets. However, the role of the increase sonnets in presenting the increase argument, or the sexual dynamic, is conditional on the Poet acknowledging their non-erotic subject matter in the five poetry and increase sonnets, 15 to 19.

Eroticism, then, in its logical relationship to the sexual, has the same function in the *Sonnets* as it does in the *Large Glass*. In the *Large Glass* this is indicated by the non-consummation of the sexual possibility. In the *Sonnets*, a sonnet cannot logically be sexual. The inclusion of the sexual dynamic is made under the logical precondition presented in the five poetry and increase sonnets. In both cases the activity of the artist or Poet is characterised as erotic.

The appreciation of the fundamental distinction between the sexual and the erotic enables Duchamp and Shakespeare to create works of art at a mythic level without generating the contradictions of traditional mythologies based on the priority of the male over the female, and the mind over the body. By incorporating the sexual into the set of *Sonnets*, and by recognising the erotic logic of his poetry, Shakespeare is able to present a philosophy that accounts for both the aesthetic and the ethical.

The pattern of 14s

Ignorance of the *Sonnet* philosophy has led to the confusion over the function of the increase sonnets. The role of sonnet 14 as the last of the purely increase sonnets is not recognised by commentators. John Kerrigan notes that sonnets 15 to 19 have a similar theme of poetry and increase. But he does not draw the obvious conclusion that sonnet 14 is the last of a coherent group that has continued uninterrupted from the first sonnet.

Sonnet 14 is the pivotal sonnet in the whole sequence of 154 sonnets. Once the Poet has presented the division of nature into the sexual dynamic of female and male, and then, in the first 14 sonnets, the logic of sexual union, he can begin to explore the erotic dynamic and the logical relationship of truth and beauty.

The structure of the *Sonnets* appears to 'multiply' out of sonnet 14. The complete set of *Sonnets* is a multiple of 14.

$$154 = 14 \times 11$$

The sequence to the youth is a multiple of 14,

$$126 = 14 \times 9$$

as is that to the Mistress,

$$28 = 14 \times 2$$

Or, diagrammatically (Diag 5),

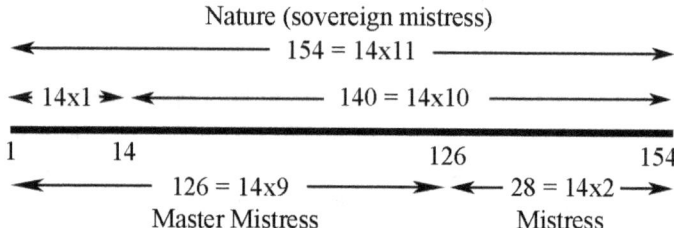

DIAG 5: **Sonnet *numbering based on sonnet 14***

The relationship established through multiplication is in keeping with the idea of multiplying through increase. There is no similar meaningful relationship in the simple addition of 14 to sonnet 14 to form sonnets 28, 42, 56, 70, 84, etc.

The number 14 is significant in that the number 5 symbolises humankind: $14 = 1+4 = 5$. The numbers 10, 11, 9, 2, and 14 also have symbolic functions in the sequence. Just as 10 or 1 stands numerologically for the ideal, so 11 is the antithetical or the ideal returned to reality. In the *Sonnets*, 11 is associated with 'Nature' as the ultimate auditor of the ideal. The number 154 accommodates both of the ideal and the real. The number 9 is 1 short of unity. The number 2 stands for shadow or darkness and equates to the role of the Mistress in the set. And there are 28 or a lunar number of sonnets in the Mistress sequence.

So numerologically, sonnet 14 is the generative sonnet for the major structural systems in the *Sonnets*. It is the pivotal point about which the whole sequence of 154 *Sonnets* generates its meaning. That meaning arises because the *Sonnets* successfully relate truth and beauty to the erotic out of the sexual dynamic.

Sonnet 14 is the hinge point around which the relation of increase, as the biological, and truth and beauty is established. Without increase there is no truth and beauty. Logically, truth and beauty arises out of the increase dynamic. Truth and beauty would not exist but for the increase dynamic.

> **As truth and beauty shall together thrive**
> If from thyself, to store thou wouldst convert:
> Or else of thee this I prognosticate,
> **Thy end is Truth's and Beauty's doom and date.**
> (Sonnet 14.11-14)

The aesthetic and ethical dynamic of the *Large Glass*

The *Large Glass* deliberately provokes the aesthetic experience of profound intuitions through artistic effects. Duchamp evokes deep realisations about the priority of the female over the male and the logic of the relation between the sexual and the erotic.

Before Duchamp published his *Green Box* in 1934 and before Andre Breton wrote his synopsis, *The Lighthouse of the Bride*, in 1936 (translated into English in 1945), the *Large Glass* was appreciated largely for its visual qualities. The publication of the notes of the *Green Box* confirmed Duchamp's intention to focus on the aesthetic, with many of the notes involving puns or poetic devices. But the notes also express the determining conditions for Duchamp's aesthetic intent and expectations. That they are able to do so gives an insight into the suppressed ethical dimension of the *Large Glass*. Inevitably many of the notes express the ethical dynamic in Duchamp's primarily aesthetic project.

The aesthetic and ethical dynamic of the *Sonnets*

Whereas Duchamp's stated intent was to focus on aesthetics to the exclusion of language, Shakespeare deliberately considers both aesthetics and ethics. In the *Sonnets*, aesthetics, or the awareness of sensations, is called beauty. It is archetypically the process of 'seeing'. Ethics, or the relation of ideas in language (whether true or false, good or bad), is called truth. It is archetypically the process of 'saying'.

As in Duchamp's *Large Glass*, the male in the *Sonnets* is logically dependent on the Mistress for his existence and understanding. It is in the Mistress sequence that the beauty and truth dynamic is given its most coherent formulation. The Poet gains his understanding of beauty and truth from the Mistress. The Mistress sonnets are the natural repository of the possibility of beauty and truth. In keeping with the primacy of the sensory over language, first beauty (sonnets 127 to 137) and then truth (sonnets 137 to 152) are considered.

In the Master Mistress sequence the dynamic of truth and beauty is introduced in sonnet 14 and is then the principal theme for all the sonnets from 15 to 126. To advise the youth of the relation between increase and truth and beauty the Poet recounts what he has learnt from the Mistress of beauty and truth in the Mistress sonnets (127 to 154).

The Mistress sonnets are the source of the beauty and truth dynamic because the female is logically prior to the male. Beauty and truth derive unconditionally from the Mistress but are available only conditionally to the Master Mistress. For the Master Mistress to comprehend the truth and beauty dynamic he must appreciate the logic of the increase argument and the logical relation between increase and truth and beauty. The Mistress is the logical source of the two possibilities.

The word truth is not mentioned in the 14 increase sonnets until the last few lines of sonnet 14. Because the increase sonnets consider the physical processes of the sexual dynamic it is appropriate that only beauty be named until the end of sonnet 14. Because Shakespeare preserves the role of truth for the function of language, or things said, he substitutes the word wisdom for truth in sonnet 11. So line 5 reads 'wisdom, beauty, and increase' instead.

The appearance of truth and beauty in lines 11 and 14 of sonnet 14 prepares the way for the presentation of the dynamic in the remaining sonnets.

> But from thine eyes my knowledge I derive,
> And constant stars in them I read such art
> **As truth and beauty shall together thrive**
> If from thyself, to store thou wouldst convert:
>   Or else of thee this I prognosticate,
> **Thy end is Truth's and Beauty's doom and date.**
>   (Sonnet 14.9-14)

Sonnet 14 states the logical relationship of increase to truth and beauty. It states that increase ('store') is prior to truth and beauty. Knowledge or judgment derives, not from the stars, augury, etc., but directly from inter-human interaction. Such knowledge is derived from the 'constant stars' that are the eyes. The couplet gives the consequence for truth and beauty if the logic of the increase argument is not appreciated. If nobody increases, especially those capable and inclined to sexual activity, then there would be no truth and beauty because there would be no human beings.

Significantly, the words 'truth and beauty' occur in the last line of sonnet 14, that is, in the last line of the increase sonnets. From the beginning of sonnet 15 onward the remaining sonnets examine aspects of the truth and beauty dynamic, beginning with the preconditions presented in sonnets 15 to 19 for the logical relation of poetry to increase. From sonnet 20 on the youth is presented with the logic of truth and beauty as the basis for love and understanding.

While in most instances the words truth and beauty appear in separate sonnets throughout the youth sequence, truth and beauty periodically appear together to reassert the truth and beauty dynamic as the cornerstone of the Poet's erotic logic. By structuring his presentation around the dynamic of truth and beauty Shakespeare ensures that his arguments are consistent, and that the relationship of body and mind has the correct multiplicity.

From sonnets 127 to 136 only beauty is mentioned. Sonnet 127 begins the analysis by mentioning beauty six times. The ten sonnets explore beauty as sensation in many of its possibilities. Any sensation is an aspect of beauty as demonstrated in sonnet 130 where the five senses are brought into play. Throughout the beauty sonnets the Mistress does not say anything. She is literally sensed. Sonnet 137 is transitional between beauty and truth. It mentions both beauty and truth using the archetypal meanings of 'seeing' for beauty and 'saying' for truth.

Sonnets 138 to 152 mention only truth, with the first line of sonnet 138 having the Mistress 'swear' or say that she is made of 'truth'. From this point on what she says is the focus of the sonnets until sonnet 152, which is pervaded by the most deliberate forms of saying, 'swearing' and 'perjury', and which also mentions truth twice. (Sonnets 153 and 154, as well as sonnets 128 and 135/136, have structural functions within the numerology of the whole set.)

This very brief outline of the truth and beauty dynamic in the *Sonnets* should be sufficient to demonstrate Shakespeare's intent to consider both aesthetics and ethics. The priority of the female over the male is explicitly reinforced by the presentation of the logic of the beauty and truth dynamic in the Mistress sequence. The priority of increase over truth and beauty is indicated by the derivation of the increase potential through the Mistress from nature and positioning of the increase argument at the beginning of the Master Mistress sequence.

The template for beauty and truth derives logically from the *Nature* and *Increase templates*. In the Mistress sequence beauty or aesthetics, as the dynamic of unmediated sensation or 'seeing', is based on non-difference ('indifference' as Duchamp calls it) or the undifferentiated sense of what is 'best or worst' (sonnet 137). Truth or ethics, as the dynamic of 'saying', is based on 'difference', or the capacity to determine right and wrong. If aesthetics is unmediated perception and ethics is the relation of the true and the false, then the logical form of the relation between beauty and truth is represented in Diag 6.

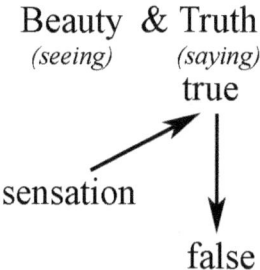

DIAG 6: **Beauty and truth template**

In the Master Mistress sequence the Poet, who has gained a mature understanding of beauty and truth, addresses the illogical understanding of truth and beauty in the youth. Because the youth does not appreciate the logic of increase for human persistence then his understanding of beauty and truth is awry. As a consequence he does not understand the logic of truth and beauty where the true and the false combine in the mind to give an intensified sensation of an idea, the most elevated sensations of which in the mind are called the ideal, or God. The Poet impresses the logic of truth and beauty on the youth to forestall the worst consequences of unbridled idealism. The relationship is represented in Diag 7.

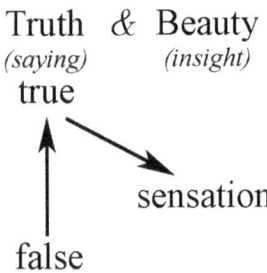

Diag 7: Truth and beauty template

Body and mind: the Nature template

Shakespeare's *Sonnets* show how to relate the sexual/erotic dynamic to the aesthetic/ethical dynamic. It should be clear already that the sexual aspects of the dynamic combine the nature/sexual division and the increase process. The *Nature female/male template* and the *Increase template* can be combined to form the *Body template* that represents the logic of human nature as sexual beings.

As the nature/increase dynamic is the logical condition for human continuity then it also determines the correct multiplicity between the body and the mind, between the world and language. The logical dynamic of the increase argument echoes the pattern for the *Nature female/male template*. The *Nature template* gives the logical relation of nature and the sexual possibility. The basic form of the increase dynamic is the relationship of female, male, and child. The *Increase template* gives the logical relation for human persistence. When combined they form the logical template for the body (Diag 8).

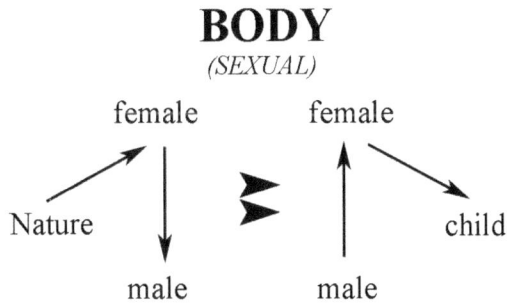

DIAG 8: *Body or sexual template*

The next move is to combine the template for beauty and truth or the process of translating sensations into ideas, with the template for truth and beauty or the process of translating ideas into sensations of the mind. Because the resulting *Mind template* has the same logical multiplicity as the *Body template*, but differs in that it lacks the procreative function of the nature/increase dynamic, it is logically erotic (Diag 9).

The genealogical multiplication of the *Increase template* and the syllogistic multiplication of the *Truth and beauty template* both generate branching structures of the same logical pattern. The English language recognises this in the use of words such as 'conception' and 'relative' for both the biological and the logical processes.

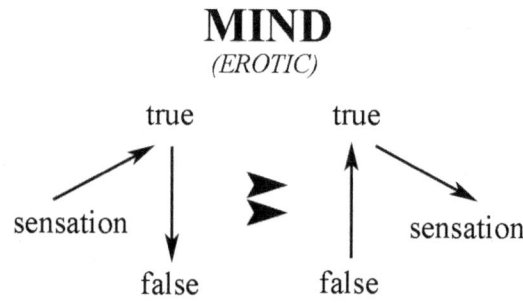

DIAG 9: **Mind or erotic template**

The *Truth and beauty template* is derived from the basic relation of female and male to nature. The consistency of the pattern from the whole of nature to the processes of understanding suggests Shakespeare accomplished what Wittgenstein failed to do. Shakespeare presents a structured system with the correct multiplicity to represent the relation between language and the world. The critical element absent from Wittgenstein's philosophy is the intermediate stage of the sexual/erotic dynamic.

It is only necessary then to combine the *Body* and *Mind templates* to represent the logic of human understanding in nature. The *Nature template* can represent the logic of the human condition within nature (Diag 10).

WILLIAM SHAKESPEARE: THE NATURE TEMPLATE

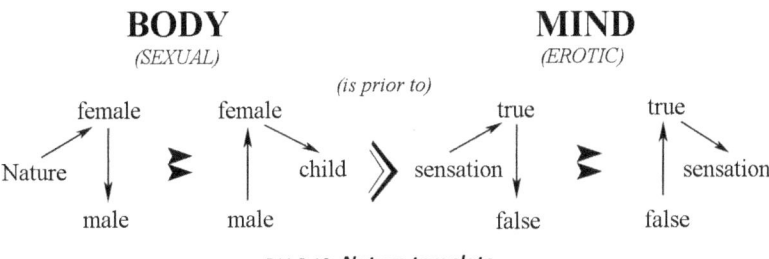

DIAG 10: **Nature template**

Or the *Nature template* can be worded to represent the *Sonnet* entities (Diag 11).

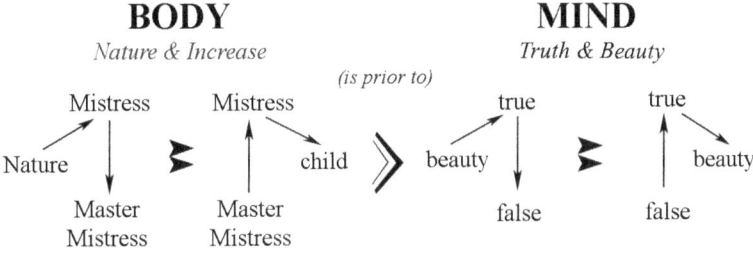

DIAG 11: **Nature template (Sonnets)**

Shakespeare's achievement is unique in the world's literatures and is in advance of any existing philosophy because it represents the logic of humankind within nature comprehensively and consistently. His ability to appreciate how the sexual/erotic logic of human existence and persistence relates to the aesthetic/ethical dynamic of the mind gives his plays and poems an unequalled veracity to life at a mythic level of expression.

The role of the Poet

In the *Large Glass* and in Duchamp's other works there is no representation of the artist. The Occultist Witnesses in the *Glass* are a function of the Bachelors, and the pseudonymous character *Rrose Selavy* does not have the complexity to be an alter ego for the artist of the complete works. The case is different for the *Sonnets*. The Poet is a ubiquitous presence throughout both Mistress and Master Mistress sequences and is in command of the philosophy of the whole set and consequently the philosophy of all the plays and other poems. He is Shakespeare's intended alter ego.

For reasons consistent with the *Sonnet* structuring, the Poet is first introduced in sonnet 10 as 'I', 'my' and 'me'. He then occurs hundreds of times in the first person in relation to the Master Mistress and the Mistress. Appropriately, the first mention of the Poet as Poet (where 'Poet' occurs twice) is in sonnet 17, which is the central sonnet of the poetry and increase group. The word Poet occurs four more times (in sonnets 32, 79, and 83) in relation to the activities of the Alien Poets.

The Poet expresses the unity that occurs when the Master Mistress acknowledges the Mistress and their logical relation to nature. From his unified perspective the Poet engages with the Mistress to determine the conditions for beauty and truth and advises the Master Mistress on the logical conditions for a mature understanding. By becoming 1 with the Mistress the Poet regains his connection to nature but as a male his acquired unity does not give him an understanding of the whole of nature. This is reflected in the way his numerological value of 145 is the sequential version of the number for nature, 154.

The Poet both appreciates the natural dynamic and gives expression to its natural logic. The transitional sonnets 15 to 19 acknowledge both his appreciation of the relation of increase to truth and beauty and the relation of the sexual to the erotic. They address the issue of the poetic medium in which the relationship between body and mind is considered. The Poet acknowledges his role as the writer of the verse in this particular form of verse, the sonnet. He articulates the relation between 'Nature, the sovereign mistress', and the Master Mistress and Mistress required for a mythic level of expression.

The mythic dynamic of the *Large Glass*

The *Large Glass* presents the logical conditions for a mythic level of expression in art. The structure of the *Large Glass* articulates the basic pre-conditions for any of the worlds mythologies.

The whole of the *Glass* represents the female dimension as the logical source of the differentiation of the whole into female and male components, the Bride and the Bachelors. This structural division establishes a consistent basis on which to explore the artistic possibility. It prioritises the female over the male as the basis for a consistent mythic expression. The Bachelors are totally dependant on the Bride for their existence.

The *Large Glass* recognises its own status as a mythic artwork by casting the Bride and the Bachelors in an erotic relationship. During the complex mechanical ballet represented on the *Glass* the Bride and the Bachelors do not, and logically cannot, consummate their sexual relationship. Their desire for each other remains erotic or an unconsummate state of mind. Artistic expression in any medium either features an erotic relationship between female and male or it relies by default on its expression in the mythology of the culture. When it is not expressed directly in the work it remains an unexpressed or unintended given. Any artwork is logically parenthesised as non-sexual or non-biological.

The *Large Glass* is the mythic source of all Duchamp's works including the *readymades* because it is an inventory for the logic of myth. The female priority and its necessary eroticism provide the mythic 'platform' for all his works. For an artwork to be mythic it must not only express the logical relation of the female and the male in nature, plus the relation of the sexual to the erotic, it must also be a consistent artistic expression of the artist's appreciation of the complete dynamic.

As a citizen of the twentieth century Duchamp creates his work from the products of the science and technology of his day. The mechanical ballet of the *Large Glass* is a hilarious mechanism that deliberately heightens sensation and converts to sensations or aesthetic effects aspects of the rational world.

Once the female/male dynamic in art is acknowledged as being logically non-sexual, and the erotic is acknowledged as any form of desire, then, within the context established by the mythic artwork, anything goes. There is logically no restraint on the possible effects other than the tacit recognition of the basic conditions for the mythic. But because Duchamp precluded the ethical, he had to limit his output to ensure everything he did was an undiluted expression of the mythic preconditions for the aesthetic.

By characterising art as logically erotic and as predominately aesthetic Duchamp was able to present the logical conditions for mythic expression and so avoid creating a new mythology. In the *Large Glass* and related works he demonstrated the way to work at a mythic level without confounding the relation between the body and mind as is the case with idealistic philosophies and their related religions. The humour in his work is the necessary antidote to the claims by religious believers that their mythologies represent the true state of the world, instead of accepting that their mythologies are an irresistible expression of erotic desire. Bernini's auto-erotic divinely inspired *St Teresa in Ecstasy* captures the syndrome perfectly.

The mythic dynamic of the *Sonnets*

The structure of the *Sonnets* explicitly recognises the logical conditions for human expression at the mythic level. The whole set of *Sonnets* represents Nature as the sovereign mistress. From the vantage of human understanding nature is logically female. Even in Shakespeare's day it would have been apparent that the male derives biologically from the female. Anatomical investigation of external and internal physiology of the human female and male was fairly advanced in the sixteenth century. Such research would add weight to the anecdotal evidence for the priority of the human female over the male. Even the logical inconsistency of biblical mythology would lead to the realisation that nature was logically female.

When Shakespeare calls Nature the 'sovereign mistress' he is not substituting a secular pseudonym for the name of a traditional Goddess. The absence of capitals from the words 'sovereign mistress' in sonnet 126 in Q suggests they have a logical function. The sovereign mistress is the logical progenitor of the human female and male. She bears a logical relation to the two sequences into which the *Sonnets* are divided. The names given to the female and male of the two sequences are consistent with the sexual derivation of the male from the female in nature. The Mistress derives from the sovereign mistress and the Master Mistress derives from the Mistress.

The names for the female and male are capitalised when they refer to distinct beings rather than the all-pervasive state of nature. This establishes the human female and male in their correct logical relation to the sovereign mistress. The positioning of the male sequence and the female sequence, their numerological relation, and the significance of their naming is consistent with the priority of the female over the male. The female determines the existence of the male. The male lacks a dimension that can only be recovered through union with the female.

If the 126 sonnets to the Master Mistress were not logically to a male, the equation of the *Sonnets* would be over determined toward the female. It would similar to having 9 females in the lower half of the *Large Glass*. So the whole of the historical debate on the nature of the relationship of Shakespeare to a mystery youth is void, and any suggestion that the first 126 sonnets should have been written to a woman is awry.

Ignorance of the *Sonnet* philosophy has led to claims that Shakespeare and a youth of his acquaintance had a homosexual relationship. But sonnet 20 counters the recurring theory of homosexuality between Shakespeare and the youth. While the homosexuality is not discussed in the *Sonnets*, the practice of homosexuality is not logically excluded. The argument of the increase sonnets is for logical conditions for the perpetuation of humankind and those conditions do no more than state the consequences if nobody increased.

After establishing the logical possibility for the sexual in nature, the *Sonnets* then present the logical relationship between the sexual and the erotic. They consider both the sexual and the erotic systematically to establish the status of mythic art as logically erotic.

The *Sonnets* do not present an increase argument to the Mistress. Because the Mistress is the primary sexual being the possibility of increase through sex is implicit in her being female. Because the male dimension is a secondary derivation from the female, and so cannot reproduce biologically (compare the residual capacity of the female in some species to reproduce by parthenogenesis), the increase argument is presented in the first 14 Master Mistress sonnets to instruct the youth in sexual logic.

The transition between increase and truth and beauty in sonnet 14 establishes the logical divide between the sexual and the erotic. The literal arguments of the 14 increase sonnets establish the philosophic basis for the erotic symbolism for the following sonnets. Sonnets 15 to 19 acknowledge the function of the increase sonnets in establishing the erotic logic of art. The literary pun on pen/penis in sonnet 16 appropriately prepares the way for the frequent erotic allusions in sonnets 20 to 154.

There is no systematic increase argument presented in Shakespeare's plays because the increase argument of the *Sonnets* provides the erotic logic for the plays. Many of the plays and poems, though, mention increase or have a theme based on increase in recognition of its empowering significance.

The inclusion of the sexual argument in the *Sonnets* not only distinguishes the erotic from the sexual, but also the ethical from the aesthetic. The *Sonnets* are an intertwined system of poetic expression and deliberate argument. The persistent argument of the 14 increase sonnets uses the ethical function of language that complements the aesthetic effect of poetic imagery. Because the sonnet form lends itself to argumentative verse, Shakespeare can combine the ethics of language with a variety of aesthetic effects.

As the *Beauty to truth* and *Truth to beauty templates* have the same logical structure as the *Nature template* and the *Increase template*, the logical conditions for a mythic level of expression established by the *Nature template* are inseparable from the ethical dynamic. The mythic expression of the *Sonnets*, and consequently of all Shakespeare's plays, incorporates the ethical. Shakespeare was conscious that when he established the logical conditions for mythic expression he automatically established the basis for a consistent aesthetics and ethics. While any mythology expresses of the logical conditions for understanding, a literal belief in a mythology confuses the sexual for the erotic. The inevitable consequence is the creation of inconsistency in the application of the dynamic of ethics and aesthetics.

Shakespeare uses the mythic philosophy in his plays to critique the negative consequences of the Christianity of his day. The consistent mythic logic of the *Sonnets* reveals the illogicalities in Christian belief and its contradictory moral injunctions. In Christian myth and dogma the male God takes priority over the female, the erotic or non-sexual is present in the Immaculate Conception, the virgin birth, in Christ's death without issue and his rising from the dead. The erotic effects are heightened by the transcendental conception of the 'word made flesh', and the ethical is compromised by moral injunctions predicated on the priority of the male God.

As with any myth, the eroticism in the Christian myth acknowledges its literary status. The eroticism points to both the sexual pre-conditions for myth and its origin from a human hand. Shakespeare acknowledges the erotic logic of his *Sonnets* and plays by incorporating the role of the Poet in the *Sonnets*. The Poet as writer not only presents the logical conditions for any mythic possibility, he is self-reflexively aware of his mythic role.

Shakespeare's Poet demonstrates the logical dynamic required for mythic expression. Comprehension of the mythic possibility is a logical prerequisite for writing myth self-reflexively. In the *Sonnets* he derives the mythic logic from the Mistress and then instructs the recalcitrant Master Mistress in the logical conditions for mythic verse. Understanding the mythic dynamic is the prerogative of any human being, but only a person with the necessary talent, female or male, can write at the mythic level of expression. Shakespeare demonstrates his mythic talent in his plays and poems.

Duchamp's limit, Shakespeare's range

Duchamp's appreciation of the mythic dynamic is limited by the absence of a representation of the artist in his *Large Glass*, and by his unwillingness to introduce ethics into his work. When Duchamp's achievement is represented in diagrammatic form the consequence of his limited explorations is apparent (Diag 12). The reduced dynamic is the logical outcome of the constraints he imposed on the mythic dynamic. Duchamp's decision to 'reduce, reduce, reduce' has an inevitable effect. The minimal nature and limited number of *readymades* is a logical product of the aesthetic focus of the *Large Glass*.

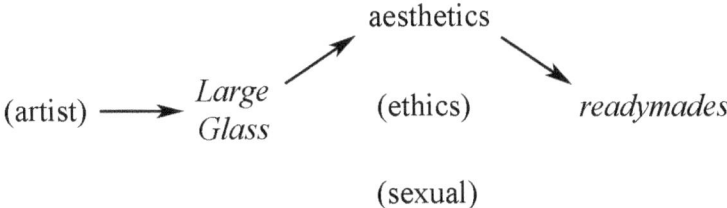

DIAG 12: *The relation of the* **Large Glass** *and the* **readymades**

Shakespeare's *Sonnets* present the complete expression of the mythic dynamic. The *Sonnets* incorporate the sexual and the aesthetic along with the ethical in their structure and organisation. Shakespeare's plays, consequently, are a logical outcome of the mythic dynamic of the *Sonnets* (Diag 13). Rather than being the 'hinge point' or the 'infra thin' as Duchamp characterised the *readymades*, they are a fulsome expression of the whole gamut of life.

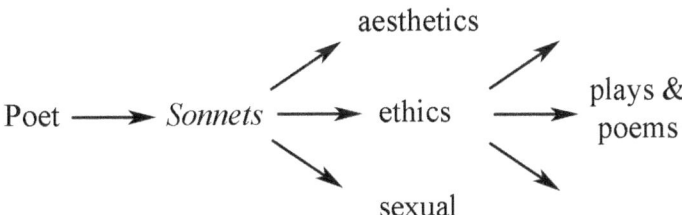

DIAG 13: *The relation of the* **Sonnets** *and the plays and poems*

Shakespeare addresses the three elements in the *Sonnets* that Duchamp does not address in the *Large Glass*. These elements are structured into the set of 154 sonnets. The Poet is present throughout as the ubiquitous 'I' who is associated with the number 145. The increase sonnets are tightly knit into the set by being associated with the number 14. Ethics or truth is inseparable from the logic of the truth and beauty dynamic in the sonnets after sonnet 14. The relationships can be represented diagrammatically (Diag 14).

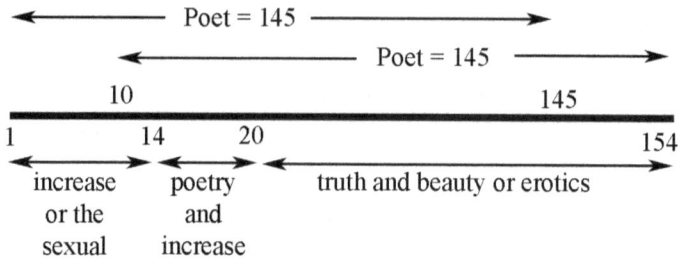

DIAG 14: *The relation of the sexual, ethics and the Poet*

Summary

The brief analysis in this chapter shows how Shakespeare incorporates the sexual, the ethical and the aesthetic into the logic of the *Sonnets*. By comparison it shows that Duchamp's *Large Glass* focuses primarily on the aesthetic. While Shakespeare and Duchamp are united in their identification of the logical conditions for any mythic expression, Duchamp's largely pictorial works limit his exploration of the full range of expressive possibilities. If anything, the inherent limitations of his preferred medium made him belligerent toward the other possibilities. For Shakespeare, the artistic is not confined to the aesthetic as it is for so many Romantic aesthetes. Duchamp identifies himself as just such an aesthete. Despite his ambition to avoid the 'retinal' and explore the conceptual, Duchamp was severely limited by his bias against language or the ethical.

CHAPTER 5

Postscript: from Shakespeare to Duchamp

When I first read Shakespeare's 154 sonnets in 1995, I had little more than an intuition that they presented a profound philosophy of fundamental explanatory power. It took five years to unveil the structure and themes of the *Sonnets* and a further five years to prepare the material for publication in 2005. And in some respects the process of understanding the implications continues at present.

With the hindsight of ten years of research and study for the 2005 publication it is evident that the insights would not have been possible without the previous twenty-five years of research into the work of Darwin, Wittgenstein, Mallarmé, and Duchamp since the early 1970s. If Darwin was essential for appreciating the relation between the body and mind, and if Wittgenstein for providing an understanding of the logic of language, it was Duchamp out of Mallarmé who provided the mythic critique essential for appreciating the full structure and organisation of the *Sonnets*.

In turn, the *Sonnet* philosophy provides the means to critique the work of Darwin, Wittgenstein, and Duchamp, and by implication most of the literature of the recent period. The comparison of Duchamp's limit and Shakespeare's range at the end of Chapter 4 can be applied equally to Darwin and Wittgenstein to better understand their achievements and their limitations.

Darwin's limit, Shakespeare's range

Darwin organised *The Origin of Species* logically to present the evidence for the evolution of species. He applied what he knew about the artificial selection of domestic animals to the possibilities for natural selection over time. He then organised *The Descent of Man and Selection in Relation to Sex* to present the argument for the logical derivation of the activities of the human mind from the characteristics of animals lower in the order than mankind. He then considered the selection of secondary sexual characteristics or the erotic aspects of behaviour.

After rejecting the Christian beliefs of his youth, Darwin based his understanding in nature. The consistency with which he conducted his scientific investigations and presented his findings led him to appreciate that the sexual dynamic is logically prior to the possibility of understanding. In *The Descent of Man* he outlined the implication of natural logic for 'mental powers' and the 'moral sense'.

On the scale of the *Nature template*, Darwin focused primarily on the first half while noting the implications for the second half (Diag 15).

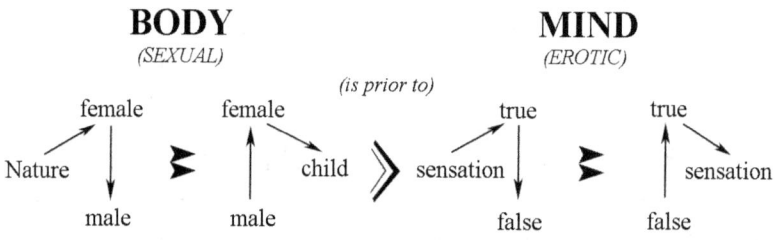

DIAG 15: ***Nature template***

These volumes have shown how Shakespeare organised his *Sonnets* to present the argument for human persistence by presenting the logic for the sexual dynamic in nature as a requirement for the continuation of humankind. The *Sonnets* present the argument for the priority of female over male and of physical increase over mental attributes as truth and beauty. They make a clear distinction between the sexual and the erotic by considering the dynamic of understanding as logically erotic. Shakespeare goes further than Darwin by articulating the logical conditions for mythic expression.

Wittgenstein's limit, Shakespeare's range

Wittgenstein's philosophy changed diametrically over his lifetime. In his early work he created a highly structured philosophy based on a symbolic logic derived from the physics of atoms and molecules. But he soon realised that he had failed to picture the relation between language and the world with the required logical multiplicity.

In his second period, his philosophic investigations of language were loosely organised around a number of organic metaphors such as nature, family dynamics, and forms of life. The published results of his investigations appear as an album of notes with a series of ideas given alternate emphasis throughout the text.

In both periods Wittgenstein claimed that ethics and aesthetics cannot be represented in language. Although he found it necessary to resort to nature to account for the logic of language he could not accept the implications for the status of the human mind.

On the scale of the *Nature template* he was still operating with the corrupt version of apologetics. The hints of natural logic in his later work are subsumed by his residual Christian belief in a final judgment, which may have led to his taking the last rights of the Catholic Church. His lifelong focus on the logic of language is a consequence of prioritising the mind dynamic in the *God template* over the nature dynamic (Diag 16).

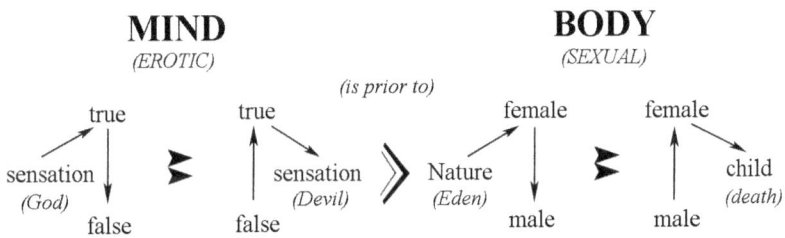

DIAG 16: **God template**

Shakespeare's philosophy remained constant throughout his life. The *Sonnets* present a precisely structured logic that takes as a given the relation between nature and the sexual dynamic of female and male. The logic of the sexual dynamic provides the logic for the possibilities of language in terms of truth and beauty. Truth and beauty recognise the logical relation between the singularity of sensations or aesthetics and the dynamic of ideas or ethics. Shakespeare's philosophy remains consistent because he appreciates the logic of myth, the highest from of expression in the language. Unlike Wittgenstein he was prepared to investigate the logic of myth.

The limitation of Thierry de Duve's formalism

It should be apparent by now that it is impossible to understand Duchamp's accomplishment by focusing on the formal implications of the phrase 'a sort of pictorial Nominalism' and the statement 'This is Art'. When Thierry de Duve addresses only a few of the *readymades* and ignores the *Large Glass*, and uses as a yardstick the limited theorising of the abstractionist Greenberg and the conceptualist Kosuth, his interpretation fails to do justice to Duchamp's achievement.

It might be possible to gain an insight into the Abstractionists and the Conceptualists from within the limitations the formalist critique places on Duchamp's work. After all, Greenberg's references to Kant and Kosuth's references to Wittgenstein are just as gratuitous as de Duve's references to nominalism and Kant.

But when de Duve interprets Duchamp's *readymades* from such a limited perspective, he reveals not the objectivity of an art historian but the parochial musings of an academic theorist. His proposal of a 'tube of paint' and a 'blank canvas' as the missing link between Abstract Expressionism and the *readymades* is telling in its presumptuousness. De Duve misrepresents an aspect of Duchamp's work and then uses it as the epitome of Duchamp's achievement. Although Duchamp also borrowed from the works of others, unlike de Duve he did so to expand the range of his own possibilities rather than severely restrict the interpretation of their work.

Unwarranted claims and inconsistencies abound in de Duve's explanations of Duchamp's work. This is despite the comparative ease with which he points out the illogicalities in Greenberg's theorising. The insurmountable problem is that his theories do not account for Duchamp's oeuvre and its persistent themes.

By comparison, when Darwin wrote on evolution his theory and the facts were largely in accord so that his theorising was logically predictive. Further scientific research has validated the theory and its broad implications. De Duve's theorising is both contrary to the majority of the facts and is woefully inadequate when applied to the larger implications of Duchamp's criticism of myth. This is not surprising when he limits the understanding of Duchamp so that he can validate a very limited tunnel of art historical taste.

The philosophic analysis presented here demonstrates how Duchamp's oeuvre operates logically and how the *readymades* operate in a way that is consistent with the whole. And the analysis leads to an appreciation of an even more sophisticated expression of the same dynamic in Shakespeare's *Sonnets*.

In the *Sonnets* the dynamic of ethics and aesthetics, the mythic dynamic, the relation of the sexual and the erotic, and the numerological correspondences and the further implications for the plays of Shakespeare, contain a logic that corresponds to the multiplicity of the logical relationship between the body and the mind. The analysis provides a unique approach to the work of Shakespeare that reveals insights never before considered.

So not only does the understanding lead to an appreciation of Shakespeare's thought, his philosophic position in turn reveals the limitations and strengths of Duchamp's work in a way consistent with the applied critique. The opposite is the case with de Duve's attempt to relate Kant and Duchamp. He takes a limited reading of Duchamp's *readymades* to Kant's aesthetics, and he uses Kant without correcting his apologetically driven shortcomings. Such a reading is light years from Duchamp's often quoted statement that he wanted to engage with ideas the way a vagina grasps a penis.

Reinstating the complete paradigm

No twentieth century artist has managed to match Duchamp's philosophic accomplishment, or even replicate it, much less understand it. Rather, the response to Duchamp has been little more than the type of literal pastiche presented in performance by Merce Cunningham's dance company in the 1950s or in the duplication of his works in the collections of the Tate Gallery and elsewhere.

The tendency toward formalist or purely aesthetic artistic expectations over the last 100 years has ensured that Duchamp's accomplishment has been misunderstood or largely ignored. Octavio Paz, as an exception, may have benefited by not having been subjected to the formalism of the tertiary academies of Europe and North America.

Duchamp was resolute in wanting no part of such a compromise. His repeated statements about his intent to recover the meaningfulness apparent in pre-modern art led to an expression of the mythic unparalleled in modern times. Duchamp's fear of the word as discourse makes it even more surprising that his understanding of the aesthetic dynamic was so logically exact. And if Duchamp stands alone in the twentieth century, then Shakespeare stands alone in the last few millennia in having expressed the same basic appreciation of the basis of life even more consistently and comprehensively.

Shakespeare's *Sonnets* have been completely misunderstood because even more than Duchamp he moved beyond the apologetic paradigm that has so conditioned expression over the last few thousand years. Shakespeare surfaces as a model for the positive and progressive attitude toward life that the life and work of Duchamp so brilliantly expresses.

Duchamp appreciates, notwithstanding the decline of interest in the mythological, that the mythic nevertheless expresses the highest level of philosophic understanding. An understanding of the philosophic basis of myth is essential for a complete understanding of what it means to be human. He shows, and Shakespeare shows more fully, just how the mythic dimension can be given effective expression in the modern world. Duchamp gives a graphic description of its operation in his *Large Glass*, and shows how to connect the mythic with objects from everyday life in the *readymades*. Shakespeare, in his *Sonnets*, gives an exact expression of its operation and in the plays gives a dramatic expression of its presence in the lives of every person.

Conclusion: the quaternary dynamic

Darwin, Mallarmé, and Duchamp point the way to a level of understanding not currently available in tertiary institutions worldwide. Their work presents with philosophic consistency what many other thinkers have been attempting to comprehend for a number of centuries. Thinkers such as Wittgenstein and most of those whose work is discussed in the essays in Part 2 of this volume, and particularly Riane Eisler, have shown the courage to question the traditional paradigm on which tertiary institutions were founded around AD 1100. The essays consider both their achievements and the degree to which the residuum of the traditional paradigm has fatally constrained their desire to see the world aright.

The comparison of Duchamp and Shakespeare over these pages, and the critique of Thierry de Duve's attempt to understand Duchamp philosophically, suggests that a systematic level of learning above tertiary is now required. The creation of the quaternary level of systematic learning seems a natural consequence of the findings presented here.

A comparison of the thinkers who feature in this letter

The equations indicate the degree of philosophic awareness of the *Nature template* demonstrated by each contributor.

    Bold   indicates a high degree awareness of the category.
    (Brackets)   indicate a misplaced understanding of the category.
    Absence   ( ) indicates an ignorance of the category.
    The sign >   indicates natural priority.
    The sign (>) indicates a reversal of natural priority.

(i) William Shakespeare

    Nature /Increase   >   **Truth and Beauty**.

(ii) Charles Darwin

    Nature /Increase   >   **Truth** and **Beauty.**

(iii) Ludwig Wittgenstein

    Nature/(Increase)   (>)   (**Truth**) and (**Beauty**).

(iv) Marcel Duchamp

    Nature/Increase   >   Truth and **Beauty.**

(v) Octavio Paz

    ( )/(Increase)   >   (Truth) and **Beauty**

(vi) Emmanuel Kant

    ( ) /( )   (>)   (**Truth**) and (**Beauty**)

(vii) Thierry de Duve

    ( ) /( )   (>)   (Truth) and (Beauty)

PART 2

10 Essays

1
Marcel Duchamp

Preamble

For nearly a century avant-garde artists have looked to the work of Marcel Duchamp for inspiration and direction. Scores of art movements have attributed whole or part of their motivation to his *readymades* and other ephemeral works. Yet, ironically, while the deeper meaning of Duchamp's works has resisted exegesis and remains shrouded in mystery, the movements derivative of his work have already been categorised and shelved by art historians.

The status and the relevance of the art movements generated by the avant-garde have been debated extensively in public and in the literature. But despite the persistent expectation of invention and criticism, by the end of the twentieth century the pursuit of the avant-garde had stalled in the self-referential stasis of post-modernism. The idea that anything can be called a work of art, supposedly under the influence of Duchamp, has become such a clichéd defense of artistic licence that it is worth asking how current practice relates to Duchamp's original intent.

The *Large Glass* and the *readymades*

The pivotal recognition must be that Duchamp did not intend his *readymades* and other ephemeral works to be understood apart from his major works, *The Bride Stripped Bare by Her Bachelors, Even,* or *Large Glass*, (1913-26) and *Etant donnes* (1946-68). He went to great lengths to emphasise the unity of his life-long vision. He ensured his most significant works were collected together in the Philadelphia Museum of Art and spent considerable energy constructing a comprehensive portable museum of miniaturised replicas. If Duchamp is to be believed and his intentions are to be understood, it is necessary to see the *Large Glass* as central to all he did and that none of the other works should be considered apart from it.

In a recent talk in the Duchamp room at Tate Modern the young woman presenter, despite having Richard Hamilton's copy of the *Large Glass* sited in the middle of the room, focused on the small collection of recently acquired *readymade* multiples and a couple of paintings by Picabia. It took a question at the end of her talk from a member of the audience to elicit a comment on the *Large Glass*. Her embarrassed reaction and inability to say anything coherent typifies the failure of scholarship to penetrate the meaning of Duchamp's complete oeuvre.

The content of the major works has not been given expression in the movements that attribute their inspiration to the influence of Duchamp. Occasional attempts to use the imagery of the *Large Glass* by artists such as Echaurren Matta or Merce Cunningham, have resulted in the trivialisation of the work's content. At best it can be said that the *Large Glass* and *Etant donnes* have provided an umbrella for intuitive responses to Duchamp's other works.

Aspects of the *Large Glass* have been discussed when the work was replicated by Ulf Linde or Richard Hamilton, or when it was analysed by Arturo Schwarz, John Golding, and others. So far, though, there has not been a movement based on their suggestions that respects the female/male dynamic of the whole *Glass*. Even Octavio Paz, the writer credited with the most insightful comments on the *Large Glass* and *Etant donnes*, was only able to suggest a general relation between the works and traditional mythologies (as does Calvin Tomkins in a final note of exasperation in a recent biography[1]).

The *Large Glass* and myth

To overcome the hiatus it is necessary to remember Duchamp's frequently declared intention that he wished to recover the basis of artistic expression from the Renaissance and earlier periods of art. When Duchamp looked back to the Renaissance and earlier, he saw works of art that derived their content from the overarching mythology of the biblical and Greek mythologies. A closer examination of the mythic content of the *Large Glass*, then, should reveal both why it has been held in such high regard and why it has been so misunderstood.

Duchamp's statements that the *Large Glass* provides the basis for the meaning of the *readymades* is given greater point if the *Large Glass* critiques and corrects the inherent logic of traditional mythologies, and if the *readymades* are specific instances of its expression. So, to understand the *Large*

Glass, it helps to visualise it as an overarching umbrella embodying a consistent mythic appreciation within which Duchamp's other works operate (and hence the works of all who have been influenced by him). If this were the case, the enduring influence of the *readymades* would be explained, as would their unfingerable quiddity.

So what in the *Large Glass* is similar to traditional mythologies and what is different? What has Duchamp done that no other artist of the twentieth century has done, including Picasso, Matisse, Miro, Beuys, Warhol, and others? What makes it possible for Octavio Paz to evaluate the contributions of Picasso and Duchamp and assign Picasso to the past/present and Duchamp to the present/future?

The mythology central to Western thought and art over the last 2000 years is Judeo/Christian. In it a male God creates the world or nature ex nihilo, forms man and then woman, puts a negative value on sex, and institutes an understanding of good and evil (ethics) that sustains his priority. The mythological status of Genesis and the Gospels is a consequence of talented prophets and evangelists who wrote a cosmology or story of origins in which Adam and Eve and Christ are created by non-sexual means as a metaphor for the limitations of human understanding.

Ironically, however, Judeo/Christian believers claim their mythology provides a true representation of the origins of the world. In their mythology God has priority over the world or nature. God and his apologists participate in an inversion of the natural dynamic by giving the 'word' of God priority over the 'flesh' of mankind.

The mythic logic of the *Large Glass*

Compare then the relationships in the *Large Glass*. The whole of the *Glass* is female and represents the world or nature, which is prior to the formation of the human female (in the top half of the work), and the formation of the male from the female, who do not consummate their relationship. Because Duchamp's primary concern is the logic of myth, he leaves the sexual outside the *Large Glass*, in what he calls the 4th dimension and, as an aesthete, he refrains from expressing an understanding of good and evil.

So Duchamp's world is not logically male but female, it is not created by a male God but is self-subsistent, and the female is given priority over the male who exhibits his complete dependency on the female. Duchamp's artistic expression is mythic because in the world of the *Large Glass* there is no sexual consummation between female and male. The artist (Duchamp) creates the artwork out of his mind (as did the prophets and the evangelists), and he acknowledges its conceptual genesis by having its entities act non-biologically.

What Paz and others have not fully recognised is that the *Large Glass* gives a profoundly logical critique of traditional mythologies, whose priorities are contrary to the logical conditions prevailing in nature. Judeo/Christian belief inverts natural logic and makes life dependant on art. Duchamp reverses the traditional mythologies by re-establishing the logical priority of life over art. The gradual but terminal collapse of the biblical paradigm over the last 500 years, because of its internal inconsistency and its external injustices, is the inevitable consequence of believing that biblical myth expresses much more than the logical limitations of human understanding.

Once it is appreciated that Duchamp's *Large Glass* captures the mythic logic behind all mythologies, (Paz: 'the criticism of myth and the myth of criticism'[2]), and recovers the logical order of evolutionary priority of nature, female, male, and the role of the artist who is capable of expressing the understanding, then it can be seen that he articulates the logical conditions for any mythic expression consistent with the dynamic of life.

Understanding Duchamp

The insuperable difficulty artists and commentators have had acknowledging Duchamp's achievement has been due to the residuum of the biblical and similar paradigms in the culture. It is as if the culture is not yet ready to accept a logically workable expression of the mythic conditions for an unprejudiced understanding of life.

So, once it is appreciated why Duchamp based the *readymades* on the *Large Glass*, it is possible to see how the *readymades* have become stranded between traditional expectations and the logic of a global awareness in which the contingencies of human life are dependent on a fruitful relationship with nature. Duchamp's relevance has not waned because the content of his complete oeuvre is, as Calvin Tomkins suggested in the 1970s, 'ahead of the game'.[3] Again, ironically, the 'mystery' in Duchamp's work possesses a surprising clarity and precision that exposes the traditional mindset as irredeemably mystified.

The twenty-first century has not caught up with the implications of Duchamp's work. The current confusion and scepticism in the avant-garde is symptomatic of its inability to cross from a discredited and inappropriate paradigm to one logically consistent with nature and with humankind in nature.

The extreme irony of the separation of the *readymades* from the *Large Glass* by the avant-garde (an irony Duchamp anticipated) becomes even more extreme when Duchamp is compared to the only other thinker to have articulated systematically the logical conditions for all mythology, and hence the logical conditions for life on earth.

Duchamp and Shakespeare

In the *Sonnets*, Shakespeare anticipates Duchamp by 300 years with a more comprehensive appreciation of the logic of myth. (Shakespeare experienced the inconsistencies of biblical thought in the religious atrocities of his day.) The *Sonnets* express the logic of life not just for artistic expression (aesthetics), but also for any form of language (ethics).

Like Duchamp, Shakespeare's understanding is based on the priority of nature, the priority of the female over the male, the logic of increase, the priority of the sexual over the erotic, and the consequent logic of beauty and truth or aesthetics and ethics. And like Duchamp with the *Large Glass* and its accompanying *Notes*, Shakespeare articulated his philosophy in his *Sonnets* to provide the mythic logic on which all his other works were based. Because they both recover natural logic, the logical structure of the *Large Glass* is the same as that of the *Sonnets*.

For those ready to graduate beyond the failure by twentieth century thinkers to penetrate Duchamp's works (epitomised by the post-modern malaise), and the even greater failure of 400 years of academicism to understand the works of Shakespeare, these volumes explore the mythic logic of Duchamp and Shakespeare (and other thinkers who worked to recover the natural logic of life such as Darwin, Wittgenstein and Mallarmé). The logical precision and comprehensiveness evident in Duchamp and Shakespeare, and apparent in Darwin and Wittgenstein, create an opportunity to institute a systematic understanding beyond the level currently available in tertiary institutions world-wide.

2

Stephane Mallarmé

Preamble

The poetry of Stephane Mallarmé (1842-98) offers one of the purest examples of the mind working at its highest pitch. Despite his reputation as the most obscure of all symbolist poets, once the mind attunes to Mallarmé's deeply realised meaning, no other recent poetry so singularly reconciles the world, human nature and the act of writing.

Mallarmé's progress toward a profound symbolism, though, was not without difficulty. As he deepened his understanding of the logic of poetry, beyond the contradictions in his Christian faith, he experienced what he called the 'abyss'. Only gradually did he find a way beyond the influence of his family's resolute Catholicism to a mature expression of the relation of poetry to life. So it is possible to follow his trajectory from the psychological trap of an idealistic faith to his philosophic expression in poetry of the logical basis of religious symbolism.

When in 1864 Mallarmé precociously announced, in a letter to his friend Henry Cazalis, a new method for writing poetry, he did not anticipate the personal crisis it would precipitate. His insight that he should 'paint not the thing, but the effect that it produces'[1] brought him face to face with the contradictions in biblical belief. After all, the sacred entities or 'effects' in biblical mythology were religiously held to be prior to the 'things' in the world.

Mallarmé's insight was that any writing depends on 'effects' generated within the mind by 'things' in the world. But beliefs based on biblical writing had, for psycho/social reasons, turned the natural process on its head. They had accorded the 'effects' generated by the mind priority over the 'things' in the world.

Mallarmé overcame the 'abyss' when he dismissed the psychological comfort of the biblical promise and accepted his logical role as a creator of 'effects'. In bypassing the notion of God as the ideal creator he was reclaiming the right for poets to evoke the world in the symbolism of their work without prejudice.

As Mallarmé moved beyond the psychology of biblical belief, he rejected the death-orientated male-based idealism of the Old and New Testaments. Critically, though, for the extraordinary depth of meaning in his later poetry, as he freed himself from subservience to the male God, he did not reject the logical function of the ideal. And neither did he merely substitute the idea of God with an abstract Hegelian Ideal. Instead, he rediscovered the sexual basis of the ideal as it is generated in the erotic dynamic of the mind.

Mallarmé's poetry, and things in the world

Mallarmé's poems use for their symbolic effects quite ordinary and everyday things such as windows, sunsets, fans, tombs, birds, stars, female and male, voyages, and even the words and books with which the poems are made and presented. He does not presume to reproduce those things realistically, abstractly, or metaphysically. Rather he realised that language and ideas transform 'things' into logically different 'effects'.

In one of Mallarmé's earlier poems, *The Windows*, he uses the everyday familiarity of light and sight passing through a set of windows to comment on the illusory effect of poetry compared with the things in the 'world below' that is 'master'. The illusory image of an 'angel' that appears on the window momentarily excites his mind to thinking he can be 'reborn' beyond the glass. But such an 'obsession' through 'art or mysticism' is a fantasy caused by the 'effects' of a poem being illogically divorced from 'things' in the world.

The Windows

Tired of the dreary hospital and of the stale incense rising in the
banal whiteness of the curtains towards the **vast crucifix weary
of the empty wall**, the **dying man** cunningly straightens his old back,
drags himself and, less to warm his decay than **to see sunlight**
on the stones, goes to flatten his white hairs and the bones of his
thin face at the windows which a bright lovely sunbeam wishes
to bronze.
And his mouth, feverish and **starving for the blue sky**, just as in
its youth it went to breathe in its treasure, **a virginal skin of long
ago! dirties with a long bitter kiss** the warm golden panes.

He lives intoxicated, forgetting **the horror of the holy oils**, the **tisanes**, the clock and compulsory bed, the cough; and when evening bleeds among the tiles his eye, on the horizon choked with light,
sees golden galleys, beautiful as swans, sleeping on a river of purple and perfumes, rocking the rich, tawny lightning of their lines in **a vast indifference laden with memory**!
So **seized by disgust of man and his hard soul**, wallowing in happiness where only his appetites eat, and persisting in the search for this filth to offer it to **his wife suckling her little ones**,
I flee, and I cling to all the casements from whence **one turns one's shoulder to life**, and, **blessedly**, in their glass washed with **eternal dews gilded by Infinity's chaste morning**,
I look at myself and **see myself as an angel**! And **I die, and I love – whether the glass be art or mysticism – to be reborn**, wearing
my dream like a diadem, in **the earlier heaven where Beauty flowers**!
But alas! **the world below is master**: its obsession comes to disgust me sometimes even in this certain shelter, and **Stupidity's impure vomiting** forces me to stop my nose in face of the blue sky.
Is there a way, O **Self familiar with bitterness**, to **break the crystal insulted by the monster** and to escape, with my **two feather-less wings** – at the risk of **falling throughout eternity**?[2]

In *The Windows*, Mallarmé dismisses, beginning with 'stale incense' and the 'vast crucifix weary of the empty wall', the Christian expectation of redemption ('banal whiteness') and transcendence ('hard soul'). The idealised vanity of escaping angel-like through the glass is rewarded with an Icarus-like fall through broken 'crystal'. In its place, Mallarmé presents his new awareness of the priority of 'things' over 'effects' through metaphors of sunlight, blue sky, the wife 'suckling her little ones', and concludes with the triumph of avoiding the psychological abyss of 'falling throughout eternity'.

In another well-known sonnet, *The Virginal, Living, and Beautiful Day*, the image of a swan caught in ice carries both the erotic idea of the swan's neck immobilised in ice, and the inability of the words on the page to emulate the actions of a living swan that would answer the call of the seasons. In other poems Mallarmé uses the doubled imagery of cranial/pubic hair. The play of light on the hair attracts the poet but when within the hair he feels impotent. He also uses the image of a fan a number of times to suggest both a surface that conveys ideas through images and the pubic area where the poet experiences frustration because writing a poem is not a sexual act.

Mallarmé's poetry and the sexual

The imagery of Mallarmé's poems coheres for the reader if it is remembered that the poet is decidedly conscious of the sexual dynamic, but is writing down its erotic equivalent. Mallarmé evokes the thing through the effect without the psychological diversion of fantasising a separate world or an omnipotent God. He does not invoke a self-contained realm of fantasy, as did other Symbolists, to escape from the natural relation of thing and effect. Rather the evocation of worldly things through erotic effects in his poetry reveals that otherworldly fantasy is a psychological condition because its 'effects' are divorced from their logical connection with 'things'.

Mallarmé's long poem *Afternoon of the Faun*, for instance, examines the logical relationship between the erotic imaginings of the mind and the sexual world from which those imaginings arise. The poem mentions the 'ideal error of roses' and the 'the cold blue eyes of the most chaste' as erotic imaginings that have their origin in the sexual activity to which poetry can only allude.

> *Afternoon of the Faun*
>
> I desire to perpetuate these nymphs.
> So bright their **light rosy flesh** that it hovers in the air drowsy
> with **tufted slumbers**.
> Did I love a dream? My doubt, heap of old night, ends in many
> a **subtle branch**, which, remaining the **true woods** themselves,
> proves, alas! That alone I offered myself the **ideal error of roses** for
> **triumph**. Let us reflect…
> or if the women that you tell of represent a **desire of your**
> **fabulous senses**! Faun, illusion flows like **a weeping spring from the**
> **cold blue eyes of the most chaste**: but the other, **all sighs**, do you
> say that she contrasts like the day breeze **warm on your fleece**? No!
> Through the motionless, **lazy swoon** suffocating with heat the cool
> morning if it **struggles**, there murmurs **no water not poured by my**
> **flute** on the **thicket** sprinkled with melody; (lines 1-20)[3]

The evocation of the erotic through the continual use of imagery derived from the sexual provides the logical underpinning for Mallarmé's exploration of the relation of body and mind. The Faun is the poetic beast who signals the moment when 'things' in the physical world become the 'effects' evoked in the mind.

Mallarmé's unwillingness to accept the traditional religious priority of the conceptual over the physical led him to search for another way to express the 'effect' he experienced when he confronted the whiteness of the untouched page. As he could not avoid referring to things or events, and as he could not ignore the role of the word on the page, he needed to remedy the psychological insistence of the abyss he experienced when he challenged the presumptions of faith.

The answer lay in the logical relation between his human mind and things in the world. He saw, for instance, that the naming of the constellations of the Zodiac imparted human meaning to the universe. As the light of the stars might be from stars now dead, then the signs of the Zodiac served purely human ends[4]. The seamlessness of the way in which Mallarmé's poetry combines its effects is a consequence of the logical reintegration of body and mind in his understanding. The poet is conscious of his pen's movement across the paper as he makes the marks that demonstrate the logic of their derivation from the bodily dynamic.

Mallarmé's poetic logic differs significantly from that of other Symbolists with whom he has been associated, and who credited him with leadership. Because Mallarmé accepts that the physical world is prior to the conceptual operations of the mind, then religious fantasy reveals itself as a secondary psychological effect. His decision to focus on 'effects' is not a flight from the objective world but a realisation that if beauty was all that existed only poetry could give it 'one perfect expression'. Conceptual processes differ logically from physical ones. In a letter to Cazalis he said,

> Beauty alone exists and it has only one perfect expression, Poetry. Everything else is a lie - except, in the case of those who live the life of the body, for love, and, for that love of the mind, friendship.[5]

Unlike Descartes, Mallarmé found that it was the 'life of the body' or 'love' and the 'love of the mind' or friendship that constituted certainty or did not 'lie'. The body is the locus of meaning, as it must be if meaning has a human reference. As he said in a letter to Eugene Fefebure,

I think the healthy thing for man – for reflective nature – is to think with his whole body; then you get a full harmonious thought.... When thoughts come from the brain alone..., they are like tunes played on the squeaky part of the first string (of a violin)'.[6]

Similarly, the philosopher Ludwig Wittgenstein in his later work found himself having to accept the logic of the body. The insistence of natural logic is evident in Wittgenstein's use of such terms as 'family resemblances' and 'forms of life' to characterise language and certainty, and in the statement, 'it is there – like our life'.[7] The poem, as Mallarmé saw it, becomes an expression of certainty or a bulwark against chance, because it attains through its erotic logic the mental equivalent of the state of the 'body', and by extension the universe. He realised that the logic of language identifies doubt and knowing as mental processes, and that certainty is a function of the body because the body does not 'know' or 'doubt'. Certainty is the cessation of knowing and doubting when the priority of the 'body' is accepted. His insight is consistent with his certainty of having been born and so of the sexual dynamic, which consequently generates the erotic dynamic of the mind.

Mallarmé's poetry and the erotic

Standard dictionaries define 'eroticism' as desires or thoughts in the mind, whereas they define 'sexual' in terms of the biology of the body, or the relationship of male and female involving fertilisation and conception and birth. Eroticism, then, is etymologically distinct from and posterior to the sexual or biological.

Mallarmé arrived at a simple poetic method for realising the traditional erotic acknowledgment of embodiment in poetry. Such acknowledgment is evident in the eroticism of God's creation of Adam and Eve in Genesis, in the virgin birth and death and resurrection of Christ, or in the non-biological birth processes in Greek mythology.[8] Mallarmé forged a logically consistent expression that accepts the priority of the body and its effect on the mind.

Mallarmé knew he could not reproduce the sexual in the conceptual realm of poetry because that would contradict the priority of the biological experience. (The double meaning of reproduce and conceptual indicates something of the logical relation between the sexual act and the erotics of language.) The biology of conception is a physical event not accessible through poetry. Simply put, the human child is not born of the mind. The mind is not a womb. Mallarmé knew it would be sufficient to allude to the sexual (with its preparatory desires and consequent detumescence) through erotic suggestion to create an abiding 'effect' of the 'thing'.

The sexual/erotic dynamic is evident in poems such as *Another Fan*.

Another Fan
Of Mademoiselle Mallarmé

O DREAMER, that I may **plunge into pure and pathless delight**,
know how to keep **my wing in your hand** by a subtle falsehood.
A twilight coolness comes to you at each fluttering, whose
captive stroke delicately pushes back the horizon.
Vertigo! Behold space **shivering like a vast kiss** which,
driven mad by **coming to birth** for no one, can neither **gush forth** nor calm itself.
Do you feel the **savage paradise** like hidden laughter flow
from the **corner of your mouth** to the **bottom** of the **unanimous fold**.
This is the **sceptre of rose-coloured** shores stagnant over
Golden evenings, this **white closed flight** which you place against a **bracelet's fire**.[9]

Mallarmé creates not just a sensory experience as in Impressionism, or an abstract arrangement as in Cubism, or an emotive outpouring as in Expressionism. His poems elicit rather a body-dependent aesthetic consistent with the erotic logic of the mind. The effect is to generate a kinesthetic experience in the conscious mind, just like the kinesthetic or 'muscular effort that accompanies a voluntary motion of the body' (OED). The cerebral cortex is excited and, consequently, the whole body is suffused.

The sexual body is the given. Logically, the body, simply by being there, is the basis or stage for the aesthetic effect. The conceptual part of the process satisfies the erotic mind that, as Mallarmé knew, generates an uncompromised, deep, and enduring aesthetic expression

The erotic element in traditional mythologies has the same logical function, except that the beliefs based on those mythologies confound the aesthetic experience by claiming that the 'effect' is prior to the 'object'. The illogical prioritising of the 'spiritual' leads inevitably to illogical prejudices against the body as in Descartes' defence of his Christian belief, and in all Christian apologetics.

Mallarmé's poetry and writing

Mallarmé's faith in the 'love of the body' ensures that his poetry or aesthetics is determined by erotics. Eroticism is the subject of his longer poems *Herodiade* and the *Afternoon of the Faun*, and is an inescapable presence in other sonnets and poems that are based on realistic images or events.

A poem written on a piece of paper, while erotically active, is sexually impotent, however beautiful or absolute it seems. The differing logical functions of body and mind give rise to metaphors of sterility or impotence in poetry. When the sterility of a poem is acknowledged, poetry can convey its content without prejudice to the body. And the content then has an aesthetic and ethical consistency.

So the theme of impotence in Mallarmé's poems is not, as some commentators would have it, a psychological or religious frustration in the face of the absolute. Rather, it is the logical state of a poem written by a human being who is primarily a sexual being, which means being born and so defeating chance. Despite its suggestiveness, ultimately a poem is an 'effect' and not a sexual 'thing'.

When, for instance, Mallarmé's typographically experimental poem *Un coup de dés* is seen from the vantage of the poet, pen in hand, sitting over a white sheet of paper, the placement of the words on the page reflect an image of the poet engaged in the writing process. The imagery captures the poet confronting the 'whiteness' of the paper with his 'fist', his 'virgin index' (finger) or 'feather', etc., and his 'arm', 'feet', 'corpse', 'beard'. All are images within his visual field as he sits at his writing table.

En coup de dés

A DICE THROW
NEVER
even cast in eternal circumstance
from the depth of a ship-wreck
whether the Abyss whitened **at slack tide and furious beneath an** inclination to hover **desperately with wings (its own) fallen back in advance from a** difficulty in trimming its flight **and covering the spoutings cutting off the leapings**
resumes very far into the interior the shadow buried in the depth **by this alternate veil**
to the point of adapting to the span

its gaping depth inasmuch as the hull of a vessel leaning to one or the other side.[10]

The blank paper becomes a screen or theatre on which images of the 'sea', 'shipwreck', etc., are generated by the poet in a somewhat fragmented way as he strives to set down words, and as words already in place suggest further ideas. As he strives to order 'his' universe, he attempts to abolish chance by creating the logical masterpiece on the paper in front of him despite the fact that 'every thought (still) gives off a dice throw'. Once finalised on paper, though, the 'thought' of the night sky becomes the constellation of words committed to the paper in front of his eyes. Once aligned with the natural logic of thought they are beyond the influence of chance.

Un coup de dés as a poem cannot be a sexual act. It is after all merely words on pages. The page is part of its meaning and the words locate that erotic meaning in themselves and not in the things they refer to, whether a Mariner, a Shipwreck, the Sea, or the Stars. By compounding the latent eroticism of the imagery with the imagery as the whiteness of the page and the 'virgin index', etc., Mallarmé introduces the idea of chance in a way that capitalises on its human equivalent in the logic of the possibilities in biological conception.

Mallarmé reaffirms his certainty in the 'love of life' by 'recreating' its beauty in a poem. When he crafts a poem that corresponds to the logic of life, the logical effect enables an escape from the perturbations of chance, or from the psychology of the abyss.

Ironically, of course, the 'perfect' poem that 'defies' chance has an erotic basis that forever trades on the certainty of the sexual process. This must be the case for the living human being who constitutes the audience for the poem. The mind alone, though it re-creates certainty, cannot logically determine it. Mallarmé's poetry points to the logical basis of words and writing in the sexual dynamic behind the eroticism of any mythological tract.

Mallarmé and Marcel Duchamp

The French artist Marcel Duchamp (1887-1968), following the lead of Mallarmé, also wanted to return art to the service of the mind, away from the painterly or 'retinal'. For him the Impressionists, the Expressionists, or the Cubists whose influence he transcended, were not sufficiently above their senses, their forms, or their subjectivity to represent ideas aesthetically.

He was interested not so much in how sensations enter the mind, or how emotions condition the mind, or how the mind reads abstract shapes, but rather how the mind generates content in art, and more specifically content at the level of myth.

Only when Duchamp acted in accord with the erotic logic of the mind could he choose an everyday object and, with a slight change, confer on it an aesthetic resonance free from psychological baggage. The objects he called *readymades,* which began to appear in 1913, resonate with aesthetic significance because they were conceived according to the natural logic of art. In 1912/13 he had already given expression to the logical conditions for a natural aesthetic in the mythic arrangement of the relationship of female and male in his major work *The Bride Stripped Bare by Her Bachelors, Even,* or the *Large Glass.*

Duchamp's appreciation of the significance of Mallarmé's accomplishment was crucial for the mythic achievement of the *Large Glass.* His comment on Mallarmé is relevant: 'A great figure. Modern art must return to the direction traced by Mallarmé: it must be an intellectual, and not merely an animal expression'.[11] Of the many influences on Duchamp, only Mallarmé's understanding of the logical relation of body and mind gives Duchamp's work its abiding profundity. From Mallarmé, Duchamp imbibed the perfect balance between everyday common taste and supreme aesthetic sophistication.

Marcel Duchamp explicitly identifies eroticism as the element in his work about which he would always be 'serious' and which he uses as a 'platform' for the *Large Glass.* His 'serious' attitude to eroticism contrasts with the humour, irony, contradiction, punning, etc., he otherwise used to 'avoid seriousness'.

Many commentators regard Duchamp's irreverent Jarryesque and Roussel-like mechanisms of humour, irony and chance as central to his achievement. For others his interest in geometry, perception, and the mechanical world take priority. Duchamp's work, though, is as free as he was of any of the technological dependencies, the psychological 'problems' and the 'metaphysical' conceits that commentators have presumed on to sustain their interpretations of his work.

The logical priority Duchamp gives eroticism identifies it as the basis for his aesthetic enterprise. Most commentators have recognised eroticism as a significant element in his oeuvre, but because they critique his work on the basis of lesser priorities, the pivotal function of eroticism has not been understood. Rather, his sexual references have been interpreted in alchemical, mythological, or psychological terms (for instance, Arturo Schwarz the symbolism of alchemy, Octavio Paz the mechanical portrayal of love, and Thierry de Duve the minimal gesture of naming). The philosophic, or the deeply aesthetic status of Duchamp's eroticism, has not been investigated.

Duchamp's *Large Glass* expresses the logical relation of the sexual and the erotic. Although both the Bride and the Bachelors 'reveal' or expose themselves to each other and experience desire, their relationship is not and cannot be consummated. They must and do express themselves auto-erotically.

Consequently, Duchamp's *readymades* are imbued either visually or verbally with the same erotic logic as the *Large Glass*. After all, Duchamp said that eroticism was the basis for all of his work. Just like Mallarmé, and even more famously, Duchamp introduced chance into his working processes, and just like Mallarmé, and unlike most of his disciples, chance was always conditional on the sexual/erotic relationship.

Mallarmé's focus on aesthetics

Why then, if Mallarmé and Duchamp's understanding of aesthetics is so incisive, is their work considered difficult or esoteric? Mallarmé's decision to 'paint not the thing but the effect that it produces', and Duchamp's profound distaste for ordinary 'language', leading to his subversion of language for aesthetic ends, create difficulties for an understanding of their ideas. The problematic moment would seem to be when they bring to focus the eroticism of everyday language as they evoke the deeply symbolic or the mythic logic of the mind.

The esoteric dimension in the work of Mallarmé and Duchamp is a consequence of their disinterest, or even hostility in Duchamp's case, to the 'difference' or the oppositional dynamic of propositional language. Neither Mallarmé nor Duchamp develops a language-based ethics, where ethics involves the give and take in everyday language (expressed in Genesis as the 'knowledge of good and evil'). Both were aesthetes who reveled in aesthetics and spurned ethics.

In the logic of language, words differentiate the sensations that enter the mind through the body from the world. There is a logical transition from unmediated sensory experiences to deliberate linguistic communication. In mythological terms the move is represented in Genesis when Adam and Eve lose their sense of unity with nature to become 'like God' in having 'the knowledge of good and evil'.

As clearly articulated in the philosophy of Ludwig Wittgenstein, the process of differentiation in language establishes the logical difference between 'things' perceived and 'objects' of thought. In his *Tractatus*, Wittgenstein identifies the operation of negation as basic to the possibility of a proposition. The proposition 'p' simultaneously identifies both the object of thought and everything in thought that is not the object, or 'not p'.

Duchamp intentionally inverts the logic of differentiation that is central to Wittgenstein's analysis of the logic of language. He establishes the 'beauty of indifference' when the polarised objects of language are reunited in a singular image or a verbal pun. In a note to the *Large Glass*, Duchamp talks of losing 'the possibility of recognising 2 similar objects'.[12]

Duchamp captures the aesthetic moment succinctly in his aphorisms 'beauty of indifference' and 'irony of affirmation'. They both refer to the operation where the propositional difference through negation is nullified by a further negation. Duchamp refers to the moment of indifference as the 'rendezvous' which invokes the experience of an 'aesthetic echo'.

Ironically, Wittgenstein, despite his clarity as to the logic of language in the *Tractatus*, decided that both ethics and aesthetics belong in the realm of the aesthetic. Under the influence of traditional metaphysics, he put both ethics and aesthetics beyond language in the realm of the 'unspeakable'. While Wittgenstein thought ethics and aesthetics were one and the same, Mallarmé and Duchamp's distaste for the everyday volitional processes of language and its ethical logic led them to focus primarily on the aesthetic. They, however, were at least logically consistent in their allocation of art to aesthetics and language to ethics.

But, in a further irony, even though Mallarmé and Duchamp were determined to remain within the logic of aesthetics, when they explained their ideas in notes and letters they had to use propositional language. Their drive for aesthetic incisiveness in their poetry and art could not completely circumvent the logic of ethics or propositional language.

Duchamp, for instance, wished to work beyond the possibility of consciously deciding between good and bad taste, a language-bound set of choices. He knew that in the logic of the singular moment of aesthetic experience in art taste is eliminated. But despite his ability to avoid the perpetual argument between good and bad taste, he had no interest in articulating the logic of ethics from which he was escaping.

Fifty years before them, in the *Descent of Man*, Darwin had argued for the evolutionary development of the moral sense from naturally occurring affections such as sympathy. His evidence for the derivation of the moral faculty from human progenitors points to the logical connection between aesthetics and ethics.

Mallarmé and William Shakespeare

A measure of Mallarmé's awareness of the logical relation of the erotic to the act of writing is evident in his references to Shakespeare. His sonnet, *The Clown Punished*, begins with the image of the eye. In Shakespeare's *Sonnets* and his poems and plays there is continuous call on the eroticism of the mind's eye, which is logically derived from the sexual eye of the body. And significantly for a poem that examines the drama of sexual/textual frustration, Mallarmé evokes the name Hamlet.

The Clown Punished

Eyes, lakes with my simple **intoxication to be reborn** other than the **actor**, who, with his **gestures as with a pen**, evoked the **disgusting** soot of the lamps, I have **pierced a window** in the **wall** of cloth.
Limpid, treacherous swimmer with my leg and arms in many a bound renouncing the **evil Hamlet!** It is as if I began **a thousand tombs** in the **waves** to disappear into them **virgin**.
Merry gold of the cymbal **beaten with fists**, all at once **the sun strikes the nakedness** purely breathed from my cool **mother-of-pearl**,
When you passed over me, **rancid night of the skin**, not knowing, ingrate! That it was my **whole anointing**, this **rouge drowned** in the **deceitful water of glaciers**.[13]

The clown is punished because he attempts to treat the poem as more than a series of effects. His 'simple intoxication to be reborn' parodies the expectation of religious idealists that they will be resurrected or reincarnated. The clown wants to be 'other than the actor' but notices that his gestures, like writing, evoke nothing but 'soot of the lamps'.

The clown imagines he has literally (as if sexually) 'pierced a window' in the 'wall of cloth'. The clown's desire to have more than what a poem can logically deliver renders him virginal. His vigorous efforts to attain transcendence entomb his fantasies beneath the waves.

In the clown's blind frustration he renounces Hamlet as 'evil'. But Mallarmé knows that Hamlet's failure to avoid his fate is likewise a consequence of his frustration at Polonius' pious expectation for himself and Ophelia (the 'wall of cloth'), and more seriously at Claudius and Gertrude ('rancid night of the skin') whose acts were contrary to natural logic. The clown's attempt to imitate the sun serves only to remind him of his 'nakedness'. What he hoped would be an 'anointing' or the glorious last rites before he ascended to heaven, is reduced to the logic of his rouge or penis drowning in the coldness of the white page.

Only a 'clown' could expect to be 'reborn' in the fantasies engendered on the page created by the 'gestures as with a pen'. A poem is an artifact that logically refuses to satisfy the sexual expectations of the clown. The sense of erotic frustration at the impasse of the 'wall of cloth' (read page), is conveyed again and again in the suggestive symbolism of impotency. The poem's litany of sexual metaphors leaves no doubt that Mallarmé was using the 'thing' of the sexual dynamic in nature to create an intensified erotic experience of the proscribed 'effect' in poetry.

Mallarmé's reading of Shakespeare correctly appreciates that immortality through verse, or any sense of immortality, be it the Platonic or biblical ideal, is the result of a misunderstanding of the logic of the written/spoken word. Shakespeare argues endlessly for an understanding of the priority of increase in nature over truth and beauty, or the logic of the mind in the *Sonnets* and in the poems and plays.

In the caption above his long poem, *Igitur*, Mallarmé acknowledges the erotic logic of poetic experience when he states: 'this story is addressed to the intelligence of the reader which stages things itself'. The central image of *Igitur*, of the poet descending stairs into the crypt of his ancestors, looks back to the descent of Hamlet into the genealogical impasse of Claudius' crime, and anticipates Duchamp's painting *Nude descending the Staircase*.

Igitur acknowledges the influence of the play and anticipates the painting in its critique of the unrealisable fantasies of idealism and its extensive use of sexual metaphor to establish the logical relation between life and art. Throughout the poem Mallarmé uses many words and phrases that critique the absolute. They range from 'the absolute at dead centre', 'indifference', 'reciprocal nothingness', 'malady of ideality', 'neurosis boredom (or Absolute)', 'frightful sensation of eternity', 'Absolute has disappeared', 'mirror absolutely pure', 'isolated from humanity', 'believing in the existence of the sole Absolute imagines he is everywhere in a dream', 'ashes of stars', and the 'empty flask' or 'madness' leaving the 'castle of purity'.

More importantly, Mallarmé uses a range of sexual metaphors. He evokes the sexual in 'a vague quiver of thought', 'hair languishing', 'stripped of any meaning', 'plunged into the shadow', 'sterility', 'miscarried', 'a pendulum about to be extinguished', 'stifle the guest irremediably', 'gasping', 'friction of a superior age', 'volume of their nights', 'pinnacle of myself'. He continues with 'pulsations of my own heart', 'the same rhythmical sound', 'disengage my dream', 'hairy stomach', 'torture of being eternal', 'curtains invisibly trembling', 'burrow in the curtains', 'gray shiver', 'saturated and weighted draperies', 'act useless', 'monsters rigid in their last struggle', 'one-horned', to the impotence of the 'empty flask'.[14]

As Mallarmé says in the introductory lines, *Igitur* as a poem is 'simply word and gesture' in which 'the family was right to deny it (the Absolute) its life – so that it stayed (or kept at bay) the absolute'. Mallarmé demonstrates that a poem that refuses to be deceived by its own seductiveness, while losing its appeal for those who live for fantasy, gains immeasurably in veracity and consistency. His symbolism is profound both because it touches the depths of the sensational mind and because it sustains its integrity in the process. In this he resembles Shakespeare, even if he does not rise to a mythic level of expression.

Shakespeare's *Sonnets*

In his *Sonnets* Shakespeare articulates the logic of aesthetics more precisely than do Mallarmé and Duchamp in their work. In sonnets 127 to 152 he shows that sensations from the world are differentiated into ideas (beauty into truth), and then in sonnets 20 to 126 that ideas are recombined into sensations of the mind (truth into beauty). As aestheticians of poetry and art, Mallarmé and Duchamp focus on the second possibility. Like Shakespeare, though, they gain their consistency by accepting the priority of nature and the sexual dynamic.

The complete dynamic from nature to the aesthetic experience in poetry and art can be rendered schematically from the logical structure of the *Sonnets*.

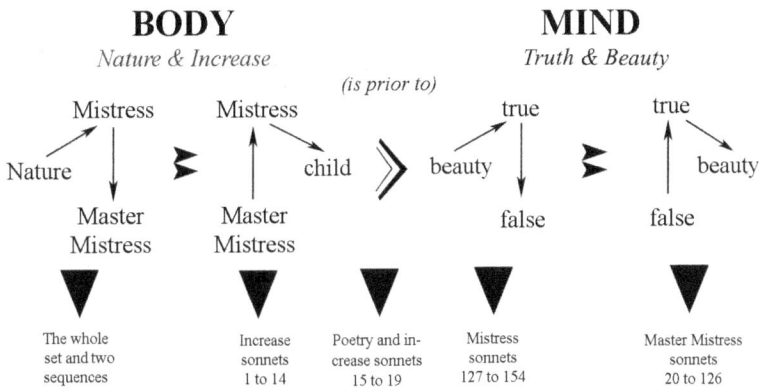

Nature template (Sonnet numbers)

In his complete philosophy Shakespeare goes further than Mallarmé and Duchamp because he also articulates the logic of ethics or the dynamic of true and false in language. In the Mistress sequence, sonnets 127 to 137 are devoted to the aesthetic of primary sensations and sonnets 138 to 152 present the logic of truth or ethics derived from those primary sensations. Shakespeare's account of both aesthetics and ethics out of nature gives his work a completeness lacking in the esoteric poems and art of Mallarmé and Duchamp.

In the *Mind template*, taken from the *Nature template* for the *Sonnets*, the logical relationships are evident. Primary sensations enter from the left, where they are differentiated through the dynamic of language into true and false. Then sensations of the mind, such as absolute beauty, God, etc., are formed to the right by the recombination of ideas into singular effects.

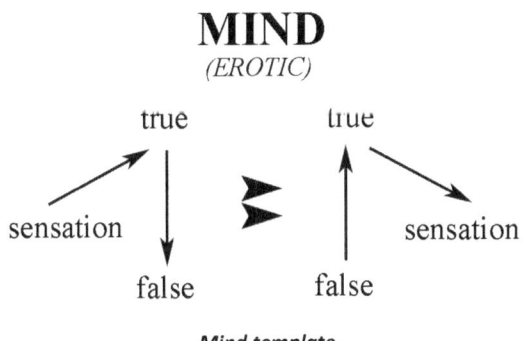

Mind template

When Mallarmé talks of representing the effect and not the thing he short-circuits the logical difference between the aesthetics of primary sensations and the aesthetic experience generated in the mind through the unifying of ideas. He jumps from primary sensations through to the secondary sensations of the mind.

The primary and secondary sensations are both singular effects unmediated by thought. The difference is between the effects generated by the senses and the poetic or artistic effects generated in the mind. When Duchamp talked of the connection between the sense of smell and the aesthetic echo in art he showed his awareness of the logical connection.

Shakespeare establishes the logical relationship between primary and secondary sensations by first articulating the logic of the sexual dynamic in nature and the logical requirement to increase for the persistence of humankind. The logical relationship in nature acts as a given for the isomorphic relationship of beauty and truth in the mind. In the work of Mallarmé and Duchamp the *Body template* is a barely indicated given.

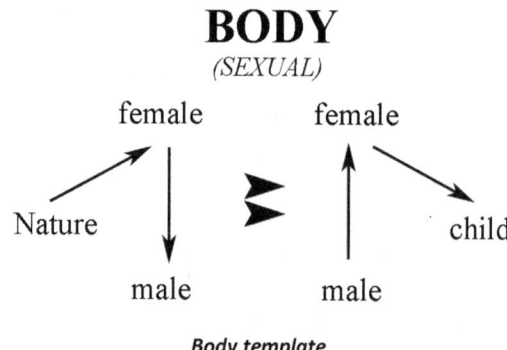

Body template

Shakespeare establishes the logic of the sexual out of nature in the first 19 sonnets and explores the logic of the erotic in sonnets 20 to 154. The first 19 sonnets provide the key to appreciating Mallarmé and Duchamp's logical insights into aesthetics. They predate Darwin's explanation of the development of the moral faculty in the *Descent of Man*. They also reveal the strengths and weaknesses in Wittgenstein's analysis of propositional logic. Shakespeare's articulation of the logical difference between aesthetics and ethics corrects Wittgenstein's illogical consignment of them both to the realm of the 'unspeakable'.

The *Sonnets* not only address the logic of ethics or truth and aesthetics or beauty by accepting the priority of the body, they also state that the sexual process is prior to understanding truth and beauty or erotics. Mallarmé and Duchamp did appreciate the logic of the erotic but they do not explicitly incorporate a statement of the priority of the sexual dynamic in their poetry or art. At best Mallarmé, in the letter to Cazalis, and Duchamp, in a letter to Carrouges, when forced to define the irreducible concerns in their work, do allude to the significance of human persistence.

Following Mallarmé's lead, Duchamp argued that other artists, such as the Impressionists, Expressionists, Cubists and Futurists, were limited in their expectation of the aesthetic. They were too focused on the first part of the *Mind template*, which represents incoming sensations and their illusory effects.

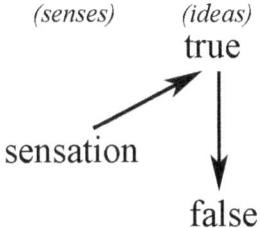

Beauty to truth template

Like Mallarmé, Duchamp realised that the more he focused on secondary sensations the more his art would be a product of the intellect. He wanted to put art at the service of the mind.

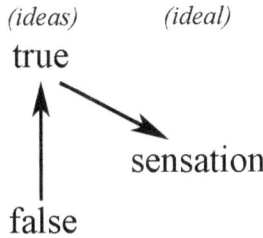

Truth to beauty template

The *Sonnets* show how the specialised interests of Mallarmé, Duchamp, and Darwin can be reconciled, and the errors of Wittgenstein be rectified.

An acceptance of the priority of the body (and so nature) over the mind for human understanding aligns their philosophic expectations with Shakespeare's natural logic. A combination of their specialisations from the nineteenth and twentieth centuries postdates by 300 years the philosophic comprehensiveness and consistency of the logic in Shakespeare's set of 154 sonnets.

Conclusion

The logical relationship of the sexual and the erotic in human persistence suggests the sexual provides the logical basis for all thought processes. Only the body with its sexual dynamic has the appropriate multiplicity to account for the logic of the mind.

Mallarmé and Duchamp, by accepting the logic of eroticism, are free of the contradictions that arise with a Descartian 'disembodied' mind. Mallarmé's early experience with the inconsistencies and contradictions in traditional biblical belief led him beyond the psychological or mind-determined view of the world through the abyss of doubt to the certainty of a philosophic view based in nature. Leo Bersani acknowledged Mallarmé's achievement when he felt constrained to leave aside his psychological hat in the *Death of Mallarmé*.[15] He recognised Mallarmé deserved a purely philosophic approach to penetrate his eroticism.

When the *Nature template* is flipped about something of Mallarmé's problem is revealed. To correct the consequences of millennia of male God contradictions he needed to recover the natural logic of life in his poetry.

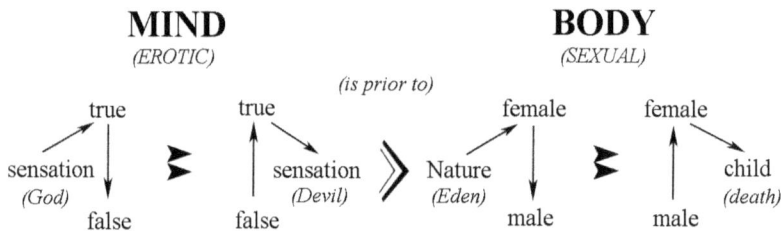

God template

Mallarmé's achievement is exemplary when viewed against the attempts by his contemporaries to break the psychological hold of biblical mythology taken literally. Although other poets and artists have rejected the traditional inconsistencies, they have then resorted to the psychology of scepticism, or turned to mysticism or other arcane beliefs and practices. Only Marcel Duchamp fully appreciated Mallarmé's philosophic level of insight and gave it a consistent mythic expression.

3
Sigmund Freud & Carl Jung

Modern psychology

In the late nineteenth century, in response to the psychiatric demand following the decline of the Judeo/Christian paradigm as a credible worldview, Freud and then Jung (among others) developed their therapeutic practices. At a time when faith in the efficacy of traditional religious insights into psychological predicaments was failing, secular psychology was seeking recognition as a scientific discipline.

Traditionally, biblical mythology had provided a series of dogmatically prescribed givens in which a male God created the world, where Adam the first male was created prior to the female, where procreation and death were created as the punishment for 'sin', and where the absolute, as the unknowable 'Word', assumed priority over the dynamic of true and false in language. But, unfortunately for the unknowable Word, the critique of biblical theology by Hume and others in the seventeenth and eighteenth centuries showed the transcendental 'He' or God was no more than a psychological preoccupation of prophets and evangelists temperamentally at odds with the natural world.

Freud and Jung sought redress for the psychological consequences of the inconsistencies in biblical mythology by turning to archetypal expressions of psychological relations in other mythologies. For instance, Freud used the myth of Oedipus to account for the psychological consequences of sexual dysfunction, and Jung analysed the world's mythologies to locate archetypal symbols that might ease the post-biblical experience of psychological alienation.

The logic of myth

To discover why Freud and Jung fell out over their division of the mythological pie, and why neither of them could appreciate the mythic depth of

Shakespeare's *Sonnet* philosophy, a different attitude to mythology is required. It is not sufficient to see the mythic either as a pharmacy for psychological problems or as a source of cathartic symbols. The mythic level of expression has the philosophic function of articulating the logic of expression while expressing the logical relation between humankind and nature.

Despite the confusion of imaginative and empirical ideas in biblical mythology, biblical prophets and evangelists appreciated, at least intuitively, the logical role of a mythology. Their illogical configuration of the relationship between nature at large and human nature unintentionally expresses the logical limitations of the spoken or written word. Biblical writing intuitively acknowledges that the mythic logic of human expression is erotic, or an expression of conscious desires. It correctly represents 'God the Word' as logically erotic and so distinct from the biological or sexual.

Even philosophers as critical of biblical theology as Hume and Kant were not prepared to explore the biological illogicality that arises when biblical myth invents a male God who in turn creates the female from the male. They remained beholden to the prevailing Judeo/Christian worldview, which proscribed the possibility of investigating the erotic logic of its mythology by enshrining the status of the heavenly pantheon in self-validating commandments and dogmatic infallibility. Biblical mythology maintained its function as a psychological refuge in a hostile world by forbidding investigation of its empirical inconsistencies. The long-term effect was to create even deeper psychopathic problems that required a different approach to the psychological when the irrationality of belief became untenable.

Freud and Jung: the differences

So Freud and Jung were faced with a double problem. Their patients manifested the usual psychological pathologies due to inheritance or to ingrained experience. But they also suffered from the psychological consequences of the vacuum or abyss following the loss of faith in Judeo/Christian mythology. Part of the confusion in the writings of Freud and Jung comes from not appreciating the difference between naturally occurring defects of mind and the estrangement from a discredited mythology.

Instead, Freud and Jung were responsive to different components of the Judeo/Christian mythology. Freud's disposition led him to focus primarily on sexual dysfunction and to suggest that neuroses and psychoses were consequent on sexual issues. Jung's inclination, while initially beholden to

Freud's focus, was to see the post-biblical psychological malaise as a failure to appreciate the archetypal significance of the signs and symbols in mythological expression. Typically, for instance, when Freud and Jung focused on dreams, Freud looked for symptoms of sexual significance, and Jung looked to interpret dream imagery in terms of archetypal symbols.

The failure, then, of biblical theology to survive the philosophical investigations of the seventeenth and eighteenth centuries had its counterpart in the fragmentation of twentieth-century psychology into competing factions that lacked the relative unity of the more coherent and comprehensive biblical mythology.

Freud and Jung's attempts to derive a comprehensive theoretical understanding from their analyses of specific psychological disorders prevented them from developing a consistent philosophy at the level of myth that would correct the logical deficiencies in the Judeo/Christian paradigm. So, predictably, they were unable to articulate a coherent mythological level of understanding and expression to provide their twentieth-century clients with a consistent philosophic connection at the level of the mythical to the logical conditions of their lived experience.

Because Freud and Jung's individual inclinations led them to focus on a limited portion of the full mythical relationship between nature, sexual beings, and the dynamic of the mind, they were not able to develop an overview of the logic of the mythic level of understanding. Without a systematic understanding of the logic of myth within which to locate their individual interests, they became antagonistic toward each other's intense focus on different parts of the old mythologies. Ironically, the sectarian conflict that typifies Judeo/Christian belief, because of its illogical inversion of nature and myth, became a conflict across mythologies for Freud and Jung because of their inability to determine the logic of myth.

Nothing in the above statements should be less than obvious to anyone who is aware of the collapse of traditional mythologies and the divergence of the interests of Freud and Jung. Freud's work has been continued and critiqued by others, with sexual issues remaining central to their practice. Similarly, Jung and his disciples have collected and investigated the various mythologies with their associated signs and symbols, in the hope of attaining a unified theory of mythical expression. But there are no logical insights in the work of Freud and Jung or their followers that offer a resolution to biblical inconsistencies, or to their personal differences.

The works of Shakespeare

To unravel the logic behind Freud and Jung's contributions and disagreements, a systematic overview at the level of mythic expression is required. Only when a consistent methodology is applied can their preferences for the sexual or the symbolic be explained and their similarities and differences reconciled.

The limitations of Freud and Jung are revealed when their analyses of Shakespeare's works are compared with the comprehensive mythic philosophy available in his *Sonnets*. Shakespeare is the only thinker to purposely articulate the logical conditions for any mythology and so is the only thinker able to provide the required level of mythic logic for a systematic overview. Freud and Jung's ignorance of the philosophy of the *Sonnets* meant they were unable to comprehend the logic at the heart of Shakespeare's work and so were prevented from finding a resolution to their own differences.

It is only necessary to examine Freud and Jung's attempts to understand the works of Shakespeare to appreciate the inadequacy of approaching the plays and poems with psychological rather than philosophic expectations. Their psychological analyses of the motivations or disorders of key characters lack credibility both because they are not able to contextualise the characters in the logical framework provided by the *Sonnet* philosophy and because in the absence of Shakespeare's overarching logic they commit the fallacy of attributing to Shakespeare some of the symptoms observed in his characters.

In *The Interpretation of Dreams*, in the chapter 'Material and sources of dreams',[1] Freud applies his theories derived from the myth of Oedipus and other sources to the relationship between Hamlet, his mother, and Ophelia. The irony is that Shakespeare creates such characters to examine the illogical consequence of believing that mythologies represent the world rather than an acceptance that the role of myth is to reflect the world by articulating the logical conditions for understanding. Because Freud's understanding is limited by his continued adherence to aspects of the illogical mythical expectations, he does not appreciate Shakespeare's philosophic argument for which the dramatic characters are argument places.

In 'The Battle for Deliverance from the Mother', from *The Psychology of the Unconscious*,[2] Jung looks to Shakespeare's *Julius Caesar* to support his theoretical position. His illogical expectations are already signaled, though, in the chapter heading. His premise of male flight from the 'Mother' is contrary to the *Sonnet* logic where the Master Mistress learns to reconcile himself to the biological priorities of the Mistress so he can express his relation to the world logically. While Jung gives attention to the role of the female in his psychological analyses, he remains a defender of the inconsistencies of the traditional paradigm by not challenging the priority given to the male. He expresses his prejudice when he says he prefers the 'brightness of the ideal' to the 'dark nature of the biological'.[3]

The *Sonnet* logic

The templates generated in Volume 1 to represent Shakespeare's logic can be used to show where Freud and Jung were heading in their critique of the Judeo/Christian tradition, and why they were still unable to move beyond its inconsistencies to a clear expression of the mythic possibility.

The *Nature template* derived from the *Sonnet* logic establishes the basis from which to investigate the illogicality of the mind-set which Freud and Jung were trying to move beyond. It represents the logical basis of understanding toward which they were intuitively struggling.

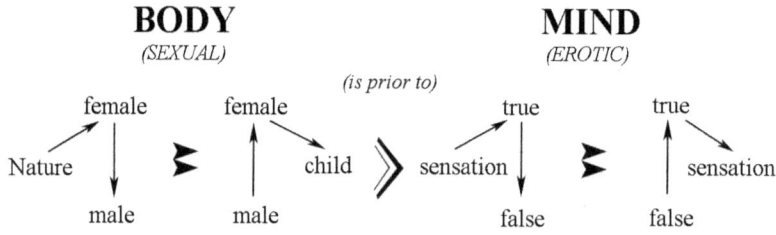

Nature template

When the template for natural logic is reordered to represent the illogical Judeo/Christian paradigm within which Freud and Jung were educated and from which they were attempting to liberate themselves, the resulting template reveals the inversion and distortion to which natural logic is subjected when a mythology is given priority over the natural world.

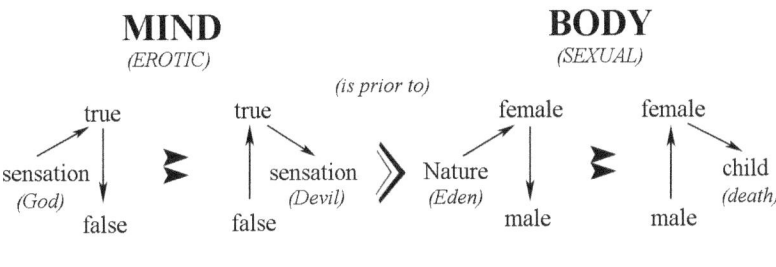

God template

The difference between Freud and Jung can be identified by realising that Freud focused on the body or sexual side of the *Nature template* for natural logic.

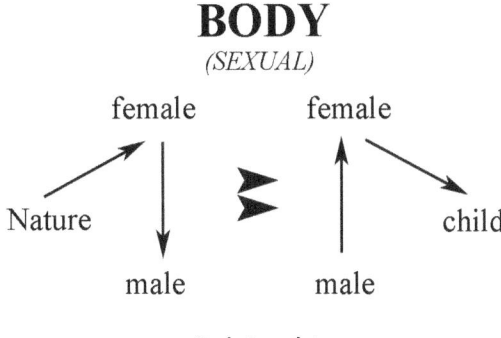

Body template

In Freud's attempt to rectify the traditional misconfiguration of the *Nature template* by recovering the priority of the body dynamic, he imported aspects of the mind dynamic into his considerations of the sexual. He looked for myths that could explain sexual dysfunction and, because he was foreshortening the *Nature template,* thought of the sexual and the erotic as interchangeable.

Jung's idealistic disposition led him to focus on the mind or erotic side of the *Nature template*.

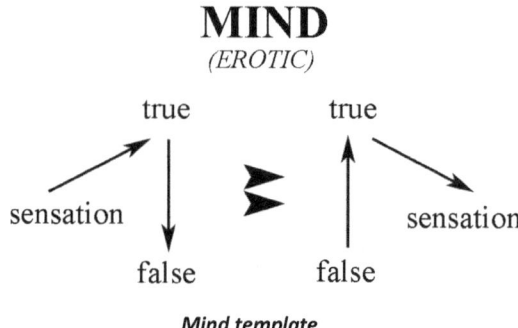

Mind template

Jung correctly maintained that he did not dismiss the sexual in his rift with Freud, but the sexual became an appendage to his traditionally sympathetic fascination with the right hand side of the *Mind template,* which completes the logical condition for mythic expression. Ironically, both Freud and Jung felt they were justified in their selection of a portion of the *Nature template,* but the effect for each was to atrophy the other side of the template. They were right in as much as their individual concerns were warranted but they were wrong in as much as they were ignorant of the complete dynamic of natural logic. In the broader view, Freud's primary focus on the pre-conscious mind complemented Jung's focus on the post-conscious mind.

If Freud and Jung had been successful in rectifying the illogicality of the traditional paradigm by reformulating the corrupt Judeo/Christian paradigm to allow their natural logic or birthright paradigm to resurface they would have had little difficulty appreciating the brilliant philosophic achievement of Shakespeare's *Sonnets.* But, because remnants of the old paradigm persisted in their thinking, they failed to do what Shakespeare had done successfully 300 years before them.

Neither of them was able to move beyond their intuition that the Judeo/Christian world-view was awry in representing the logical relation between the body and the mind. Freud did sense that the old mythology denied the body its natural priority. Because of the logic of the sexual in human experience, Freud validly related the denigration the sexual dynamic in biblical mythology to the sexual dysfunction and disorders he observed in his patients.

Of the two thinkers, Freud was closest to recovering the logic of the sexual dynamic in the *Sonnet* philosophy. He remained confused, though, about the logical distinction between the sexual and the erotic. He was unable to appreciate the difference between the sexual as the biological and the erotic as mind-based desire. Hence he was not able to separate the logic of human sexual persistence in nature from the logic of the operations of the mind expressed in a culture's mythology.

Because Jung rejected the logical priority of the sexual, he was further than Freud from appreciating the need to completely reconstitute biblical priorities. Because he still gave priority to the mind over the body, his contribution was limited to demonstrating that mythologies express archetypal relations and constants. His greater idealism meant he sympathised with the overt idealism of the biblical myth, which entails relegating the sexual to a necessary function of the body without wishing to accord it its logical status for the human mind within nature.

The case of Marcel Duchamp

Many art movements in the period 1910 to 1968 claim Marcel Duchamp as their guiding light, but of particular interest is his role as an involuntary father figure for the Surrealists. The founder of the Surrealists, Andre Breton, attempted to recruit Duchamp to the movement but he remained aloof, only participating occasionally in some of their events.

One of the reasons for Duchamp's wariness would have been the Surrealists uncritical acceptance of the psychoanalytical investigations of Freud and Jung. While Duchamp's oeuvre resists Freudian and Jungian analysis, the deliberately symbolic works of Dali, Miro, Ernst, and Magritte are fair game for psychological and alchemical readings. Their work, unlike Duchamp's, remains illusive, enigmatic, or simply obscure. It is not possible to work through their symbolism to discover a consistent expression of the logic of art.

By contrast, an investigation of Duchamp's *Large Glass*, *Etant donnes* and his *readymades* reveals ever deeper levels of philosophic coherence. Whereas a jump from the symbolism of the Surrealists to Shakespeare's mythic expression is unrewarding, Duchamp's aesthetic achievement leads logically to the comprehensive mythic philosophy of the *Sonnets* and plays.

The inadequacy of the psychological reading for understanding the logic of Shakespeare's plays is reinforced by the inappropriateness of applying either Freudian or Jungian analysis to the works of Marcel Duchamp. Because Duchamp's *Large Glass* has the same logical structure as the *Sonnets*, psychological theories about its operation and meaning are unavailing.

When Freudian style analysis is applied to the *Large Glass* psychologists inevitably attempt to account for the logic of the erotic relationship between the Bride and the Bachelors as a symptom of sexual dysfunction in Duchamp. They say Duchamp must have been either masturbatory or incestuous to have created the sexual/erotic dynamic of his work.

Such psychoanalysis completely misses the logical critique Duchamp makes of the inconsistencies of traditional mythologies through his recovery of the logic of mythic expression. Because Freudian psychology does not involve a logical correction to the female/male priorities, it shifts the critical content of the *Large Glass* to a reflection on the mental health of the artist. But, as a few Freudian analysts do acknowledge, Duchamp was one of the sanest persons to have lived.

Jungian style analysis does not accuse Duchamp of sexual dysfunction. Instead, it looks to his symbol system to discover relationships between ancient mythological symbols and those in the *Large Glass*. Because Jungian analysis is pan-mythical in outlook it is not able to consider Duchamp's critique of traditional mythologies in the *Large Glass*. Instead it turns hopefully to the formulaic symbol systems of arcane practices such as alchemy to explain the significance of Duchamp's iconography.

Jung's lifelong fascination with alchemical practices has led his followers to look for alchemical correspondences in Duchamp's work. But because Duchamp's work provides a philosophic critique of such practices, which are themselves illogical consequences of the inconsistencies of traditional mythologies, Jungian analysis misses the logical heart of Duchamp's achievement. Duchamp was quite explicit in rejecting attempts to associate his work with traditional alchemy. He did not deny that it was possible to find alchemical elements in his work but insisted that the logical function of his work had nothing to do with such psychological practices.

The attempt to accuse Duchamp of sexual dysfunction and alchemical interests is reminiscent of two of the typical accusations brought to the person and the works of Shakespeare. But the accusations about Shakespeare's sexual life are rebuffed when the logical function of the *Sonnets* is revealed, and sonnet 14 specifically rejects idealistic alchemical fantasies. The similarity of the difficulties Freudian and Jungian analysis has with Shakespeare and Duchamp reinforces the limitations of their psychological insights when confronted with the compelling logic of the *Large Glass* and the *Sonnets*. Duchamp, like Shakespeare, was recovering the natural logic of life as the context for art.

Conclusion

Freud and Jung were treating patients who were sexually traumatised and mythologically bereft. Freud centered his work on the consequences of the sexual and Jung's forte was in the erotic or post-sexual mind. Out of his sexual focus Freud was unable to account comprehensively for the mythological as an expression of the deepest human logic. Jung considered the mythological primarily as sign and symbol, as he attempted to recover the mythological dimension of biblical thought but for a global consciousness. Ironically for Freud and Jung's psychological approach, the world's mythologies became a resource for a universal psychological panacea.

Freud was correct in identifying the sexual as logically prior to and hence constitutional of mind-based potentialities, but was wrong to put greater emphasis on the sexual over the erotic. Jung was right in acknowledging the importance of myth in human expression but was wrong to prioritise the ideal over nature.

The inability of Freudian and Jungian analysis to penetrate the logic of the works of Shakespeare and Duchamp indicates their illogical commitment to the psychology of the tertiary methodologies that explicitly or tacitly give priority to the ideal over nature. Only by appreciating the quaternary achievement of the *Sonnets* and plays of Shakespeare and the *Large Glass* and other works of Duchamp, can a logical perspective be gained to see clearly what Freud and Jung were up to, and what is required if they were to understand Shakespeare and his works.

4
James Joyce & T. S. Eliot

Although the worldviews of T. S. Eliot and James Joyce differed profoundly, they were united in their misunderstanding of the logic of mythic expression. Eliot's lifelong commitment to a single mythology and Joyce's increasing need to accommodate all mythologies were of no avail when they attempted to understand the mythic logic of Shakespeare's works.

While both Eliot and Joyce drew on the works of Shakespeare for inspiration and evaluation, their individual trajectories reveal attitudes at odds with the mythic logic articulated in his *Sonnets*. Their works exemplify opposing approaches to mythology that the *Sonnet* logic rejects and transcends.

The singular approach of T. S. Eliot

Throughout his career T. S. Eliot (1888-1965) rarely strayed from the influence of his Christian upbringing. He was raised a Unitarian and made a formal commitment to the Church of England in 1927.

Eliot's unswerving commitment to the tradition of Judeo/Christian learning and 'advancement' as he called it meant that when he attempted to include other mythologies within his poetry he was unable to write with coherence and purpose. Even before he reaffirmed his Christian faith in 1927, his attitude toward other mythologies was largely formal or at best experimental, as with the use of Indian mythology in the *Wasteland*. His ad hoc interest in other belief systems resulted in poems of barely coherent parts.

Paradoxically, Eliot's most significant early achievement was his least overtly Christian poem, the *Wasteland*. And the added irony is that the poem owes its formal strength to the editorial intervention of Ezra Pound. Pound reduced Eliot's repetitious and infelicitous manuscript by over half. His intervention drew attention to the disjunction between Eliot's evident craftsmanship and his lack of a logical system to regulate his ideas.

Although Eliot's later poetry and plays are more faithfully Christian in their psychology, their intellectual disingenuousness makes them little more than apologia for his faith, or the offerings of a troubled mind for troubled minds. Eliot sublimated his anxiety within his poetics and in his prose critiques of art and society. In a twist of fate, he was instrumental in consigning his wife to an asylum when by some accounts she was sane enough to question his pretences.

When, in *Notes Toward the Definition of Culture*, Eliot debates the relation between culture and religion, he uses the opportunity to justify his recommitment to a traditional belief. He says he does not believe that the 'culture of Europe could survive the complete disappearance of the Christian faith' because 'if Christianity goes, the whole of our culture goes'.[1] Because he believes religion is 'incarnated'[2] in a culture, he cannot see how a culture could survive without Christianity. Yet he admits that his way of 'looking at culture and religion' allows him to 'grasp' the connections only in 'flashes'.[3] And he guilelessly confesses that 'religion…gives apparent meaning to life' by providing a fortuitous 'frame-work' to protect the 'mass of humanity from boredom and despair'.[4]

Eliot's recognition that the Christian faith fulfils a psychological role in a culture, especially as Christianity has lost its capacity to be identified with the culture as a whole, is consistent with his lack of insight into mythic logic. If he had understood Shakespeare's *Sonnets*, and hence the mythic philosophy behind the plays and poems, he would have appreciated the logical connection between religion and culture beyond the particular manifestation of the mythic in a religion like Christianity.

Eliot and Shakespeare

In his Introduction to Wilson Knight's *Wheels of Fire*, Eliot reveals his ambivalence toward Shakespeare. While he frequently acknowledges Shakespeare's 'great poetry' he also exhibits a deep antipathy toward a poet he dismisses as having 'no philosophy' and whose works have 'no design on the amelioration of behaviour'.[5] The irony is that until Eliot reaffirmed his Christianity, his poems had no systematic pattern, and after his re-commitment they still lacked logical or moral coherence.

In the Introduction, Eliot avails himself of the opportunity to compare Shakespeare with Dante. Even though he acknowledges Shakespeare's complexity and depth, he much prefers the Christian 'philosophy' of Dante's

Divine Comedy, with its moral rewards and retributions in 'hell', 'purgatory' or 'paradise'. Shakespeare seems by contrast to have only a 'rag-bag philosophy'[6] derived at random from his sources, and he 'elaborated' no system of 'morality'.

Yet, the gratuitousness of Dante's moral system does not seem to bother Eliot. After all Dante grants himself and his childhood sweetheart Beatrice unconditional entry to paradise, he consigns the 'pagan' poet Virgil to purgatory, and while there encounters a colleague who he saved from hell by procuring a last minute extreme unction. Eliot finds it difficult to understand how Dante's 'superior' Christian moral system is 'discounted' by 'interpreters', while Shakespeare's works are looked to for moral guidance. Not only does Eliot disparage Shakespeare's worth, he believes there is a philosophical pattern and moral system in biblical mythology despite the devastating critique of its claims by scientists and philosophers over the last few centuries.

However, the psychology of belief, with which Eliot assuaged his anxious mind, provides no substitute in the twentieth century for a critical awareness of the logical relationship of the mind and nature. Eliot's late Christian play, *Murder in the Cathedral*, is an anthem for his failure to achieve a coherent world-view.

The 'monomythic' ambitions of Joyce

In his early works, James Joyce (1882-1941) graduated from the youthful idealism of his *Stephen Hero*, to self-awareness as an artist in the *Portrait of the Artist as a Young Man*. Then, once he achieved a perspective on his youthful idealism, he set out in *Ulysses* to write a modern myth for Dublin by duplicating the mythical journey of Odysseus. The achievement of *Ulysses* led then, at least in Joyce's mind, to the need to write the encyclopedic history of myth, or the 'monomyth' that became *Finnegan's Wake*.

Joyce's early development from autobiography to critical self-awareness was achieved through an analysis of the romantic idealism of his younger self. Joyce, born Irish Catholic, became a searcher/researcher for a more meaningful spiritual expression at the beginning of the twentieth century.

Under the influence of James Frazer's encyclopedic catalogue of myths and Freud and Jung's exploration of the symbolism of mythologies, Joyce experienced liberation from his youthful indoctrination in Judeo/

Christian mythology. His decision to base *Ulysses* on Greek mythology began a process that ended with the attempt to assimilate all mythologies into *Finnegan's Wake*.

But Joyce, after recreating in *Ulysses* a day in the life of Dublin as a mythical journey, began to confuse the logic of myth with the history of mythologies. The distinction between myth and history is immediately apparent in the Bible where there are only two passages of mythological expression. The first, in Genesis, which describes God's creation of the world, his forming of man and then woman, with the consequent revelation of the knowledge of good and evil. The second, in the Gospels, describes the miraculous conception, birth and death of Christ. The rest of the Old and New Testaments recount legendary and historical events of the Hebrew tribes and early Christian communities.

So when Joyce decided to compile his monomyth he compounded, under the influence of the historicist patterns of Giambattista Vico, the mythological expressions from the world's cultures, with their legends and histories. Even though he had identified some of the logical characteristics of myth in *Ulysses*, his decision to record the events of a day in the Dublin of 1904 led to a confusion of myth and history, with disastrous consequences for the intelligibility of *Finnegan's Wake* as either myth or history.

Joyce and Shakespeare

Whereas Dante was Eliot's poet of choice, Joyce considered Shakespeare his greatest protagonist. He was challenged both by the self-awareness Shakespeare demonstrated in characters like Hamlet, and by the mythic depth sounded in plays like *King Lear*. Despite his regard for Augustine and Aquinas and other Christian apologists, he intuitively responded to the mythic achievement of Shakespeare's works.

But the trajectory of Joyce's development as an artist led him away from the possibility of appreciating the singular mythic logic Shakespeare articulated in the *Sonnets* as the philosophy behind all his plays and poems. Joyce's engagement with Shakespeare never rises to the philosophic heights required to appreciate the logic of myth. Instead his confrontation with the psychology of his youthful self and then his engagement with an historical moment in the life of Dublin deflected him toward repeating the logical errors of the Judeo/Christian tradition.

Stephen's deliberations on Shakespeare in the library scene in *Ulysses* provide an insight into Joyce's level of expectation. While Stephen's 'theories' cannot be read as Joyce's own understanding of Shakespeare, when they are aligned with the mythological pattern in *Ulysses* or *Finnegan's Wake* they give a measure of Joyce's limitations.

Symptomatic of the limitations is Joyce's recourse to the biographical speculations that litter the orthodox literature on Shakespeare's works. Despite Joyce's desire to penetrate the workings of Shakespeare's mind, his failure to comprehend the mythic logic available in the *Sonnets* leads inevitably to a miasma of biographical and psychological speculation.

In the library scene in *Ulysses,* Joyce has Stephen expound, with interjections from the others in the library, on issues such as authorship of the plays, the identity of Mr. W. H. and the 'dark lady', the supposed neglect of Anne Hathaway, and Shakespeare's presumed need to journey to London to discover himself (is it coincidental Joyce was in exile in Paris and Trieste?). It is indicative of Joyce's failure to achieve Shakespearean insights that he devotes a whole chapter to such spurious debate.

Particularly revealing of the inadequacy of Joyce's achievement is Stephen's play on the relation of 'father' and 'son'. Joyce's struggle to gain a perspective on his youthful idealism, and his ruminations on Shakespeare's psychological similarity to Hamlet, led him to formulate the circular metaphor of a 'father' who gains artistic maturity by giving birth to the literary 'son' who fathered the maturity. The telling irony is that by focusing on the literary relation of Shakespeare to Hamlet, and to the 'ghost' of Hamlet's father, Joyce ignores the role of Hamlet's mother Gertrude.

Joyce's exploration of an autobiographical connection between Shakespeare and Hamlet, which reflects Joyce's consciousness of his youthful self, does not account for the mythic objectivity achieved by Shakespeare in his plays. *Ulysses* demonstrates that Joyce could reflect objectively on Stephen and Bloom's path to maturity, but the discourse in the library, which presents a litany of *Sonnet* ephemera, shows that Joyce did not appreciate the mature vision evident in Shakespeare's *Sonnet* philosophy. And the absence of the *Sonnet* logic from *Finnegan's Wake* demonstrates that he never achieved Shakespeare's level of mythic insight.

A precise indicator of Joyce's failure to understand Shakespeare is the absence of significant conversation between Leopold and Molly Bloom and more critically between Steven and Molly. There is no examination in the

Portrait or *Ulysses* of a mother/son/daughter dynamic equivalent to Joyce's examination of the relation of 'father' and 'son'.

Ulysses, possibly in imitation of the conventional psychological misunderstanding of the relation of the 'friend' and 'dark lady' in the *Sonnets*, does start with the youthful Stephen and ends with the 'dark' ruminations of Molly. But there the resemblance ends. Neither Stephen nor Bloom engage with the woman who should have been central to Joyce's attempt to recreate myth. Molly begins and ends the day lying in bed. If she were to emulate Penelope's role in Odysseus' epic journey her attitude toward her 'suitors' would have been less self-indulgent and non-committal.

The mute self-reflection of Molly is in contrast to the role of the Mistress in the *Sonnets*. In the Mistress sequence, the Poet first imbibes the logic of beauty from her sensory presence (127 to 137) and then, in the verbal interaction of the second half, he learns the logic of truth (138 to 152). If Molly represents the passivity of nature for Joyce, and Gerty and the whores are the active female principle, he doubly misrepresents the logical role of the human female in relation to the male.

Joyce's unwillingness to create a credible female character, who can demonstrate the priority of the female over the male through her appreciation of the logic of both beauty and truth, leads inevitably to the mythological confusion of the *Wake*. By focusing primarily on his own experiences as a male, Joyce perpetuates the male-God illogicality of the Judeo/Christian tradition.

Joyce and Eliot

Joyce and Eliot were both determined to recover the mythological dimension in literary expression. The use of traditional mythologies in their earlier work, and their determination to engage with the mythical at a philosophical level in their later work, sets them apart from most other twentieth century writers. They differed, for instance, from Yeats whose interest in the arcane and the spiritualistic crippled his capacity to engage seriously with mythologies. Similarly the crypto-religious writings of fantasists like C. S. Lewis and J. R. R. Tolkien, with their sentimental idealism, make Joyce or Eliot seem rigorous.

At least Joyce and Eliot had an apprehension of the significance of the higher sensations of the mind. Eliot's description in *Tradition and the Individual Talent*, of the relation between 'ordinary emotions' and 'new ones' in the mind was an attempt to express the consequence of the 'concentration of a very great number of experiences' which unite in an 'atmosphere' of 'a passive attending upon the event'.[7] For Joyce, the difference between the 'kinesis' of ordinary emotions and the 'stasis' of art is the 'satisfaction of certain special feelings'. It involves a process so that 'as we come to see truth, so we come to feel emotional stasis'.[7]

Yet Joyce and Eliot seem inarticulate when their efforts are compared with the consistent logic of Shakespeare's *Sonnets*. While they both mused on the nature of the aesthetic experience, neither was aware that the *Sonnets* give a precise and comprehensive presentation of the logic of aesthetics and ethics. Sonnets 127 to 152 consider the logic of beauty and truth, and sonnets 20 to 126 consider the logic of truth and beauty. If they had been aware of Shakespeare's logic, Eliot would not have accused Shakespeare of having no philosophy and no morals and Joyce's later work would not have been stunted by its mythological presumptions.

The limitation of Joyce and Eliot's understanding of Shakespeare's natural logic can also be seen in the significance both writers give to the concept of time. In the *Four Quartets*, Eliot muses plaintively and frequently on the passage of time. He is concerned about past, present and future as well as the beginning and the end. His concern is consistent with his commitment to a death-orientated religion that many dismiss as being irrelevant to the demographics of the twentieth century except as a psychological bulwark for anxious minds.

Joyce's attempt in *Finnegan's Wake* to bring all the historic expressions of the mythological sensibility into focus in one man's dream similarly subjects the logic of myth to the exigencies of time. His reliance on Vico's temporal cycles of the human spirit, the 'Religious', 'Heroic', and 'Civil',[8] anchors his understanding of myth to temporal concepts.

It is no wonder then, that neither Joyce nor Eliot appreciated the mythic philosophy of Shakespeare works and particularly the precise articulation of mythic logic in the *Sonnets*. Shakespeare gives exact expression to the priority of nature over time (sonnet 126), and to the logical relation of birth and death, and the priority of the female over the male. Joyce and Eliot's acceptance of the supremacy of the male, whether in Finnegan's dream or in the male-God of Christianity, prevents them from understanding the philosophy of a poet and dramatist whose influence they could not avoid.

When the work of Joyce and Eliot, with their attempts on the one hand to construct a novel based on all mythologies, and on the other to recover faith in a particular mythology, is compared with that of their contemporary Marcel Duchamp, the differences are striking. Duchamp demonstrates what is possible when the illogical basis of traditional belief is challenged and rectified. It is ironical, particularly given the complex ironies in Joyce's work, that neither of them were aware of the penetrating insights of an artist regarded as the most astute aesthetic practitioner of the twentieth century.

Shakespeare's challenge to Joyce and Eliot

So far, the mythological stances of Joyce and Eliot and their regard for the works of Shakespeare have been noted. Both desired to regenerate a mythological level of expression in their writing. They differed, though, as to whether Shakespeare's works were a resource for the recovery process.

Eliot sensed a mythic depth in Shakespeare's works but dismissed the idea that he developed his own philosophy, and did not consider the possibility that he articulated the logical conditions for a mythic level of expression. Instead he turned to the Christian mythology of Dante, and renewed his own faith in the Judeo/Christian tradition. The result was a body of verse that lacks mythic resonance, despite the ever-present background of his Christian faith.

Joyce attempted to access the mythic depth available in Shakespeare's works. Even though he based *Ulysses* on Homer's *Odyssey*, he revealed his fascination with Shakespeare in *Ulysses* and throughout his works. But Joyce was not able to penetrate the mythic logic of the *Sonnets* and plays, so he remained at the mercy of a psychological and biographical level of interpretation.

To gain an insight into Joyce and Eliot's opposed attitudes to the mythological, the mythical dimension in their work can be compared with the complete mythic logic presented in the *Sonnets*. Because the *Sonnets* present the logical conditions for any mythological expression, the exercise should not only identify the elements missing from Joyce and Eliot's work but also rectify their errors. And because their works remain within the male-based psychology of the Judeo/Christian tradition, the comparisons also critique that tradition.

Shakespeare's *Sonnets* detail the relationships in nature that lead logically to a comprehensive and consistent understanding of the mythic level of expression. By taking nature as a given, and by recognising the irreducible elements in human logic, Shakespeare is able to locate the components of the world that enable the human mind to perceive, think, and then experience intensified sensations.

Once Shakespeare lays out the logical structure of human understanding within nature, he is able to structure his writings according to the same logic to reflect his awareness of the dynamic of understanding. Because his development of the relation of body and mind in his writing is consistent with the natural process of human evolution, his work automatically carries with it the logic of the mythic possibility.

The logical structure evident in the *Sonnets* can be expressed diagrammatically to show the linear relationship of the interconnected components.

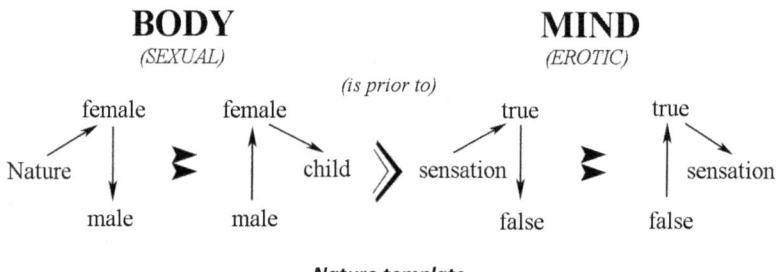

Nature template

Eliot's decision to reaffirm his Christian faith puts him diametrically at odds with Shakespeare's natural logic. Not only could Eliot not see the brilliant philosophy articulated in the *Sonnets* and apparent in all the plays, he opted for the system of Christian apologetics, and its greatest poet, Dante. Even though Eliot was operating under the aegis of a recognised mythology, he was not actively able to engage the components of mythic logic in his work. The major role he gives to time ('beginning and end') highlights his inability to appreciate the mythic components available even in his own beliefs.

Eliot's difficulties with Shakespeare can be expressed in a template that takes the components of Shakespeare's natural logic and shows how they are redistributed to accord with the priority of the male God over nature. Ironically, while the diagram for the biblical myth incorporates the literary basis of belief, it illogically presumes that the literary structure has priority over the natural logic from which it was originally derived.

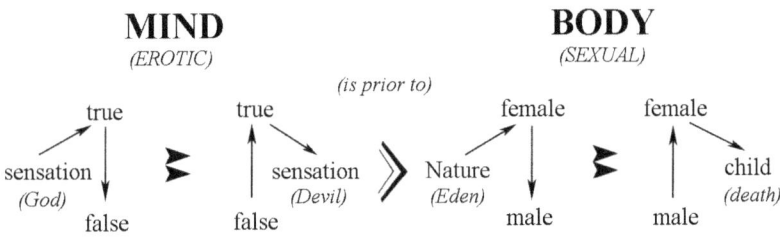

God template

The crucial inversion is the reversal of the priorities of the sexual and the erotic. In the *God template* the state of human desires comes before the sexual dynamic from which it arises. The absence of eroticism in Eliot's own writing demonstrates his ignorance of the logical priority of body over mind. A psychological fear of the sexual is apparent in his avoidance of the erotic. Eliot even states his belief that the body is an 'enminded' thing. Eliot's ignorance of the logical significance of the increase argument and its implications for truth and beauty means his work lacks both a basis in common sense and an active truth dynamic.

Joyce at least recognised that the Judeo/Christian tradition had lost its singular hold over the imagination of thinking human beings in the West. His determination to engage afresh with the mythologies of the world ensured that many of the components of mythic logic are genuinely present in his work. Instead of creating a disembodied poetry like Eliot, in the *Portrait* Joyce explores his psychological development as a male, and then in *Ulysses* gives a rudimentary expression to the relation of male to female.

Joyce is uninhibited in exploring the sex life of his characters and, whether he realised it or not, has both males and females in *Ulysses* assuage their erotic desires through masturbation rather than having sex for the purpose of increasing humankind. The eroticism in *Ulysses*, and this is particularly the case with Leopold and Molly's masturbations, seems to acknowledge the non-biological status of literature. Joyce's apparent intuitive appreciation that the eroticism in Genesis and the New Testament is auto-erotic, because myth both presents the basic logic of the world and reflects on its own non-sexual status as erotic, governs the sexual relations in *Ulysses*.

But Joyce, as demonstrated by his largely psycho/biographical approach to Shakespeare, did not appreciate the logic of the mythic level of expression. He uses natural features around Dublin as the matrix within which the action occurs, and even though Molly Bloom forms the background against which his human drama unfolds, neither nature nor the female is restored to its rightful priority, as in Shakespeare. If Joyce had understood the *Sonnet* philosophy he would have recognised the need to acknowledge the logic of increase as prior to the possibility of truth and beauty.

Joyce's inability to appreciate the philosophy of the *Sonnets* meant that his work hovers uncomfortably between the apologetic illogicalities of Eliot's resort to orthodox beliefs and Shakespeare's achievement of locating the logic of any mythic possibility. Joyce did not see that the *Sonnet* logic frees Shakespeare from the history of mythological expression, and enables everything he writes to be inherently mythic. Because Shakespeare isolates the key components for writing at will at a mythic level, unlike Joyce, he had no need to give expression to all the myths and legends and folktales in recorded history.

The comparison between the inventiveness and deep drama of Shakespeare's plays and the formal and stylistic games of the drama-less *Finnegan's Wake* is a measure of Shakespeare's philosophic brilliance and Joyce's continued subjection to the psychology of male-based idealistic egoism. (Ezra Pound summed up the syndrome with the laconic title of his journal, *The Egoist*.)

None of this would matter if Eliot was not so determined to deny Shakespeare a deliberate philosophical 'pattern' and Joyce was not so susceptible to making life easier for himself by belittling the mythic achievement of the plays. Together, along with 400 years of persistent misrepresentation either by believers wishing to deny Shakespeare his rightful standing or by well-meaning egoists who fall into the trap of psychological identification (such as Oscar Wilde in his book *Mr. W. H.*), Joyce and Eliot show in opposing ways how to get it so wrong about Shakespeare.

(Acknowledgment is given to S. L. Goldberg's *Joyce*, Oliver and Boyd, 1962. His precise summary of Joyce's achievement has proved an invaluable resource over the last 30 years. Even though this critique goes beyond Goldberg's comments by examining Joyce's relationship to Shakespeare's mythic logic, Goldberg's analysis of Joyce's trajectory from youthful idealist to ambitious mythologist provides an invaluable preparation for appreciating Shakespeare's achievement.)

5

Germaine Greer

In his *Sonnets*, Shakespeare articulates a consistent and comprehensive philosophy based in nature. By recognising nature as logically female (the 'sovereign mistress'), and by accepting the priority of the female (the 'Mistress') over the male (the 'Master Mistress') he re-establishes the logical priority of female over male.

By intentionally restoring the priority of nature over the male God of religions, Shakespeare challenges millennia of male-based prejudice. In the *Sonnets* and in the poems and plays he demonstrates that the literal interpretation of the traditional mythological priority of male over female perpetuates an inconsistency in human understanding, and perpetrates an injustice on woman.

Shakespeare's plays not only demonstrate the inconsistencies that arise when the male is given priority over the female, they also show how to recover the natural logic of female priority within the dynamic of female/male relationships. Each play, whether comedy or tragedy, dramatises the process of gender reconciliation. Typically, a play begins with an imbalance toward male-based prerogatives from which Shakespeare constructs a resolution where the natural priority of the female contextualises the conceit of male independence.

In his *Sonnets* Shakespeare recovers the natural logic that connects the biology of the female/male relationship and the mythic as the highest form of human expression. In the plays and poems he shows how to write at a mythic level without falling into the contradictions of traditional male-based beliefs.

The elevation of the male over the female in societies where there is a belief in the priority of a male God results from two basic misunderstandings. The first misinterprets the non-biological elements in the logic of myth and the second inverts the male's evolutionary function.

In the first case, myth openly exhibits its logical status as an imaginative account of origins by representing relations between female and male entities as erotic rather than sexual. The erotic logic of a mythology employs all forms of secondary sexual desire but precludes the direct biology of procreation. Hence a myth can represent human origins by having a male God who appears ex nihilo to create man from clay and then himself be born again of a virgin. But the erotic dynamic, which serves to indicate the conceptual or mind-based role of mythology, becomes a source of contradiction if it is read literally. Logically, the male God cannot be prior to the female in nature.

The second confusion arises because the male, as a consequence of the differentiation of the male sperm from the primacy of the female cell, is in effect at the leading edge of the evolutionary possibility. While the role of the male, or the masculine dimension in human understanding (in male or female), enables humankind to develop in ways not available to single sex species, Shakespeare makes the point in the *Sonnets* that it all comes to naught if, like the idealistic Master Mistress or youth, all males refuse to increase. Then, as he argues in sonnet 126, nature would prevail without humankind.

Even though male-based idealism is symptomatic of a highly competitive societal model, the belief in the supremacy of the male can create the expectation that the male will become self-sufficient or independent of the female and ultimately nature. But the idealistic scenario ignores the logical consequences of denying increase and the priority of nature and the female in nature.

In the *Sonnets* Shakespeare makes the logical point that increase is the fundamental condition for human persistence. The point is logical because he does not insist that humankind should persist, only what it should do if it wishes to persist. The logical connection between persistence and existence is descriptive not prescriptive.

The illogical representation of the human relation to nature in beliefs based on traditional mythologies affects both sex and gender. The *Sonnets* examine the tendency of the male to become isolated in his male dynamic but they also consider the consequences for the female who over-exercises her masculine persona.

Some feminists, for instance, in their drive to gain equality with men, forget the significance of the logic of human persistence. While there may be short-term benefits from such a stance, ironically the denial of the logic of increase allies them to traditional beliefs in male-based mythologies that give men priority over women.

Shakespeare also recognises (as did Darwin) that the logic of increase is prior to the possibility of human understanding or the dynamic of 'truth and beauty'. Shakespeare argues that only by acknowledging the logic of increase can human understanding achieve consistency and hence justice.

The *Sonnet* philosophy clarifies millennia of confusion. Human nature is based in nature and any male-based system of Gods or ideals is secondary and at best visionary. So the question arises as to how such misunderstandings have developed and persisted. It could be that the transmission of ideas in the medium of writing led to the reification of beliefs in a way not previously known in oral culture. Certainly, great schisms and sectarian wars have occurred and are still occurring over the too literal interpretation of words committed to paper, as in the Bible, the Koran, etc.

The consolidation of male-based religions, particularly in the Middle East, and specifically the monotheistic male-God religion of the Hebrews, coincided with the development of writing. When such religions encourage a fundamentalist belief in the mythological word, intolerance and persecution result. Thomas Jefferson, objecting to religious intolerance in Europe, acted against the iniquities of faith by separating Church and State in the fledgling United States. It might be appropriate now to enact a constitutional article to assert the priority of the female over the male.

The work of Shakespeare offers the most consistent, comprehensive and sustained challenge to the illogicality of male-based determination. Only by recognising the logical conditions for sexual persistence out of nature can the feminine and masculine gender relationship be understood and addressed. (See also essay 10 on Riane Eisler.)

Germaine Greer

This essay compares the attitude of a leading feminist to the natural logic of Shakespeare's *Sonnet* philosophy. Germaine Greer lends herself to the discussion of the relation of women's rights to Shakespeare's philosophy because in her professional life she combines a persistent advocacy of feminist issues with her status as an internationally recognised Shakespeare scholar. It should be possible to align her statements on women's issues from over the last 35 years with her statements about Shakespeare's works to see if her understanding corresponds to Shakespeare's philosophy.

It is not the intention in this essay to outline or even summarily critique Greer's writings on feminism or to examine feminism generally. Rather, the idea is to listen to her hopes for feminism and her concerns about the fate of feminism in the period between *The Female Eunuch* of 1970 and its sequel, *The Whole Woman* of 1999. Because she makes mention of Shakespeare in these volumes it should be possible to show how her understanding of Shakespeare misses his logical recovery of the female over the male, with its relevance for challenging the continued adherence to mythological beliefs inherently contrary to female rights.

In her 'Recantation' that serves as a preface to *The Whole Woman*, Greer expresses her concern that feminists of her generation were beginning 'to assert with apparent seriousness that feminism had gone too far'.[1] Yet it is she who goes nowhere near far enough in *The Female Eunuch*, *Sex and Destiny* of 1984, and *The Whole Woman* in challenging the illogicalities of the beliefs and values of a Bible-based society in which women have been denied their natural priority.

The impression gained from reading Greer's feminist writings is reinforced by her attitude toward Shakespeare in the 130-page monograph *Shakespeare* that she produced for Oxford University Press in 1986. While there is some attempt to acknowledge the significance Shakespeare gives to his female characters, Greer meekly conforms to the orthodox prejudice of passing him off as an idealist and even a Christian. Because she is ignorant of the *Sonnet* philosophy, with its logical critique of Platonic and biblical idealism, she attributes to Shakespeare an attitude and values contrary to woman's logical status and rights.

The *Sonnet* philosophy in *The Phoenix and the Turtle*

To begin to understand how Greer can be a tireless advocate for women's rights yet attribute to Shakespeare a 'Christian scepticism'[2] or suggest that Hamlet exhibits a 'Christian spirit of resignation',[3] or that *The Phoenix and the Turtle* 'is the most perfect statement of the Platonic ideal in English poetry',[4] an appropriate starting point is *The Phoenix and the Turtle*.

As Shakespeare based his philosophy in nature, he was trenchant in his criticism of the Platonic inspired claims for a prior ideal world. For Plato an ideal world must exist to account for the imperfections of life. But for Shakespeare all ideal worlds are phantasms of the human mind, which is logically dependent on nature. Instead, the evidence of his works suggests he was sympathetic to Aristotle's regard for the natural world.

So Greer's statement, while in keeping with other attempts to convert

Shakespeare to Christianity or Neo-Platonism, is diametrically opposed to the *Sonnet* philosophy and hence contrary to the meaning of *The Phoenix and the Turtle*.

Traditional attempts to patronisingly convert *The Phoenix and the Turtle* to Platonic/Christian values have not gone unnoticed. William Matchett's line-by-line examination of *The Phoenix and the Turtle* reveals not a perfect expression of Platonism, but Shakespeare's devastating critique of idealism. Matchett's reading rejects the traditional idealistic gloss on the fate of the two birds, and shows that the poem, with its original punctuation, is a satire on the birds' futile expectations.[5]

Unfortunately, while Matchett makes a number of comparisons between *The Phoenix and the Turtle* and the *Sonnets*, he is unable to show how the philosophy of the *Sonnets* informs every aspect of the poem. Instead, as with many who are at a loss to understand the *Sonnet* philosophy, he speculates that the poem comments on the intrigues of the Elizabethan court.

If *The Phoenix and the Turtle* is examined from the vantage of the *Sonnet* philosophy, then Matchett's anti-Platonic reading is readily vindicated. Consistent with the natural logic of the *Sonnets*, the poem mentions 'Nature', sexual 'Division', a sexual 'lay', 'posterity… and …married chastity', and 'Truth and Beauty'.

Greer, however, does not bother to itemise her evidence for thinking the poem is a 'perfect statement of the Platonic ideal'. Instead she turns to a 1601 account from a law student's diary, which reports that Shakespeare upstaged Burbage for the favours of a woman who frequented the Globe. To forestall challenges to her prejudicial reading of the poem she prefers to cite unverifiable student gossip, and allude to the 'bawdy strain'[7] in Shakespeare's plays.

By asserting that such behaviour is 'not in the least incompatible with Platonic idealism'[7], and by dismissing in simplistic terms as 'bawdy' the erotic logic of the plays and poems, Greer blindly promotes the orthodox view that Shakespeare conforms to the Platonic ideal.

And if, as Greer claims, the poem glorifies the eternal happiness of two birds in a 'perfect statement of the Platonic ideal', Shakespeare rebuts such a reading at every turn. The sole Arabian Bird witnesses a 'Tragic scene', 'Love and Constancy' are reckoned 'dead', 'love was slain', the two birds lie in 'cinders', their 'infirmity…was married Chastity', 'Truth and Beauty' are 'buried', and the last line laconically suggests the reader 'sigh a prayer' for the 'dead Birds'.

Ironically, those like Greer who wish to convert Shakespeare's devastating critique of idealism in *The Phoenix and the Turtle* into a 'perfect statement of the Platonic ideal' frequently characterise the poem as symbolically opaque and cryptically obscure. Rather, the poem reveals its brilliant natural logic when viewed as an expression of the *Sonnet* philosophy. (A full analysis of *The Phoenix and the Turtle* is available in Volume 3.)

Christian apologetics

Greer not only brings to her *Shakespeare* a Platonic expectation for *The Phoenix and the Turtle,* she also peremptorily presumes Shakespeare adheres to Christian beliefs and values throughout his works. Even if she is ignorant of the nature-based philosophy of the *Sonnets*, her presumption of a Christian meaning ignores the evidence of the plays, which most commentators acknowledge are based in nature rather than the male God of the Bible.

For instance, Christian sympathisers such as A. C. Bradley and Blair Leishman have to admit there is no evidence in the complete works for presuming Shakespeare was a Christian. Yet, despite the lack of evidence, they still feel compelled to convert him to Christianity by suggesting he was a closet believer. Greer even quotes Orwell as saying that 'from Shakespeare's writings it would be difficult to know that he had any religion',[8] but persists in her Christian interpretation. Having branded Shakespeare a Platonic idealist, she is far less circumspect than many in her determination to read Christian intentions into the plays and poems.[9,10]

The intention of this essay is to redress injustices done to Shakespeare by a scholar who might be expected to be sympathetic to Shakespeare's nature/female philosophy. As examples of Greer's Christian misinterpretation of Shakespeare's works are considered, it must be asked how an inveterate feminist such as Greer can be so blind to Shakespeare's prioritising of the female over the male, which challenges the self-righteousness of the male-based beliefs of religions such as Christianity.

Greer operates principally as a polemicist who uses hyperbole for immediate advantage. While her timely but overstated claims and challenges have forced her to alter her opinions over time, this essay does not discount the importance of the polemic moment. But because Shakespeare held to and argued logically for his nature-based philosophy throughout his life, it might be hoped that even a perennial polemicist such as Greer might reflect on the evidence and argument for a consistent and comprehensive philosophy in Shakespeare's works.

When Greer titles Chapter 5 of her *Shakespeare* 'Teleology', she signals her intent to interpret the play in terms of an intentional God. Throughout the chapter, which examines *King Lear* at some length, she proceeds to convert Shakespeare to Christianity. Typically she insists on the 'emergence and gradual transcendence of Lear's soul'.[11] But if the *Sonnet* philosophy is based in nature, and the natural processes brilliantly represented by Darwin, the idea of a God directed purpose is logically redundant.

Instead, according to the logic of the *Sonnet* philosophy, *King Lear* is about a conceited, paternalistic male idealist who has lost touch with the natural logic of life. In the *Sonnet* logic the goals of life are immanent in nature. Lear reveals his conceit when he demands the total love of his daughters. Lear ostracises Cordelia when she responds with the natural logic of the increase argument (1.1.*102-10*) (as does Desdemona in *Othello*, 1.3.*527-36*). Cordelia identifies love as a boon passed from generation to generation so it cannot be the sole preserve of a selfish male King who demands absolute love.

Shakespeare then takes Lear through the process of recovering his natural logic by literally exposing him to the elements and by subjecting him to the aggrieved anger of the bastard Edmund, who likewise has been denatured by his conceited father, Gloucester. Shakespeare removes the Christian allusions from the original play *King Leir*, to force his characters to face the natural world without the compensating psychology of the paternalistic idealism of Christianity.

Greer, in her revisionary misinterpretation of the play, excuses Lear by claiming he is 'senile'.[12] Neither does she appreciate the significance of the roles of Cordelia and Edmund as differing expressions of the same reaction to male-driven injustices. But most significantly she misrepresents the role of the Fool. Whereas Shakespeare removed references to God from his play, in Greer's discussion of the Fool's status she reintroduces them with a vengeance.

She begins by referring to 'Erasmus's fool in God'. Such a fool must be 'as a child, for unless we become as little children we cannot enter heaven'.[13] And she threatens, in the style of the self-serving First Commandment, 'It ill behoves man to vaunt before God of his intellectual achievements and the temporal wealth and power he has managed to secure, for all was done by grace of God and is as nothing compared to the wisdom and power of God'.[13]

She then refers to the Fool as 'a 'natural', *simple* as we say, and by extension, still in a state of nature. We are all born in this condition' (her emphasis). With further references to God, and 'born idiots...touched by God',[13] Greer completely inverts the intent of the play as a critique of the adolescent conceitedness and inconsistency of the Christian belief in biblical mythology. Instead she says, in complete contradiction of the nature-based *Sonnet* philosophy 'Shakespeare's wise fools moved, (in) a frame of reference which is profoundly sceptical and profoundly Christian'.[13]

Not content with that, she also characterises Edmund as a 'natural'.[14] Even though she has to acknowledge the ubiquitous presence of nature in the play, she avoids the inference that Shakespeare bases the play in the logic of nature by claiming there is an 'intricate play on mutually contradictory notions of what constitutes nature'.[14] She further dismisses Shakespeare's nature-based logic by maintaining 'every character in *King Lear* bandies the word 'nature', and in no two cases does it quite mean the same thing'.[14]

And when Edmund refers to nature as a 'Goddess', with Shakespeare alluding to Venus from *Venus and Adonis* who exacts nature's justice on the idealising male Adonis (and also alluding to Nature the sovereign mistress of the *Sonnets*), Greer presumes 'the Elizabethan audiences would have been shocked at such idolatry'.[14] Shakespeare, in sonnet 105, identifies idolatry as the literal belief in the primacy of the male God, so it is wonderfully ironical that Greer, the inveterate feminist, would characterise as 'idolatry' Shakespeare's decision to stage the play within the context of the natural world, and pervert his advocacy of natural logic as the basis for recovering of female rights.

Greer's frequent interpolation of the idea of God and Christian values, and her claim that they are consistent with Shakespeare's intent, is patently contrary to a more judicious reading of *King Lear*. No doubt it would please the Christian Church to have a prominent feminist who, under the guise of polemicising social injustices, is an apologist for Christian illogicalities. She effectively collaborates with the religious hierarchy of the Church in the perpetrating the priority of the male God over humankind, and particularly over womankind.

Throughout her commentary, Greer never misses an opportunity to advocate for the Christian God. From her recital of such simplistic and outmoded beliefs as 'God, when he created and continues to create all that is',[15] to the threat against 'the adequacy of reason to scrutinise the ways of God',[16] to her assertion that 'we witness the emergence and gradual ascendance of Lear's soul ... (and that) Shakespeare draws out Lear's soul, even as his mind decays',[17] to her delusion that 'Gloucester dies the joyous death of the faithful',[18] she warns that 'it would be a mistake to interpret the futility of Lear's appeals to his Gods as evidence of atheism on Shakespeare's part'.[19]

Greer's complete misreading of *King Lear* in her *Shakespeare* is symptomatic of her unwillingness to hear Shakespeare's case for the priority of nature over the male God of religion and the priority of the female over the male. She claims 'the goddess nature is an amoral pagan personification, her laws harsh and ineluctable'.[20] Nature at large is not a goddess, and do not the divine duo of God and Satan incite a worse immorality through their self-serving laws.

In *Venus and Adonis* Shakespeare argues that natural events, while capable of causing great distress, are unavoidable, whereas the evil consequences of prioritising an idealised God are completely avoidable. He argues that if excessive idealism is circumscribed (as Jefferson did to the Churches in the American Bill of Rights), then the inevitable evil of idealistic beliefs would be diminished. It is not possible to worship nature as a Goddess in the same bloody way that overly committed Christians worship their male God, totally and blindly. Greer's misrepresentation of Shakespeare's use of nature as 'idolatry' is typical of the way in which absolute male God worship perverts even a concerned polemicist for women's rights.

Shakespeare's women

Greer's willingness to associate Shakespeare's works with the God of Christianity also affects her appreciation of the role of Shakespeare's female protagonists. She pleads that 'it must be remembered that while Shakespeare's concept of virtue tends to be the active rather than the contemplative, his view of redemptive action is Christian. Christ, the paradigm for both men and women, redeemed humanity by suffering and dying on the cross'.[21] Greer's inability, in her commentary in *Shakespeare*, to free herself from the Christian prejudice against nature and the female could not be more succinctly expressed.

She deepens her association of Christianity and Shakespeare with the claim that 'the Christian concept of passive heroism places a high value on endurance, which in Shakespeare's ethic is cognate with constancy and hence truth'.[22] She goes on to suggest that 'while he may make reference to a contemporary stereotype of women as fickle as in sonnet 20, and allows both Isabel and Viola to animadvert on women's malleability, of all Shakespeare's plays only *Troilus and Cressida* deals with a genuine case of female treachery'.[22]

Not only is Greer determined to blacken Shakespeare's references to natural processes as idolatry of a pagan Goddess, she calls the primacy of the female over the male (as defined in sonnet 20) 'fickle'. She does not appreciate that if Isabel and Viola criticise 'women's malleability' they do so from completely different vantages. In *Measure for Measure*, Isabel the novice nun is a blind idealist who regains her natural logic under the tutelage of the Duke, and Viola, throughout *Twelfth Night*, applies the *Sonnet* philosophy to help Orsino and Olivia recover their natural logic. If the 'treacherous female' in *Troilus and Cressida* is Cressida and not Helen, then Greer is blind to the lesson in natural logic that Cressida teaches the overly idealistic Troilus.

When Greer turns to the '33 year separation in perfect celibacy' of the Abbess in the *Comedy of Errors*, she claims 'Shakespeare places a high value on chastity'.[23] Yet the arguments of the increase sonnets, the pleasures of the maid in *A Lover's Complaint*, the sexual love between the Duke and the novice nun Isabel, the liberation of Olivia from her 'dead love' toward brother, the marriage of Juliet at 14 in *Romeo and Juliet*, the destruction of the male celibacy of the four Lords in *Love's Labour's Lost*, and then the imposition on them of retributive celibacy by the princesses as punishment, speak to the contrary. Why, then, does Greer claim Shakespeare places a high value on chastity unless she projects her own values on to his works.

Shakespeare's philosophy

Greer seems determined to paste a male-based Christianity over Shakespeare's natural logic, just as she seems willing to plaster a false set of expectations on his women. But not only is Shakespeare made to seem a servant of the Church, who creates 'stereotypes' of women, another of Greer's refrains is that he has no philosophy or no systematic method for producing his works. This last claim is the most serious because it reduces Shakespeare to putty in the minds of those who wish to undermine his devastating criticism of religion and sexism evident in the Church, and in those elements of the State devoted to the Church.

Because Greer cannot, or for the sake of her apologetics will not, see a philosophy in Shakespeare, it is ironical that she quotes from the philosopher, Ludwig Wittgenstein.[24] Wittgenstein's philosophy, and particularly his later philosophy, is a determined attempt to rid philosophy of apologetics and return it to an expression of the relation of the world and mind and recover its role as an investigative tool into the use and misuse of concepts. If Greer understood Wittgenstein's intent she would be better able to appreciate that 400 years earlier Shakespeare approached philosophy in a similar spirit but more consistently and comprehensively.

Greer dismisses the philosophic depth that pervades Shakespeare's works through disparagement and innuendo. She bypasses the deeply philosophic disposition in Shakespeare's plays alluded to by scholars such as Coleridge, Benedetto Croce, and Lytton Strachey. Despite calling *The Phoenix and the Turtle* an expression of the Platonic ideal, she believes Shakespeare's philosophy would at best be 'philosophical or literary conceits and conventions'. She resorts to biographical speculation to claim, 'we do not even know whether the sonnets are correctly interpreted as revealing Shakespeare's life and self primarily or whether they deal principally with philosophical or literary conceits and conventions'.[25] She allows only that if Sir Walter Raleigh could write a poem to Queen Elizabeth expressing his 'loyalty in terms of love melancholy', Shakespeare must be at least that 'sophisticated'.[26]

Little can be expected of Greer's assessment of Shakespeare's philosophic depth if her highest expectation of the *Sonnets* is that they express 'conceits and conventions', and this of a playwright who penned the greatest dramas in the language that do not sink into conceits and conventions. She allows against fellow polemicist George Orwell's claim that Shakespeare had no philosophy that she would not argue Shakespeare's work contains no thought at all. She says 'it may not be possible to extract a nugget of thought, which we usually think of as a series of interrelated propositions' concluding that 'Shakespeare knew, as we have forgotten, that feeling is as intellectual as thinking'.[27]

Unfortunately, she leans on the most apologetic of poets, T. S. Eliot, to portray Shakespeare as an 'intact non-dissociative sensibility'.[27] The Shakespearean idea, she says, 'is inseparable from the mode of its expression'. But her apologetic disingenuousness ignores the persistent presence of argument throughout the *Sonnets*, and that each play is constructed as an argument with the characters as the logical premises, with mock arguments interspersed. It ignores the arrangement of the *Sonnets* into discreet argumentative parts, with the grouping of sonnets such as the 14 increase sonnets, the 5 poetry and increase sonnets, the 9 Alien Poet sonnets, and the division of the Mistress sonnets into parts that explicitly deal with beauty (127 to 137) and then truth (138 to 152), not to mention the precise numerological relationships within the set.

Greer's tendency to characterise Shakespeare as a dramatic divine, conveniently avoids his devastating criticism of excessive idealism in general and the Christian Church in particular. She allows that 'Shakespeare's perceptions were more comprehensive than those of more disciplined minds but they are not the products of intuition and Shakespeare is not merely the conduit of some kind of divine inspiration'.[28] Rather he 'was profoundly aware of and interested in intellectual issues, which he chose not to simplify, codify, reconcile, or resolve, but rather to dramatise' so that he could give his audiences the 'thrill' of an 'imaginative dimension'[28] to their daily lives.

Greer's apologetic intent and her patronisation of Shakespeare's audience cannot conceal her profound ignorance of a philosophy that more comprehensively and logically than any other philosophy argues for the priority of the female over the male and the priority of nature over the male God. She casts Shakespeare as a latter-day post-modernist post-structuralist (a tertiary mindset from which her polemical style has benefited) claiming that the 'strength of Shakespeare's position is that he refrains from coming to conclusions but leaves that to those who complete his utterance'.[24]

Greer persists in denigrating the man by denying Shakespeare the right to be anything more than a mouthpiece for commonplaces of thought. 'Shakespeare's achievement as a thinker, then, is not that he formulated original notions or erected a new system of philosophy, but that he took the commonplaces of Elizabethan thought and made them actual'.[29] In her attempt to straddle the unbridgeable divide between women's rights and male-God based Christianity she cannot help but, like the Christianity she defends, be pre-emptory and patronising.

There is no respite from her assault on Shakespeare's worth. She says, 'Shakespeare does not provide us with a map of an ethical system'.[30] What about the extensive treatment of truth and beauty in sonnets 20 to 126 and 127 to 152, and the unrelenting critique of male-based injustices in the plays and poems? She says 'there is nothing innovative in Shakespeare's idea of history, no ideology or philosophy which he imposed on the material that he organised'.[31] The commentaries on the *Sonnets* and plays in these volumes demonstrate overwhelmingly that the logical/ethical structure articulated in the *Sonnets* is the basis for all his poems and plays.

In Shakespeare's most deliberately philosophic play, *Love's Labour's Lost*, in which the four princesses challenge and correct male-based conceits, he presents the most exacting expression of the rights of women in the face of the hierarchical patronisation of the type practised by the idealising Church. But Greer, the arch feminist, does not note and approve of Shakespeare's intent to right millennia of male-driven wrong. Instead she slights the role of Jaquenetta, who carries the logical inevitability of increase through the play. More significantly, she disparages the logic of the female challenge to the 'narcissistic' lords as being their part in a 'game'. She says, 'the young lords accost the ladies of France with more evolved versions of the same convention, but the ladies treat the whole business as a game, and a rather narcissistic and misconceived game at that'.[32]

Marriage

Greer concludes her final chapter in *Shakespeare* with the subheading 'The achievement of marriage'. She claims 'for Shakespeare marriage was not simply a cliché for ending the action, although it became so in his lifetime. He was profoundly interested in the paradox of creating a durable social institution out of the volatile material of lover's fantasies'.[33] And a little later she insists 'Shakespeare was giving form to the Protestant ideology of marriage'.[34] But both these claims are contrary to the *Sonnet* logic.

Shakespeare's natural philosophy seeks to resolve not simply 'lover's fantasies' but to naturalise through the increase argument and the logic of truth and beauty the fantasies and delusions of those who believe literally in the mythological stories of the Bible and other religious tracts. Only when an attempt has been made to address religious delusions are the characters in the plays assigned a state of union appropriate to their psychological maturity.

Because Shakespeare bases his philosophy in nature, he does not lead all his characters into the institution of marriage as a holy union sanctified by the Christian Church, Catholic or Protestant. The characters in the plays who achieve a mature appreciation of natural logic do not, as Greer suggests, enter a bond where 'no other witness except God was required'.[35] Shakespeare's natural philosophy moves beyond the psychological dependence on an idealised male God.

Shakespeare's own marriage occurred after he and Anne Hathaway were pregnant with their first child. Possibly something in his youthful experience of both the logic of increase and the role of marriage led him to realise marriage that is conferred without an appreciation of the logic of increase in nature is no more than a conceit or a convenient contract.

While Greer notes that the Church had for centuries established marriage as a second rate state compared with 'virginity, celibacy and widowhood',[36] her claim that Shakespeare led his characters toward a 'durable social institution' is not consistent with the endings of plays such as *Measure for Measure* and *Twelfth Night*. These plays have been called problem plays in the literature because their endings are not consistent with Christian expectations of the type espoused by Greer. They are consistent, though, with the *Sonnet* philosophy.

Shakespeare, in his *Sonnets* and in his plays and poems, argues persistently for marriage as a possible contract between couples after they have achieved an awareness of natural logic. The first 14 sonnets, for instance, have traditionally been dismissed as 'marriage sonnets' in which Shakespeare was doing his duty by encouraging a Lord to marry. Yet the theme of the 14 sonnets is increase and not marriage. At no point do the increase sonnets encourage the youth to marry. In Shakespeare's philosophy the sexual division in nature is followed logically by the requirement to increase if humankind wants to persist and love without prejudice. Marriage, by contrast, is a social/religious contract that does not guarantee a loving or procreative union.

Greer's misreading of the *Sonnets* carries over into the misinterpretation of Shakespeare's intent in the plays. In some plays in which marriage is a possibility, one of the female characters is pregnant before the action begins, at least one of the characters has an attitude inconsistent with the logic of increase, and at least one of the characters is charged with bringing the others to an awareness of natural logic. Only then is marriage entertained as a possibility.

And consistently, in those plays, Shakespeare uses marriage either as a fitting climax for characters who have achieved a philosophic resolution of the relation to nature away from their previous capture by idealistic or religious prerogatives (Benedick and Beatrice in *Much Ado About Nothing*). Otherwise he either ensures that idealising or selfish partners are married as a punishment for their previous divorce from natural principles (Angelo in *Measure for Measure*) or, if the characters have a psychological disposition that makes it difficult for them to come to such an understanding, he acknowledges their psychological problem by allowing them a Christian marriage (Olivia and Sebastian in *Twelfth Night*).

The other possibility is reserved only for those characters who control the action and pair off with a partner who gains complete freedom in their natural understanding. In those cases the play ends with them agreeing to cohabit without a mention of marriage (Viola and Orsino in *Twelfth Night*), much like the best of de facto relationships existing now. If anything, Shakespeare should not be complimented by Greer for giving marriage a new meaning but for creating the philosophic climate in which the modern mature agreement between consenting couples prevails without the marriage sanctions and prejudices of the male God driven Church. Shakespeare's treatment of the idealising Isabel and Angelo in *Measure for Measure* typifies his desire to relieve such characters of the burden of conceit and deceit.

When Greer notes the prevalence of nature in *King Lear*, and others note its ubiquitous presence throughout all his works, Shakespeare's intent is not to institute another idolatry to replace the idolatry of the male God, but for the philosophic purpose of bringing reason and sensibility into the relationships of those characters at odds with nature.

Conclusion

In her *Shakespeare* Germaine Greer accepts the traditional misreadings of Shakespeare as a Platonist and Christian. She misrepresents the challenge to male-based conceit by many of Shakespeare's women, she misunderstands Shakespeare's attitude to marriage, and dismisses the possibility of a coherent philosophy articulated in Shakespeare's works. In doing so she remains blind to a critique of male-based prejudice that would give consistency to her vacillating polemics as a professional feminist and would eliminate her unthinking support for attempts to convert Shakespeare to Platonism and Christianity.

For instance, Greer is unable to develop Bronislaw Malinowski's Freudian analysis of the mythic basis of patrilineal Christian/Roman presumption into a critique of paternalistic morals.

> The complex known to the Freudian school, and assumed by them to be universal, I mean, the Oedipus complex, corresponds essentially to our patrilineal Aryan family with the developed 'patria potestas', buttressed by Roman law and Christian morals, and accentuated by the modern economic conditions of the well-to-do bourgeoisie.[37]

Instead, in her desire to accommodate the obvious harshness of some of Shakespeare's characterisations of religious hypocrisy in many of the plays,

Greer, at a number of points in her *Shakespeare*, offers the oxymoronic notion of 'Christian scepticism'. But even she demonstrates, through her unrelenting conversion of Shakespeare to Christianity, that belief in an ideal God cannot be conditional. And moreover, the history of philosophical scepticism since the time of Hume runs counter to Christian belief. In response, Christianity, undermined by its mass of inconsistencies, has attempted to excuse itself by asserting that all other paradigms of understanding must also be inconsistent.

Greer unwittingly buys into the charade. When she disparages some of the references to nature in the plays as idolatry, she characterises Shakespeare's philosophy, which is based on common sense and logical acuity, as another religion like Christianity. The circuitousness of her polemic is a sad reflection on her lack of confidence in nature and womanhood.

A much more consistent analysis of the history of the usurpation of women's rights is available in the writings of Riane Eisler, Merlin Stone, and Marija Gimbutas. They argue that for 30,000 years the female priority was recognised and celebrated in Goddess-based religions. Only in the last 3000-4000 years has there been a perversion to a male God based priority. While neither Eisler, Stone nor Gimbutas have fathomed Shakespeare's recovery of the logic of female priority at the mythic level of expression, their thinking is free of the oxymoronic cul-de-sacs that bedevil Greer's polemic.

Ironically, in the current climate of the recovery of women's rights, it is to males such as Shakespeare and Duchamp that the kudos goes for addressing the logical heart of the problem. They, as males, have been prepared to take responsibility for the history of male-based injustices by acknowledging the priority of the female over their masculine sensibilities. Their works exhibit respect for the logic of sexuality in nature and paradoxically they have been able to achieve a consistent level of mythic expression denied to male driven prophets and evangelists.

It is unfortunate for women's rights, then, that Greer's social criticisms and political polemic have been supported by inadequate arguments and, in the case of Shakespeare, such a bewildering blindness to his achievement. When the template for Shakespeare's natural logic is placed above a version reworked to represent the traditional male God based belief, it is apparent Greer has attempted to understand the world from the inadequacies of the *God template*.

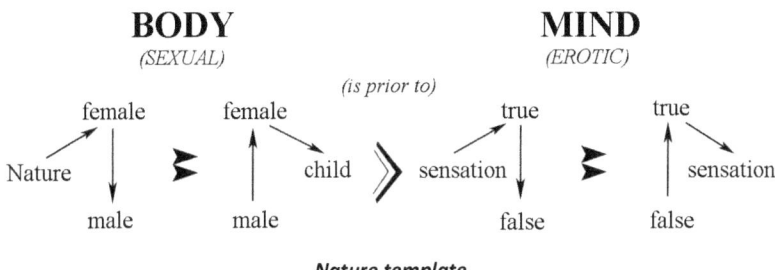

Nature template

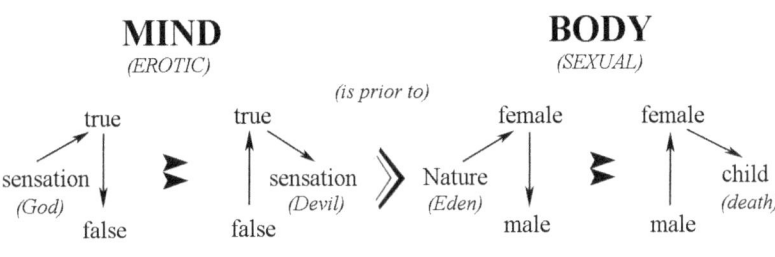

God template

The singular God at the head of the *God template* has no leverage on the world. God can only reveal his true nature by first casting out the false in the form of Satan. The dynamic of God's goodness is logically linked to the characterisation of the sensuous as evil. As in Greer's analysis, when nature is made secondary to the absolute God, it is reduced to an Eden-like state lacking the natural complexity represented in the *Nature template*.

Greer's attack on nature idolaters is ironic, considering the idealisation of nature in the Garden of Eden. But worse is the traditional prioritisation of the male over the female, which leads to the denigration of the natural dynamic of increase. In the illogical *God template*, the life of a child ends in a singular non-reproductive death that conveniently requires divine intercession to gain 'eternal life'.

Greer's determination to convert Shakespeare's natural philosophy to a male God Christian reading does an injustice both to Shakespeare and to the women whose causes she has championed. It is a sad reflection on human understanding that a person dedicated to women's rights is so willing to submit Shakespeare's female-based natural logic to a retro-active inquisition.

6

Stephen Booth & Helen Vendler

Of the ten essays in this volume, nine consider thinkers and writers whose understanding of Shakespeare is secondary to their professional roles as psychiatrists, psychologists, feminists, politicians, novelists, poets and artists.

In this essay the contributions to the *Sonnet* literature by two Shakespearean scholars is compared to give some idea of the difficulty scholars have when they are bereft of the *Sonnet* philosophy. Stephen Booth and Helen Vendler differ in their approach to the *Sonnets*, but because they consider the 154 sonnets in some detail it should be possible to compare their differences to show better what is missing from their methodologies. The essay will show that, while Booth and Vendler acknowledge their inability to determine the *Sonnet* philosophy, they unintentionally disclose the reason for their failure.

Stephen Booth

Stephen Booth's 1977 tome *Shakespeare's Sonnets*[1] is part of a recent trend that accepts the ordering of the sonnets in the 1609 edition as, if not exactly authorial, then at least not bettered by 400 years of published re-orderings. Booth acknowledges the current attitude toward the 1609 text by reproducing it alongside his modern English version.

Then, in his 400 pages of commentary, Booth documents a welter of possible meanings for nearly every word. He sources meanings from the literature he reckons was available to Shakespeare including the Bible, Greek and Roman texts (such as Homer and Ovid), the historical Chronicles, authors such as Dante and Chaucer, and his Elizabethan contemporaries.

Booth then adds many other variations of meaning including sexual or erotic or simply bawdy undertones or overtones he believes Shakespeare wished to evoke in the reader. From all his sources he builds up an encyclopaedic set of suggestions so that the reader can add the 'multitude' of potential meanings to their own interpretation of the words and phrases.

On the surface Booth's intention is an innocent one of assisting the reader understand the range of meanings in individual sonnets. He says he wishes to forestall the desire to arrive at a singular set of conditions to explain the meaning of the whole set.

Helen Vendler

In her *Art of Shakespeare's Sonnets*[2] published in 1997 Helen Vendler takes a more analytical approach. She prefaces her analysis of the poetry of individual sonnets by listing a number of other commentators who have failed to elicit from the *Sonnets* an understanding that does justice to their poetic achievement. To her mind the traditional psychological, sociological, religious, or gender-driven analyses do not account for the richness of meaning apparent when the sonnets are considered as lyrical inventions.

Vendler discusses significant features of individual sonnets such as their imaginative, structural, semantic, syntactic, phonemic, and graphic properties. She believes that focusing on Shakespeare's words and their relationships at the level of prosody she will avoid the indiscriminateness of Booth's analysis by identifying elements undeniably Shakespearean. Vendler admits she does not have a single 'expository scheme for each sonnet' and does not 'pretend to understand all the sonnets equally well'.

Like Booth, Vendler accepts the ordering of the 1609 edition and reproduces a facsimile of each sonnet above her modern English versions. She hopes that by leaving aside past prejudices, her insights into Shakespeare's poetic devices and techniques might provide the 'evidence' for future attempts to do justice to the meaning of the whole set.

Booth's 'multitude' of meanings

Booth's strategy of detailing all possible intended and unintended meanings in the individual sonnets should, it might be thought, provide an insight into the salient ideas addressed in the *Sonnets*. But that is not Booth's intention. At first he seems determined to avoid locating the singular reading that even Vendler hopes might arise from her formal analysis of the poetic structure. Instead, Booth begins by suggesting that his multifaceted approach recreates something of the experience of the 'Renaissance reader'.[3]

But on the second page of his preface[4] he suddenly apologises for 'some awkwardness' in the commentary, which is 'interrupted several times by lengthy discussions on particular topics'. Yet the first three 'topics', which discuss the 'emendations', the 'grandeur of the best sonnets', and 'spelling and punctuation', hardly warrant an apology.

The real reason for Booth's apologetic interlude is revealed in his fourth 'lengthy discussion' on the 'function of criticism' following sonnet 146. Only then does he disclose his ulterior purpose for insisting on an encyclopaedic 'multitude' of meanings.

In what Booth heralds as the 'longest of the long notes' he admits that 'a secondary purpose of this edition is to campaign for an analytic criticism that does not sacrifice…any work of literature to logical convenience or even to common sense'. Then after disingenuously apologising for 'another source of discomfort for my reader', he suggests that by not being specific about the meaning of individual sonnets his commentary 'tries to describe the physics' of how poetry goes 'beyond reason' to evoke the 'sublime'.

Booth's reason for his extreme discomfort is revealed in the long note to sonnet 146. And it seems Booth cannot wait to explain his 'secondary purpose'. After dismissing sonnet 145 as the "slightest of sonnets', he prepares for his commentary on sonnet 146, which has traditionally been viewed along with sonnets 116 and 129 as a 'Christian sonnet', by referring to three published articles, one on 'Critical Principles' and the other two on the 'Christian Sonnet'.[5] He then quotes 12 lines from a 1602 poem by Francis Davison that features a specious dialogue between the 'soul' and the 'body' to further predispose the reader toward his 'secondary purpose' for providing a 'multitude' of meanings.

Booth prepares the reader for the 'secondary purpose' of his 'longest of long notes' by belabouring his line-by-line examination of sonnet 146 with a plethora of quotations from the Bible and Christian references. And Booth's index has substantial references for entries such as 'Bible', 'Book of Common Prayer', and 'Christianity'. By contrast, reflecting Booth's ignorance of the *Sonnet* philosophy, he has no entries for 'increase', or 'Poet', or 'sovereign mistress', or 'beauty', only one for 'mistress' and a only few for 'nature'. Even Booth's preference for the word 'multitude' with its biblical overtones is revealing, as the usual term for a range of meanings is multiplicity.

When Booth begins his ten-page crusade to allow a Christian reading of sonnet 146 (and by implication all the sonnets) he argues not that sonnet 146 is Christian but that a Christian reading is equally possible alongside other readings. So he joins the many previous commentators who, for the last 400 years, and particularly since Malone's edition of the 1790s, have attempted to convert the *Sonnets* to Christianity. Occasionally a voice of sanity has been raised against the injustice, but has remained isolated in its focus on individual sonnets (such as Robert Graves and Laura Riding's study of sonnet 129[6]).

A short way into his 'note on the function of criticism' Booth belittles B. C. Southam's rejection of John Crowe Ransom's claim that sonnet 146 is a 'statement of Shakespeare's sympathetic attitude toward a commonplace of Christian doctrine'.[7] Southam recounts Ransom saying that the 'divine terms' in the sonnet are 'not particularly Christian', and there are 'few words' that would indicate 'conventional religious dogma'. Southam further rejects a claim by 'Luce' that the sonnet is 'an exact epitome of the Biblical yet lofty morality of Shakespeare's time', and expresses his own view that 'it is Shakespeare the humanist speaking, pleading for the life of the body as against the rigorous asceticism which glorifies the life of the spirit at the expense of the vitality and richness of sensuous experience'.[8]

But Booth, who is most likely conscious that Christian mythology, thanks to philosophical criticism, has been relegated to no more than one of many possible mythologies, wants it both ways. He says it is 'unreasonable and unprofitable to argue that sonnet 146 does not espouse an orthodox Christian position'.[9] But, not surprisingly, he does not want to 'homogenise' the experience of the poem by combining the seemingly opposed views. Rather he disingenuously suggests that Shakespeare's poetry is designed to accommodate irreconcilable readings.

In his desperation to engineer a Christian reading of the sonnet, Booth concludes with the 'editorial plea' that the 'metaphors (of soul and body) are the Bible's own, and they do not ordinarily give us trouble'.[10] Claiming he finds the last line of the sonnet 'moving in its sincerity' he cannot stop himself saying that sonnet 146 is, 'as readers have traditionally thought, a Christian exhortation to reject transient pleasures and gain eternal life'.[11] Then he pleads that sonnet 146 '*feels* as all inclusive as the logic of Christianity asks us to believe it is' (Booth's italics).[11]

Booth's strategy of providing a 'multitude' of readings is no more than a ploy to engineer validity for the traditionally imposed Christian reading. Booth wants Shakespeare's *Sonnets* to remain available for Christian inquisition and conversion. Despite the emendations and corruptions the *Sonnets* have been subjected to under the assault of the Christian inquisition, Booth adds further indignity by arguing disingenuously for a parallel reading. He cannot justify a solely Christian reading for sonnet 146 without avoiding the inconsistencies such a reading has with the words and the tone of the sonnet and of the whole set.

If Booth was not so equivocal in his belief that Shakespeare intended the *Sonnets* to be Christian then he might have honestly titled his book *A Christian Interpretation of Shakespeare's Sonnets*. Then readers would not be deceived by an interpretation posing as multitudinous only to find a supposedly secondary agenda that is blatantly Christian.

Vendler's 'key words' and 'couplet ties'

Vendler like Booth makes the 'words' of the *Sonnets* the primary focus of her analysis. But unlike Booth she declares no secondary agenda.[12] At least she does not use her commentary to make a special pleading. Contrary to Booth, she acknowledges that the 'speaker of Shakespeare's sonnets scorns the consolations of Christianity'.[13]

Yet Vendler is still doubly the victim of her formal analysis of what she calls Shakespeare's 'highly conventionalised lyric'.[14] She first restricts the meaning of the *Sonnets* to a level consonant with her formal analysis and then makes comments and emendations in which an undeclared adherence to the traditional Christian paradigm surfaces despite her avowal that the *Sonnets* have no such 'freight of meaning'.[14]

Vendler is aware that her decision to examine the *Sonnets* for their 'lyric' qualities relieves her of the traditional need to create 'social fictions' or make 'biographical revelations'.[14] In her view, traditional characterisations such as 'Young Man' and 'Dark Lady' turn the *Sonnets* into a 'proto-sketch for a drama rather like Othello'.[15] For her, all psychological accounts of the *Sonnet* 'story' have been frustrated by their lyrical 'indeterminacy'.[15]

Instead, in keeping with her personal predilection for poetic devices, Vendler considers the 'true actors in lyrics are words, not dramatic persons'.[15] So the drama of any lyric is 'constituted by the successive entrances of new sets of words, or new stylistic arrangements'.[15] Changes in 'topic' of 'syntactic structure' are for her among the 'strategies which constitute vivid drama within the lyric genre'.[15] Not only is the 'lyric drama' the raison d'etre for a sonnet, she also claims that 'a writer of Shakespeare's seriousness writes from internal necessity – to do the best he can under his commission…and to perfect his art'.[16]

In response to 400 years of failure to find a coherent approach to the whole set of *Sonnets* Vendler decides to examine all the sonnets piece by piece for evidence of their lyrical coherence. She hopes that by resisting the distraction of 'classical references' or 'systematic doctrines' she can give some indication of Shakespeare's 'native language'.[17]

By focusing on the lyrical aspects of the individual sonnets, Vendler imagines it is possible to hear an 'ur-language'[17] or the 'permutations of emotional response'.[18] If the poetic devices create the 'art' of the sonnets then 'Shakespeare's *Sonnets* are philosophical insofar as they display interrelationships among their parts which, as they unfold, trace a conflict in human cognitive and affective motions'.[18]

So Shakespeare as a poet is only allowed to be 'constantly inventing new permutations of internal form' just as the 'speaker' of the *Sonnets* exhibits 'intrapsychic irony'.[19] Hence for Vendler, lyric poetry has 'almost no significant freight of meaning'.[14] For her, Shakespeare's 'main intellectual and poetic achievement' is the 'hierarchizing of several conceptual models at once',[20] but those models are the cognitive and affective ur-language behind the poetic surface. Vendler's task, as she sees it, is to examine the poetic surface in detail to enable the reader to better appreciate the background 'models'.

Whereas Booth is predetermined in his need to give the *Sonnets* a Christian ur-language and creates a sham surface of multitudinousness to conceal the conversion, Vendler admits that she vaguely sees the 154 sonnets as a 'single object' that 'displays…dispersive gaps and uncertainties between the individual units', with the smaller certainties of 'single sonnets' floating and colliding on the 'large uncertainties'.[21] Despite her years of analysis of the poetic structure and hundreds of pages on 'Shakespeare's art', she still does not know 'what sort of poet is Shakespeare'.[21]

Although Vendler senses something significant within the whole set she has no idea what it is. But instead of questioning the whole basis of her understanding in the Judeo/Christian paradigm, as Shakespeare does, she focuses blithely on 'Shakespeare's art'. Ironically, textual scholars of the last few decades have attempted to blame the compositors of the 1609 edition for the 60 to 100 emendations that traditional scholarship needs to make the text correspond to their preferred reading, and like her they do not question the influence of their Judeo/Christian prejudices. Vendler gets no further than the textual scholars despite, or because of, her pedantic examination of the sonnets' poetic texture.

In a desperate attempt to connect her examination of the poetic texture of the 154 individual sonnets to the 'large certainty' she senses is beneath the whole set, Vendler identifies two patterns of words that, she suggests, unite the three quatrains of each sonnet with its couplet. The first pattern is formed by 'couplet ties', words that occur in at least one of the three quatrains and in the couplet. And the second pattern is formed of 'key words', or some variation of the words, that occur in all three quatrains and the couplet.

Vendler claims that the couplet ties are 'almost always thematically highly significant ones',[22] yet many are trite and nine sonnets do not have them. And she finds key words in only forty of the 154 sonnets and of those twelve are extremely contrived. To compensate for the fact that less than twenty-five percent of the sonnets have genuine key words Vendler invents a further category of 'defective key words' in which the connections are extremely tenuous. But the 'defective key word' sonnets, where she imagines a key word may have been 'designedly suppressed',[23] add less than thirty more sonnets to her key word list. So, less than half the sonnets have key words.

Vendler religiously ends each commentary by listing the couplet ties and key words for those sonnets where they can be found. By making such a major issue of such a trivial aspect of Shakespeare's sonnet 'art' Vendler reveals the bankruptcy of her approach. If her title reflected the true focus of her analysis it would not herald an insight into the 'art' of Shakespeare's *Sonnets*, rather it would announce a formal investigation of their craft.

Included in a pocket at the back of Vendler's book is a CD in which she reads a selection of the sonnets. Though she claims to have memorised all the sonnets, her decision to read only some of them accords with her inability to understand the meaning of the whole set. She criticises 'three readings available on tape' by actors who she feels use 'constant mis-emphasis'.[24] John Gielgud's reading, though, like hers, is notable for its lack of understanding of the *Sonnet* philosophy, and he leaves out a number of sonnets tradition has considered inferior.

Vendler and Gielgud reveal their ignorance of the *Sonnet* philosophy when, in their list of favourite sonnets, they invariably chose the most lyrical and dismiss the ones they consider less poetic. Sonnets 18, 73, 116, 129 and 146 are some of the few always anthologised but sonnets 9, 14, 77, 99, 126, 145, 153, 154 are frequently ignored or disparaged. Yet these are pivotal sonnets in the structural presentation of the *Sonnet* philosophy.

Vendler's analysis of the 'lyrical' in individual sonnets ignores the evidence for structured argument throughout the set. A number of times sonnets are joined by logical connectives, clearly defined groups of sonnets present the increase argument and the poetry and increase argument, and the group of 9 sonnets near the centre of the set dismiss the Alien Poets, who ironically like Vendler revel in rhyme and meter. Vendler's determination to examine Shakespeare's 'art' or craft and her inability to appreciate his 'content' identifies her level of understanding with that of the inadequate Alien Poets.

Not only does Vendler's ignorance of the *Sonnet* content align her with the Alien Poets, she persists with the traditional emendations, which are an indictment of 300 years of *Sonnet* misinterpretation out of the inappropriate Judeo/Christian paradigm. And, even though she claims not to presume on the ur-language of the set, she reveals her covert sympathies for Christian apology when she makes additional emendations that are contrary to the sonnet logic. In sonnet 55 she gives the word 'judgment' a capital 'J' because she thinks Shakespeare was referring to the Christian Day of Judgment. Yet 'judgment' has a quite different logical function in the *Sonnet* philosophy.

Vendler is relentless in naming every figure of speech as if Shakespeare deliberately exploited the grammarian's grab-bag of tricks. For Vendler, Shakespeare gave form to his 'cognitions' and 'emotions' by the artful use of such devices. By naming them and by noticing other regularities like the couplet ties she imagines that the hidden meaning will become more palpable.

But the naming of such features merely categorises what is inherent in language. It is more likely that Shakespeare's incredible facility with language, aided by some schooling, generated the figures of speech and word patterns. Vendler allows Shakespeare a supreme command of the craft of language, but has no idea how he is able to generate an artistic 'ur-language' of profound meaning.

Ironically, the philosophy articulated so precisely in the *Sonnets* needs a much deeper level of deliberate intention than Vendler presumes Shakespeare brought to the figures of speech, 'couplet ties', and 'key words'. If Shakespeare was as deliberate with prosody as he was with the philosophy then her findings would demonstrate a much greater degree of coherence than she is able to show in the twenty five per cent of the sonnets in which her key words are regular.

Booth and Vendler

Booth and Vendler have both been recognised for their scholarly contributions to the *Sonnet* literature. Booth's encyclopaedic set of references explores a complex range of intended and unintended meanings. Vendler provides a detailed analysis of Shakespeare's poetic tools.

But Booth and Vendler were not driven to write 600-page tomes on the *Sonnets* solely to exercise their academic talents. Booth's plea that a Christian reading be allowed and Vendler's desire to understand the 'ur-language' behind Shakespeare's 'art' reveals an interest in the meaning of the complete set. As with the musings of other commentators, Booth's 'secondary' agenda and Vendler's investigation of the lyrical surface indicate a belief that Shakespeare organised the *Sonnets* to convey more than they have been able to comprehend. The disjunction between their academic contributions and their inability to understand the *Sonnets* surfaces many times throughout the commentaries.

An indicator of Booth's difficulty is his belated rejection of the traditional emendation to the word 'wish' in the first line of sonnet 111. In his first edition he sided with the traditional editors in emending 'wish' to 'with'. Yet if Booth had understood the *Sonnet* philosophy he would have understood the relevance of 'wish'. And if Booth would accept that the overwhelming percentage of other traditional emendations are equally wrong he would be able to reject attempts to blame the innocent compositors because of the application of an inappropriate paradigm to the *Sonnet* set. But his Christian agenda blinds him to the *Sonnet* logic.

When Vendler decided to limit herself to an analysis of poetic devices, because neither the traditional literature nor she could see a way to comprehend the whole set, she did leave open the possibility that someone in the future would benefit from her work to make a breakthrough into the *Sonnet* mystery. Ironically, within two years, one of the academics whose textual theorising has resulted in the compositors being excoriated for their carelessness over the emendations outlined a case for an overview using some of Vendler's work.

Partly in response to Vendler's desire to find patterns throughout the *Sonnets*, albeit with her erratic couplet ties and key words, MacDonald P. Jackson wrote an article summarising some of the apparent patterns in the set.[25] But instead of critiquing Vendler's refusal to question the traditional paradigm in her dutiful analysis of the technical features of the *Sonnets*, Jackson takes the opportunity to further implicate the compositors. Jackson, who has been called the 'unsung hero of the sonnets' by his academic peers for his work in apportioning blame on the compositors of the 1609 edition, uses Vendler's inadequate 'key word' theory to justify another emendation.

In sonnet 152 Vendler decided that the key word was 'eye'. This is despite the fact that 'eye' occurs only in the couplet, whereas 'I' occurs in all four parts. Vendler, although she does not accept 'I' as a 'foregrounded word', in this case spies a pun with 'eye'. So building on her inverted logic, Jackson emends the 'eye' in line 13 to 'I'.

Jackson began his article by stating that key words are 'almost invariably picked up in the last two lines'. But that is a very generous interpretation of Vendler's own list that shows that only twenty five percent of the sonnets have regular key words. It is ironic that by using his reputation as a defender of the emendations to completely regularise sonnet 152 for Vendler, Jackson reveals the level of collaboration at the heart of traditional *Sonnet* scholarship.

Shakespeare's *Sonnet* philosophy

Stephen Booth and Helen Vendler's laborious efforts at least recognise that the *Sonnets* deserve serious analysis and that the 1609 edition remains the default text despite the editorial interference of the last 400 years. The tacit admission that *Q* still has credibility after 400 years of denigration and misattribution is evidence of the inadequacy of the reasons for doubting its authenticity.

It is a commonplace refrain in Shakespeare studies that he based his plays and poems in nature. And the evidence from even a cursory reading of the *Folio* and *Q* supports that expectation. Commentators such as Bradley and Leishman have had to admit, against their fervent wishes, that there is no evidence in the works that Shakespeare was a Christian.

Booth and Vendler fail to comprehend the *Sonnet* philosophy because of their traditional prejudices. In particular, if the Christian prejudice is so inadequate for understanding Shakespeare then why do they not examine the possibility that the *Sonnets* are based in nature and the sexual dynamic? Despite Booth's readiness to comment on all the shades of sexual references and Vendler's acknowledgement of such meanings, Booth draws no conclusions from their ubiquity and Vendler passes over the many figures of speech that show Shakespeare's interest in nature and his use of sexual/erotic imagery.

Because the *Sonnets* can be shown to articulate Shakespeare's philosophy, by setting out the logical relation between nature/female and male and the possibility of understanding as truth and beauty, Booth's diversionary tactic of covering every eventuality and Vendler's academic exercise in poetic devices are shown to be disingenuous.

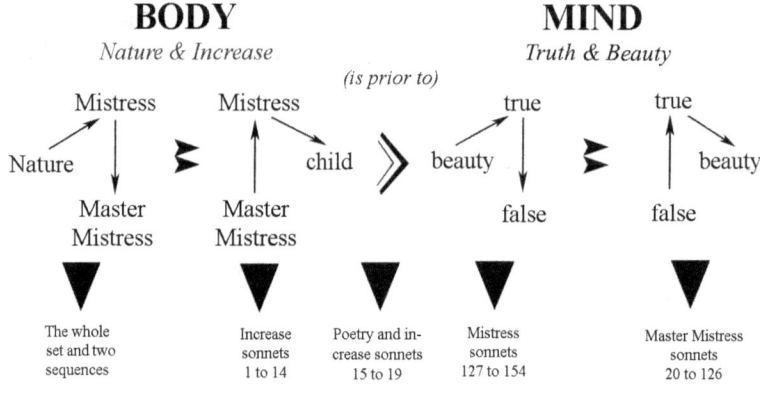

Nature template (Sonnet numbers)

The presentation in these volumes recognises the commonplace that nature is the basis for the philosophy Shakespeare structures into the *Sonnets*. Once the logic of the whole set as nature and the two sequences as Mistress and Master Mistress is recognised then the logical development of the dynamic of understanding or truth and beauty out of nature and the sexual dynamic can be shown to be consistent with the division of the Mistress sequence into the beauty dynamic (127 to 137) and the truth dynamic (137 to 152), and the Master Mistress sonnets that present the increase argument (1 to 14), the poetry and increase argument (15 to19), and the extensive discussion of truth and beauty (20 to 126).

As Booth and Vendler fail to recognise even these basic elements of the *Sonnet* logic, they have no chance of saying anything incisive about individual sonnets, the imagery of the sonnets, the individual words, figures of speech, etc. Because they are blind to Shakespeare's natural logic they do not even mention the basic structure of the *Sonnets*. Their commentaries are driven by a prejudice against nature and a preference for the anti-nature theology of Christianity.

The problem for commentators such as Booth and Vendler is that Shakespeare begins where their level of understanding ends. Shakespeare as the consummate poet would have been aware of most of the shades of meaning Booth attributes to his words. And with his grounding in rhetoric and grammar he was most likely aware of the types of figures of speech Vendler uses to analyse his verse. For lesser artists the dictionary of symbology and the grab bag of technical devices might exhaust their creative impulse. But artists such as Shakespeare and Duchamp move beyond formal and technical exploration to set down the logic of 'content'.

They not only employ imagery that shows their insight into the dynamic of nature or to convey the deeper resources of their imagination, they have a complete grasp of the logical conditions for content at the highest possible level of artistic operation, the mythic. Shakespeare and Duchamp not only understand the operation of the mythic, their works incorporate the fact that they do understand. The reflexivity of the *Sonnets* and the *Large Glass* at the level of the mythic makes it impossible for those with lesser expectations to determine their meaning.

Because Booth and Vendler operate at a level well below Shakespeare, their attempts to understand his work appropriately focus on aspects of his work he would have considered rudimentary, such as the encyclopaedia of imagery and the dictionary of special effects. Ironically, the only way they can show their awareness of the inadequacies of their approach is to insist on the Christian reading as an option or on a non-interpretative reading with Christian trimmings. They are unwilling to claim that Shakespeare was a Christian as the overwhelming evidence indicates he was not. The fact that Booth and Vendler are rated as two of the more incisive readers of the *Sonnets* shows how inadequate the awareness of artistic practice at the mythic level is and how abysmal are the available interpretative tools in the culture.

Because Booth and Vendler fail to understand even a small portion of the *Sonnet* logic and because they hold a high status as professors in the tertiary hierarchy, the case for a level of learning above tertiary is argued for eloquently by their ignorance. The institution of a quaternary level of systematic learning is a potential consequence of showing that Shakespeare's *Sonnets* articulate the logical conditions for any mythic expression.

The *Nature template* derived in Volume 1 is the standard for quaternary pedagogy. Not only do Booth and Vendler not arrive at its formulation in the *Sonnets* they barely recognise its components and show by their preference for the Christian mythology that they invert its logic to favour the male God illogicality.

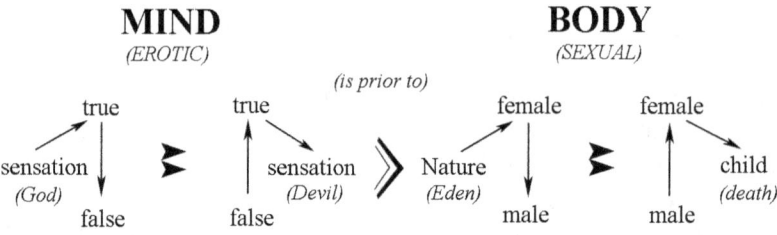

God template

But, contrary to Booth's ardent hope and Vendler's uncertainty, the natural logic of the *Sonnets* encompasses the male-based idealism of Christianity in the sequence to the distracted idealistic youth. Because the *Sonnet* logic encompasses the male-based God of the Christian myth, Booth and Vendler's desire to validate only that part of the whole set distorts the consistent and comprehensive philosophy of Shakespeare's *Sonnets*. Booth's desire to have an alternate reading is only possible if he accepts that Shakespeare incorporates his male-based God within the Master Mistress sequence. And Vendler's desire to read some words as Christian misses Shakespeare's correction of the traditionally inverted meaning of those words when he applies his natural logic.

7
Friedrich Nietzsche & Ludwig Wittgenstein

Ludwig Wittgenstein: from atoms to human nature

These volumes acknowledge Ludwig Wittgenstein's (1889-1951) contribution to the philosophic attitude required to understand Shakespeare's natural logic. Particularly significant was Wittgenstein's decision to abandon atomic physics as a model for representing the logical relationship between language and the world in favour of a model based in 'nature', 'family resemblances', and 'forms of life'. His acceptance that the human mind is based in natural logic provides an example of the shift needed to begin to appreciate the *Sonnet* philosophy.

When Wittgenstein moved from the strict formal logic of the atomic model of the *Tractatus* to a more human-based model in *Philosophical Investigations* he tried in vain to recover the precision of the earlier work. Unlike Shakespeare in the *Sonnets*, he did not arrive at a clear and systematic expression of the natural logic of life.

The critique of Western metaphysics in these volumes has questioned the shift in traditional philosophy from the macro-world of male God metaphysics to the micro-world of atomic physics. When Wittgenstein realised that neither Kantian style metaphysics or Russellian atomism could provide the correct multiplicity to account for the logical relation between language and the world he developed his ordinary language approach. But despite the change he could not bring himself to accept all its implications. In his lectures on religious belief he revealed a residual commitment to Christian dogma that continued until his death, when he received the last rites.

And despite Wittgenstein's move toward natural logic he was unable to comprehend the works of Shakespeare. He could only imagine they had worth because of the value they had in the estimation of authors he did admire. Given the persistence of Wittgenstein's religious belief it is not surprising he could not appreciate even the little of what others saw in Shakespeare.

This essay considers the relationship between Wittgenstein's life work and his residual Catholic idealism to better understand why he was unable to appreciate the natural logic of the *Sonnets* as the philosophy behind Shakespeare's plays and poems. And because Wittgenstein's *Tractatus* and posthumous publications such as the *Philosophical Investigations* do not mention his Catholic beliefs, the essay compares their covert influence on his philosophy with the overt rejection of the Christian God in Nietzsche's philosophy with its deliberately prophetic style.

Friedrich Nietzsche: from male Gods to nature

This essay explores the irony that Friedrich Nietzsche's (1844-1900) overt rejection of Christianity and Wittgenstein's covert acceptance of it were driven by the same residual idealistic fear. Nietzsche's rejection of the macro-world of biblical Gods did lead to an acceptance of the priority of nature and the processes of life as basic to a sound philosophy. Wittgenstein arrived at a similar position in his later philosophy. But their inability to appreciate the logic of the female/male dynamic in nature, and their unwillingness to consider the logic of the sexual dynamic for human persistence led to inconsistencies in their understanding of the logic of good and evil.

Both Nietzsche and Wittgenstein were strongly influenced by Arthur Schopenhauer's notion of the transcendental 'Will'. Nietzsche's belief in an aesthetic state of mind 'beyond good and evil' and Wittgenstein's understanding that 'aesthetics and ethics are one and the same' but beyond language, derive from Schopenhauer's semi-secular idealism.

Similarly, while Wittgenstein had little to say about the status or role of myth in a culture, probably because of his covert adherence to the Christian myth, Nietzsche had much to say despite his overt rejection of Christian mythology. His understanding, though, that 'art is a kind of play' because 'life is best conceived as child's play'[1] and, as he says in the *Birth of Tragedy*, music has the power to give birth to myth,[2] reveals an ignorance of the level of language skill required to express mythic logic.

Nietzsche, like Wittgenstein, did not understand Shakespeare's philosophy. Nietzsche was unaware of the mythic dynamic articulated in Shakespeare's *Sonnets* and of the way in which the plays achieved their mythic depth. And incredibly for a supposedly insightful philosopher, throughout his life,

Nietzsche believed that Shakespeare was Francis Bacon. That Nietzsche gave credence to the Shakespeare identity debate reveals the abysmal level of his understanding of Shakespeare's works. Also revealing was his single-minded drive to find instances of a 'will to power' in the plays. For instance, in *Julius Caesar* he focused on Brutus' apparent 'will to power', to the exclusion of other characters and the overall plot.

Something of Nietzsche's own mental condition surfaces when he speculates on the psychological difficulties he thought the author of the *Sonnets* would have experienced to write with such 'gloominess'. Not surprisingly, Nietzsche's rash claims reveal a mind further removed from the *Sonnet* logic than even Wittgenstein, who was at least frank in admitting incomprehension before Shakespeare's works.

So this essay compares the analytic examination of the logic of language by Wittgenstein with the anti-Christian, pro-nature, pro-life philosophy of Nietzsche to better appreciate Shakespeare's achievement. As some critics have had difficulty reconciling Wittgenstein's change in direction between his early and later thought, and others have had difficulty reconciling the positive and negative influences of Nietzsche's thought, the idea that Nietzsche and Wittgenstein were constrained by similar prejudices may provide some insights.

Vestiges of the male God

Nietzsche was forthright in dismissing the Judeo/Christian claim for the primacy of the biblical God. By heralding the idea that 'God is dead' he overtly challenged the inconsistencies and injustices that arise when such a God is given priority over nature. He correctly recognised nature and the forces of life as the logical entities within which to contextualise the psychology of religion. As Robert Wicks says, just as 'some Christians find solace in the prospect of participation in an otherworldly kingdom of God after their bodies die, Nietzsche found solace in the possibility of participating in the universal life forces that permeate the here-and-now, earthly world of the living'.[3]

Ten years before he proclaimed the death of the male God of Christianity in the *Gay Science* in 1882, Nietzsche had published his first book *The Birth of Tragedy*. Greek tragedy provided him with two Gods with which to represent the opposing tendencies in human understanding. Apollo represented the intellectual or 'idealising' tendency and Dionysus the sensory or 'animal' tendency. And Nietzsche persisted with the characterisation of mental dispositions in terms of two male Greek Gods until his mental health failed in 1889. Ironically, then, despite his replacement of the life-negating Christian God by life-affirming Greek Gods, he persisted with a representation of mental dispositions as male Gods.

Nietzsche's determination to look to nature for the basis of meaning was foiled by an uncritical acceptance of Apollo and Dionysus as the representatives of mental dispositions. Nietzsche's decision to use the two male Gods reveals a deep prejudice against the female both in that Apollonian characteristics are unequivocally male and the attribution of female characteristics to male Dionysus doubly emphasises the prejudice.

As Robert Wicks notes, there is only one 'juncture' in the *Birth of Tragedy* where Nietzsche does mention the female.[4] Yet while Nietzsche does talk of 'mother nature' using terms such as immoral, exploitative, and violent, and that 'truth' should be 'gently coaxed from her', his model woman is Helen of Troy who represents an ideal of 'sweet sensuality'.[4] To reconcile his preference for the idealised Helen he contrasts her with the terrifying Medusa or Baubo, who personified the female genitals.

So not only does Nietzsche replace the male God of the Bible with two male Greek Gods, his representations of the female predominately prioritise the male and when they do consider the female they make a division not dissimilar to that between the biblical Virgin Mary and outcasts like Eve and Mary Magdalene.

Nietzsche approaches the logic of human understanding with a prejudice against the female. His prejudice prevents him from characterising the feminine and masculine dimensions of the human mind logically. And despite his desire to acknowledge the state of nature and conform to the processes of life, his male prejudice removes the possibility of recognising the biological priority of the female over the male.

It is not surprising then that Nietzsche's prophet Zarathustra is unquestionably a male and his 'superhuman' is referred to, like the biblical God, as 'he'. Nietzsche also compares the superhuman with strong male leaders from history, again ignoring the logical relation of female and male. The tendency of some to read superhuman as supermale is not surprising as logically Nietzsche did not move beyond the gender contradictions of the Bible. It is not sufficient to denounce theism by avowing atheism. Without addressing the deeper issue of the logical relation of female and male Nietzsche's denouncement of the male God of the Bible is mere cant.

Nietzsche's overt recognition of the illogicality of religious claims gives his philosophy its declamatory and uncompromising tone. Having dismissed biblical precedent he assumed the role of prophet, particularly through his alter ego Zarathustra. Nietzsche's rejection of the singular male God, however, led not to greater insight into aesthetics and morality, but, because he lacked an appreciation of the logic of myth, to inconsistencies not dissimilar to those he dismissed.

For his part, Wittgenstein's philosophy was dramatically conditioned by his covert adherence to Christianity throughout both periods of his career. His acceptance of Catholic extreme unction on his death bed was the final act in a lifetime in which he considered entering a monastery and was unable to accept the Darwinian idea that human mental propensities were derived from other mammalian species. He believed they must have another source.

Wittgenstein's covert Catholicism, like the overt Catholicism of Descartes and the overt Protestantism of Kant, kept him from challenging the logic of the priority of the male God. Constrained by the psychology of his beliefs he never examined the logic of the female/male dynamic as it impacts on language and particularly how it is basic to the mythological expression of his religious faith.

Wittgenstein's covert belief never surfaces in his philosophy. Instead he saw philosophy as a process of delimiting the role of language the better to appreciate the realm of metaphysics, which he characterised as the unsayable. Yet when his first period of philosophy based on atoms and molecules collapsed under its internal inconsistencies his later work drew closer to Nietzsche in its acceptance of nature and life as the ultimate criteria for the logic of thought. But like Nietzsche, Wittgenstein remained confused about the logic of aesthetics and ethics.

Aesthetics and ethics

Nietzsche and Wittgenstein's confusion about the logic of aesthetics and ethics derives from their inability to free themselves completely from the influence of the male God religions of the last 4000 years. Even though they both moved toward an understanding of the logic of life based in nature, their view of nature was afflicted by residual aspects of male God beliefs.

The traditional male God was believed to be both the repository of ideal goodness and the creator of the world with all its pain and violence. When Nietzsche proclaimed that God was dead, because he recognised that belief in the God of tradition led invariably to social and political injustices and prejudices, he ironically carried over some of the illogical characteristics of male God belief into his characterisation of nature and life.

Nietzsche recognised that the conflict between belief in an other-worldly ideal God as creator of this world and of the apparent evil in the world creates the 'problem of evil'. Because aspects of life involve pain and violence, Nietzsche's solution was to call all life 'immoral'. He hoped to eliminate the problem of evil by embracing the whole of life as immoral. He envisioned humankind coming to terms with an indifferent universe by professing *amor fati* or a love of fate.[5] When humankind eschewed an idealised eternity or a perfectible world, they would achieve solace by living moment to moment.

To overcome the paradox that life must be viewed as immoral if the death of God is to be sustained, Nietzsche reckoned that the distinction between 'good and evil' should be removed to enable a person to gain equanimity with the world. If truth was to be attained then the difference between those things considered good and the evil must be dissolved. Nietzsche's 'superhuman' was one who acted as if good and evil was not their concern when they exercised their will to power.

Nietzsche considered the natural consequence of removing the distinction between good and evil would be an 'aesthetic justification' of life and existence. Music, for instance, could have a redeeming quality. So, to overcome the iniquities of the Christian system of morals handed down as the word of God, Nietzsche proposed an understanding beyond good and evil in which the mind could regain its cultural health by listening to music or imbibing the aesthetic experience of a Greek tragedy.

It is ironical that Nietzsche's 'genealogy of morals' dismissed a rational view of the world in favour of a poetic approach. Nearly 300 years before, Shakespeare had precisely articulated a genealogical and rational philosophy in the poetry of his *Sonnets*.

To complement the aesthetic experience as a way of connecting with the here and now, Nietzsche fostered the idea of 'eternal recurrence'. Nietzsche's alternative to an eternal life spent with God, or forever in the fires of hell as promised by Christian dogma, was the prospect of the world of experience being played over and over throughout time. He considered eternal recurrence as the 'highest formula of affirmation'[6] of life, a life which paradoxically could be lived in equanimity by achieving a state of mind 'beyond good and evil'.

Wittgenstein was as confused as Nietzsche about the role of aesthetics and ethics for humankind within nature. In the *Tractatus* he not only says that 'aesthetics and ethics are one and the same',[7] he places them in a mystical realm beyond the reach of language. He refused an ethical function to propositional language despite spending a considerable amount of space analysing the logic of language using truth tables that evaluated propositions according to their truth and falsity.

Wittgenstein's attitude that language was unable to convey the meaning or value of the world, because aesthetics and ethics were located in the unspoken world, confuses the unspoken impetus that is life with the everyday use of language to determine the most appropriate attitude or action to ongoing events. His commitment to a male God mysticism blinded him to the logic that decision making through language is the ethical process. It is only necessary to reflect that ethics committees principally use language and not music when they arbitrate points of conflict.

When Wittgenstein says aesthetics and ethics are one and the same he confuses the aesthetic impulse, which logically remains unworded, with the ethical processes of language. Wittgenstein's belief in an absolute God, who logically cannot say anything and so is inseparable from other aesthetic impulses, commits him to say aesthetics and ethics are the same.

Wittgenstein remained affected by the illogicalities of his faith in his later philosophy. If in his early work the aesthetic and the ethical were beyond language, in the later version, after the possibility of an extra-language world collapsed, he conceived of aesthetics and ethics as at the boundary of the speakable world.

Nietzsche and Wittgenstein were both determined to recover philosophy's task of representing the logic of human understanding in terms of the natural world. While each was prepared to disavow the illogicalities of 2000 years of Judeo/Christian apologetics neither was able to appreciate that the crux of the problem lay at the heart of the logic of the male-based biblical myth. Nietzsche disavowed the idea of God ('God is dead') without redressing the illogicality of the priority of the male God over the female. Wittgenstein pared down his Roman Christianity to the residue of fear of a final judgment but never addressed the status of its male God and so was constrained by the illogicality of prioritising the male over the female.[8]

The logic of myth

Neither Nietzsche nor Wittgenstein understood the logical conditions for mythic expression. Nietzsche rejected traditional expressions of mythology and disingenuously suggested that the mythic could be conveyed by music. Ironically, Wittgenstein's honesty was a consequence of his literal adherence to biblical mythology. In his few comments on Shakespeare, Wittgenstein acknowledged his inability to appreciate why others such as Milton rated Shakespeare as the greatest dramatist and poet of all time.

Yet not only did Shakespeare write plays of acknowledged mythic depth, his *Sonnets* set out the logical conditions for any mythic expression. Shakespeare appreciated that for a work of art to achieve a mythic level of expression it needed to convey the logical relation between nature and human nature. It needed to express something of the origin of the world and the place that humans as sexual beings occupied in the natural world. But more significantly it needed to express the relation of the operations of the mind to humans as sexual beings within nature.

Mythic expression not only expresses the logical relation between nature and sexual beings and the mind, it also recognises that the presentation of the relationships is in the medium of language or writing. And it is not sufficient to understand the logical conditions for mythic expression. The artist or writer needs to be capable of giving effective expression to the relationship.

Shakespeare's *Sonnets* are witness to both his understanding of the logic of myth and his ability to evoke the mythic level of experience in his poetry and prose. By giving effective expression to the mythic conditions for the relation of nature and humankind he moves beyond the limitations of all previous mythologies that gave expression to the logic of myth but then mistake the mythic expression for the logical conditions of life prior to its expression in language.

Crucial to the logic of myth is the recognition that the myth itself does not substitute for the world that it represents in words. The distinction is expressed in myth in the logical relation between the sexual and the erotic. The sexual relates to the unwritten world and the erotic to the world as represented in the form of language. In traditional mythologies the logical expression of the erotic central to all myths is illogically taken to be prior to the sexual. The philosophic expression in myth is subverted by the psychology of fear and belief to a status prior to the sexual in nature.

When Shakespeare set out his nature-based philosophy in the *Sonnets* to articulate the logical conditions for any mythology he recognised the logical implication of distinguishing between the sexual and the erotic was to acknowledge the sexual division in nature between the female and the male. Only by structuring into his *Sonnets* the logical priority of female over male could he begin to account for the logical conditions for any mythology.

Understanding Shakespeare

Wittgenstein was unable to see beyond his limited understanding of nature into Shakespeare's nature-based philosophy. It is worth recalling his thoughts on Shakespeare from Part 1, Chapter 2.

> It is remarkable how hard we find it to believe something that we do not see the truth of for ourselves. When, for instance, I hear the expression of admiration for Shakespeare by distinguished men in the course of several centuries, I can never rid myself of the suspicion that praising him has been the conventional thing to do; though I have to tell myself that this is not how it is. It takes the authority of a Milton really to convince me. I take it for granted that he was incorruptible. – But of course I don't mean by this that I don't believe an enormous amount of praise to have been, and still to be lavished on Shakespeare without understanding and for the wrong reasons by a thousand professors of literature.[9]
>
> My failure to understand him could (then) be explained by my inability to read him easily. That is, as one views a splendid piece of scenery.[10]
>
> I do not believe that Shakespeare can be set alongside any other poet. Was he perhaps the creator of language rather than a poet.
>
> I could only stare in wonder at Shakespeare; never do anything with him.[11]
>
> The reason why I cannot understand Shakespeare is that I want to find symmetry in all this asymmetry.[12]

If Wittgenstein was circumspect about his understanding of Shakespeare, Nietzsche seemed in no doubt about his ability to see into the mind of a fellow poet and philosopher. Yet, as indicated above, Nietzsche's statements about Shakespeare and his *Sonnets* and plays are abysmal and wilful. Nietzsche's view of himself as prophet and moralist is revealed for all its hubris when viewed against the consistent logic of Shakespeare's *Sonnets* and poems and plays.

Because Nietzsche looked for characters in Shakespeare's plays who seemed to conform to his image of the superhuman ideal, it is not surprising he should focus on plays like *Macbeth* or *Julius Caesar*. In *Daybreak* he expresses his conviction that Shakespeare would have felt exactly as Macbeth did, with a 'joy' of 'raging ambition'.

> Whoever thinks that Shakespeare's theatre has a moral effect, and that the sight of Macbeth irresistibly repels one from the evil of ambition, is in error: and again he is in error if he thinks Shakespeare himself felt as he feels. He who is really possessed by raging ambition beholds this its image with joy…Can the poet have felt otherwise?[13]

Nietzsche's simplistic identification of poet and character to make Shakespeare into an exemplary superhuman, begs the question as to why Shakespeare experienced such feelings only for the characters Nietzsche personally sympathised with. Nietzsche says nothing of the overarching philosophy of the whole play within which Macbeth's 'superhuman' ambition is contextualised.

In a note Nietzsche wrote a few weeks before he lost his mind, he says that 'if I seek my highest formula for Shakespeare, I always find that he has conceived his type as Caesar'.[14] And Nietzsche's sister, Mrs. E. F. Nietzsche, reports that,

> The tragic friendship relation that Brutus had with Caesar he (Nietzsche) found the most astounding that was ever written; to him Shakespeare had dedicated his best tragedy. Independence of soul – that is here the remarkable thing. No sacrifice can be too great.[15]

She goes on to say that 'this tragedy directly led my brother to believe that the poet whom we call Shakespeare is perhaps indeed Lord Bacon'. Nietzsche's excessively psychological reading of Shakespeare has its counterpart in Freud's belief that Shakespeare was the Earl of Oxford. The critique of Freud's understanding of Shakespeare given in Chapter 3 of this volume highlights the inadequate psychologism in Nietzsche's philosophical style. In *Ecce Homo* Nietzsche says,

> We are all afraid in the face of Truth; and while I recognise that I am instinctively certain and sure of this, that Lord Bacon is the creator, the self-torturer of this most gloomy sort of literature.[16]

And again,

> Long are we without adequate knowledge of Lord Bacon, the first realist in every great sense of the word; what he has done, what he has desired, what his experiences have been.... And to the devil with you, Messrs. Critics! Suppose I had baptised my 'Zarathustra' under a strange name, or instance that of Richard Wagner, and the sagacity of two centuries had not been sufficient to guess that the author of 'human, all too human', the visionary of Zarathustra is…![17]

Nietzsche not only believed Bacon was Shakespeare, he ascribes to his Bacon/Shakespeare the psychological turmoil he sees in Brutus.

> Perhaps he too had his dark hours and evil angels, like Brutus. But whatever of that sort of similarity and common relations it may have yielded, Shakespeare before all that figure and virtue of Brutus, threw himself to earth and felt himself unworthy'.[18]

Nietzsche has no compunction about translating such emotion 'back to the soul of the poet who wrote it'. If, as the article by Ebenhof suggests, Nietzsche calls on the historic relation between Bacon, Essex and Shakespeare to account for the intensity of the drama of *Julius Caesar*, then he not only accuses Shakespeare of being psychologically indulgent but that his play was written as an indirect account of the political fortunes of his contemporaries.

Nietzsche, who did suffer psychological problems, applies his psychological reading to the poet of the *Sonnets*. And revealing of his inability to extricate himself completely from his Christian past, he attributes to the writer of the *Sonnets* a 'Christian gloominess'.

> In addition there remains a misery kept secret and thus more deeply rooted: for not everyone possesses the courage of Shakespeare to confess his Christian gloominess on this point in the way he did it in his Sonnets.[19]

Shakespeare's natural logic

Shakespeare avoids the illogicalities that occur in the thinking of Nietzsche and Wittgenstein. Their inability to take account of the female/male dynamic in nature, riddles their writings with inconsistencies and reduces many of their philosophical ambitions to little more than psychological posturing. Shakespeare avoids their dilemma by structuring the female/male priority into the *Sonnets* at the first level of differentiation.

Because Shakespeare acknowledges the priority of the female over the male and the logical consequence that humans must increase to persist, he is able to develop the arguments of the *Sonnets* consistently toward an expression of the logic of the erotic. Because the erotic logic of myth always inter-relates the female and male, and consequently the feminine and the masculine, its basis in the sexual dynamic needs to be accepted before it is possible to express a consistent form of mythic content.

Despite their willingness to acknowledge the primacy of nature in aspects of their writings, Nietzsche's doctrine of eternal recurrence and Wittgenstein's Christian fear of a final judgement are but metaphorical expressions of the logic of the increase argument. And whereas Nietzsche acknowledges the gender relationships of feminine and masculine only through the feminine aspect of Dionysus, Wittgenstein takes no account of the gender dispositions of the mind.

In sonnet 22, immediately after sonnets 20/21 introduce the erotic logic of truth and beauty, Shakespeare recognises the gender dynamic central to mythic expression. The recognition of the gender dynamic is pivotal to Shakespeare's development of a consistent philosophy. The *Nature template* captures the interrelationships between the bodily division of female and male and the gender distinctions in the mind.

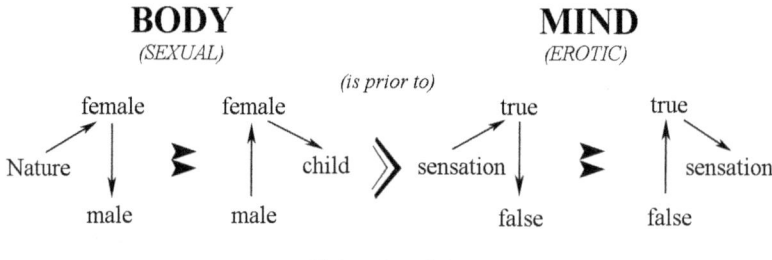

Nature template

Nietzsche does not acknowledge the logical priority of the female over the male from the body portion of the template. Neither does he appreciate the logic of increase or the critical function of the poetry and increase sonnets which state the preconditions for developing metaphorical ideas on the logic of the body dynamic. Then, because he does not understand the inter-relationship of sensory input to the mind, the dynamic of true and false in the mind, and the consequent heightened sensations of the mind, he has an inadequate appreciation of the 'moral' function of mind, and little idea of the logic of mythic expression. And by proclaiming that 'God is dead' he effectively amputates the right-hand side of the *Nature template*.

Nietzsche's concept of will to power ironically locates the motive force of human ethics within the aesthetic or beauty dynamic of the mind. His concept of the will attempts to transcend both the mind and nature, but by negating the ethical function of language it leaves the will as indeterminate as an unmediated God as the source of the ideal created in the mind. Nietzsche's attempt to locate 'good and evil' outside language, and to equate the mythic with music, all point to his confusion resulting from the complete dismissal of the concept of God and his failure to appreciate that a nature/life based philosophy logically prioritises the female over the male.

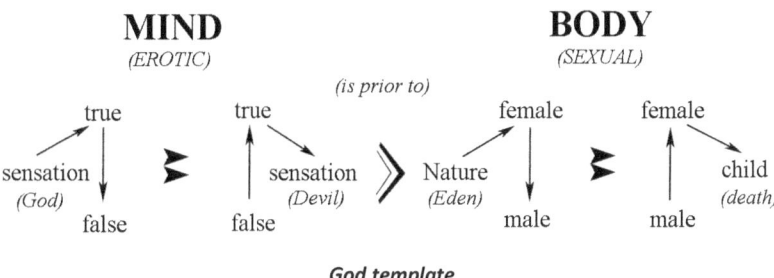

God template

It is little wonder then that Nietzsche does not understand Shakespeare despite his desire to convert him to his superhuman model of human ambition. Nietzsche equivocates between the natural logic of the *Nature template* and the *God template* that inverts all the values of natural logic.

Nietzsche's overt proclamation of the death of God coupled with his reluctance to acknowledge the priority of the female over the male is a classic example of the inability of theism and atheism to achieve consistency in relating the logic of nature to the logic of the human mind. As Duchamp well knew, the question is not whether God exists. Once the priority of the female is recognised and nature is accepted as the logical basis for human potentiality and understanding, then God as a male or any female Goddess, as beings who are generated erotically and who generate erotically, are logically derived from the human mind.

Wittgenstein's difficulties are similar to Nietzsche's. He attempted to recover a natural logic of language in his later philosophy after demonstrating the inadequacy of the idealistic atomic model in the *Tractatus*. But his covert Christianity prevented him from accepting the logical consequences of his extensive investigations into the criteria and certainties that act as preconditions for any use of language. So he, like Nietzsche, equivocated between the powerful indications of natural logic in his enquiries and his residual commitment to Christian dogma.

It is possible to show, as it is with Nietzsche, how Wittgenstein failed to consider aspects of the *Nature template* or actively disparaged them and how he attempted to compensate for the absence of the elements essential to a consistent and comprehensive philosophy by reverting to the inverted form of the template. The consequence was a confounding of natural logic and a profound confusion about the aesthetic/ethical dynamic of the mind.

Ironically, Nietzsche and Wittgenstein's confusion about the relation of the *Nature template* to the *God template* has given their writings an untoward value in the post-modern tertiary institutions, where the consequences of post-Christian scepticism have achieved their most debilitating effect. The work of Shakespeare, Darwin, and Duchamp demonstrate the way to avoid the illogicalities of biblical apologetics without succumbing to the post-modern malaise.

8

George Lakoff & Mark Johnson

George Lakoff is a cognitive scientist based at the University of California, Berkeley, and Mark Johnson is a philosopher currently at the University of Oregon. Together and separately they have produced a number of books that argue, largely on the basis of empirical evidence, for the dependence of the mind on bodily functions and dispositions. Their work challenges what they call '2500 years of objectivist tradition' in which the mind has been viewed as transcendental and prior to the human body.

In books such as *The Body in the Mind* (1987)[1] by Mark Johnson, *Women Fire and Dangerous Things* (1987)[2] by George Lakoff and co-authored books such as *Metaphors We Live By* (1980)[3] and *Philosophy in the Flesh* (1999)[4], they examine the way language is used and show that the majority of human communication relies on metaphorical expressions that are so deeply embodied in human experience that only by accepting the priority of the body over the mind can the phenomenon be explained.

In *Philosophy in the Flesh* Lakoff and Johnson scrutinise the objectivist tradition relentlessly to show that for 2500 years philosophical thought has been based in wishful thinking rather than the natural logic of language. They use their findings to critique traditional philosophy that has based its speculative metaphysics on the illogical presumption that the mind is prior to the body.

This essay considers the contribution of Lakoff and Johnson to the post-Darwinian transformation in attitude to both language and the mind. Darwin had demonstrated the priority of the body over the mind through his scientific examination of the process of natural selection in evolution. As a consequence of Darwin's insights many philosophers have rejected the tradition of justifying metaphysical claims and now accept the natural logic of bodily priority. Lakoff and Johnson make special mention of Maurice Merleau-Ponty and John Dewey who base their philosophies on the understanding that 'our bodily experience is the primal basis for everything we can mean, think, know, and communicate'[5]

But the essay also considers the difference between Lakoff and Johnson's claim that philosophy is a process of 'inquiry' best conducted by 'empirically responsible philosophers' who propose philosophical theories, and Ludwig Wittgenstein's idea that philosophy continually reiterates the logical conditions of life. If the logic of life is subject to ongoing empirical research, as Lakoff and Johnson suggest, the implication is that until scientists finalise their research no one can appreciate the logic of life.

Yet many people remain at ease with themselves and the world throughout their lives, and no doubt many in the past have understood the natural dynamic of life. The four thinkers who feature in these volumes (Darwin, Mallarmé, Duchamp, and Shakespeare) despite working at the highest pitch of intellectual achievement, were by all accounts philosophical about life.

The essay examines Lakoff and Johnson's limited recognition of Wittgenstein and questions why they decide not to examine his work when they examine the contributions of other philosophers in the second part of *Philosophy in the Flesh*. It then considers their determination to see philosophy as a form of scientific inquiry into the mechanism of language without subjecting the mythological language of male God biblical faiths to a similar scrutiny.

Lakoff and Johnson's reluctance to inquire into the culturally significant language of myth and its sexual/erotic logic, despite the allusion to the 'word made flesh' in the title of *Philosophy in the Flesh*, raises questions as to the depth of their challenge to the objectivist tradition of the last 2500 years. It is no surprise that Christian philosophers such as Augustine, Aquinas, Descartes, and Kant never questioned the logic of the biblical mythology because they were seeking to justify it using formal philosophical processes. But ironically Lakoff and Johnson's insistence that philosophy like science is based in theories leaves them unable to do justice to the metaphor in their title.

Four hundred years ago Shakespeare articulated the consistent mythic logic of his *Sonnets* to correct the corrupt form of mythology in the biblical texts. He shows that the logical elements for a consistent philosophy sought by Lakoff and Johnson are available, though scrambled, in any mythology.

The essay will first consider the four books by Lakoff and Johnson mentioned above, and then examine the relationship of their ideas to Shakespeare's philosophy.

Metaphors We Live By

In *Metaphors We Live By*, Lakoff and Johnson present numerous examples of metaphorical language to demonstrate that a large part of human communication is based on metaphor. Unlike the traditional view of metaphor as an accessory to language used only to evoke poetic insights or account for events not otherwise understood, Lakoff and Johnson's investigation shows that everyday language is riddled with metaphoric references. The use of metaphorical structuring in human communication is so pervasive they suggest that 'metaphor plays a very significant role in determining what is real for us'.[6]

So instead of being incidental, the occurrence of metaphor in language is systematic. The instances of metaphorical structuring can be quite complex with one form of metaphor 'hiding' another. For instance, in the meta-language used to reflect on the use of language, their research identifies three metaphors: 'ideas are objects', 'linguistic expressions are containers', and 'communication is sending'.[7] Lakoff and Johnson give a number of examples of such metaphors in use, most of which are used unconsciously in the give and take of daily discussion.

Metaphors We Live By discusses a range of ways in which metaphors enter language as a consequence of bodily activity in the world. Language uses many 'orientational metaphors' that correspond to bodily dispositions. The words up, down, front, back, side, face, etc., are used universally to express intention, emotion, decision and many other mental states. Lakoff and Johnson describe the prevalence of 'ontological metaphors', 'personification', and discuss the role of 'metonymy' in which a part stands in for the whole.

The interlacing of the various metaphorical expressions corresponds systematically to aspects of human experience. The structure and coherence of metaphors in language is a direct consequence of the structure and coherence of everyday activities. While sentences expressing immediate human requirements such as 'pass the salt' or 'salt is good' have no metaphorical content, the distinctive capacity of humans to use language to convey more complex ideas and desires is firmly grounded in the use of metaphor. And just as factual sentences depend on bodily activities, the language of metaphor is also based in bodily interaction.

Because the majority of human communication is based on metaphorical language derived from bodily experience, Lakoff and Johnson say that such metaphors are 'grounded by virtue of *systematic correlates within our experience*' (authors' italics).[8] They then use their empirical findings to critique traditional philosophical 'theories'. When they examine the notion of 'truth', for instance, they find their understanding has elements in common with 'correspondence theory', 'coherence theory' and 'pragmatic theory' and 'classical realism'.[9]

But for Lakoff and Johnson their 'experientialist theory of truth' takes it as a 'given' that (summarising their points) the 'world, cultures and people are as they are', that 'people successfully interact with the world', that 'human categorisation is constrained by reality', that it 'extends classical realism's focus on objects to people', and that 'human concepts correspond to interactional properties and not inherent properties'. They then critique the 'myth of objectivism', in which the 'world is made up of objects', and the 'myth of subjectivism', which prioritises individual 'feelings and intuitions'.[10] They see their experientialist theory of truth reconciling Plato's objectivist fear of metaphor with Aristotle's appreciation that metaphor makes it possible to 'get hold of something fresh'.[11]

But Lakoff and Johnson do not offer a comprehensive philosophy of life based on their empirical investigations. Instead they end their book with a chapter on 'understanding'.[12] They show how the 'experientialist account of understanding provides a richer perspective on...interpersonal communication, self-understanding, ritual, aesthetic experience, and politics'.[13] As this essay progresses and the comprehensive structure of Shakespeare's *Sonnet* philosophy is brought to bear on such musings, the consequence of Lakoff and Johnson's high expectation of scientific theories and their misunderstanding of the status of myth will emerge.

Women, Fire, and Dangerous Things

In *Women, Fire, and Dangerous Things*, Lakoff continues the work begun in *Metaphors We Live By* but in greater detail and with greater attention to variations across cultures. The title *Women, Fire, and Dangerous Things* derives from the one of the four distinctive classifications of things in Dyirbal, an Australian aboriginal language. The three items are in their second category *balan*, which includes 'human females, water, fire and fighting'.[14]

The principal focus of Lakoff's investigation, though, is still the contrast between traditional 'objectivism' and 'experientialism'. He first 'defines' the 'issue' that contrasts objectivism with experientialism. He asks if 'meaningful thought and reason concern merely the manipulation of abstract symbols and their correspondence to an objective reality, independent of any embodiment' or 'do meaningful thought and reason essentially concern the nature of the organism doing the thinking – including the nature of its body, its interactions in its environment or its social character'.[15]

Lakoff begins by considering the importance of categorising to the process of understanding and so for the possibility of understanding what makes us human. Compared with classical categorisation based on 'abstract containers' with things inside or outside, most human categorisation is done automatically and unconsciously and includes every type of entity. He introduces the work of Eleanor Rosch who questions the assumption that all members of a category are the same or that they are unaffected by the peculiarities of the beings doing the categorising.

In his second chapter Lakoff introduces the themes he will discuss. To show the influence of human embodiment on categories he will consider family resemblances, centrality, polysemy, generativity, membership gradience, centrality gradience, conceptual embodiment, functional embodiment, basic-level categorisation, basic-level primacy, and metonymic reasoning. All the themes are united under the umbrella of 'cognitive models', which structure thought and are used in 'forming categories and in reasoning'.[16]

It is not the intention in this essay to give any more than an indication of Lakoff's exhaustive investigation of the embodiment in human language. His book not only provides detailed evidence for such embodiment and argues for experientialism against classic objectivism, it provides three extended case studies of 'recalcitrant' ideas that classical techniques have been unable to account for adequately.

Of interest to the findings presented in these four volumes is the acknowledgment Lakoff gives Wittgenstein for his groundbreaking notion of 'family resemblances' to characterise the properties found in conceptual categories. But Lakoff avoids the logical overview Wittgenstein brings to his understanding of the function of philosophy as a set of already existing logical conditions that do not need to be proved or found but that are frequently obscured from view. Lakoff's contrary belief that only empirical investigation will reveal the logic of life and philosophic investigation is unavailing will be critiqued as the essay continues.

The Body in the Mind

In *The Body in the Mind* Mark Johnson explores the role of the imagination in the language dynamic. He wants to correct the 'total absence of adequate study of imagination in our most influential theories of meaning and rationality'.[17] The problem can only be addressed by overturning the 'widely shared set of presuppositions that deny imagination a central role in the constitution of rationality'[17]. The presumptions of the objectivist tradition, with its 'one correct God's-Eye-View', reduce the world to 'objects' that are 'independent of human understanding'.[18]

The empirical evidence from 'studies in many different disciplines' including cognitive science have demonstrated that 'human understanding is required for an account of meaning and reason'.[19] He lists categorisation, framing of concepts, metaphor, polysemy, historical semantic change, non-Western conceptual systems and growth of knowledge as phenomena that challenge objectivist assumptions. As Hilary Putnam says, 'any adequate account of meaning and rationality must give central place to embodied and imaginative structures of understanding by which we grasp the world'.[20]

Johnson illustrates the notion of 'embodied imaginative understanding' by considering two types of imaginative structure, image schemata and metaphorical projections. He defines an image schema as a 'recurring, dynamic pattern of our perceptual interactions and motor programmes that gives coherence and structure to our experience'.[21] *The Body in the Mind* explores some of the more 'important embodied imaginative structures of human understandings that make up our network of meanings and give rise to patterns of inference and reflection at all levels of abstraction'.[22]

Against the background of the objectivist tradition and continuing objectivist expectations among many philosophers Johnson sees two 'especially controversial aspects in the view'[23] he is developing about the centrality of image schematic structures. The first is their 'apparently nonpropositional, analog nature', and the second is their 'figurative character, as structures of embodied imagination'.[23] His intention is to build a 'constructive theory of imagination and understanding that emphasises our embodiment'.[24]

After providing a brief examination of objectivist theories of meaning and rationality, with mentions of Descartes, Kant, Frege, Donaldson, and others, Johnson concludes that image schemata have no place in objectivist theories because they are 'too bodily' and because they are not 'sufficiently rule-governed'.[25] His procedure throughout the rest of the book is to consider 'embodied patterns of imagination', the 'role of bodily experience in reason', the 'pervasiveness of image schemata', and he then applies his theories to 'meaning, understanding, and imagination'.[26]

This is not the place to review Johnson's detailed case for the embodiment of the imagination. It is sufficient to say that his arguments are in accord with the attitude to the body/mind relationship articulated in these volumes. But, as mentioned before, his insistence that philosophy is based in theories restricts his ability to consider questions of the highest level of imaginative engagement, the mythic. The absence is apparent in the last couple of pages where he sketches a 'non-objectivist account of truth' and then on the last page, through the agency of Hilary Putnam, he considers the 'coherence of our beliefs'.[27]

Putnam's idea is that a 'whole system of statements' is rationally acceptable through its 'coherence and fit', with 'experiential beliefs' and 'theoretical beliefs…deeply interwoven with our psychology'. The resulting objectivity is an 'objectivity for us' as against the 'God's-Eye-view' of religion. Johnson says he goes 'beyond Putnam's focus on beliefs' to stress the importance of the 'public nature of image schematic and basic level structures of understanding' to provide a 'shared human perspective' that is 'tied to reality through our embodied imaginative understanding'.[27]

This essay will show that only by understanding the function of the deepest level of imaginative expression, the mythic, can the relation of the psychology of beliefs and a sound philosophy be gained.

Philosophy in the Flesh

Philosophy in the Flesh begins by acknowledging those 'empirically responsible philosophers' who draw on the 'best available empirical psychology, physiology, and neuroscience to shape their philosophical thinking'.[29] Then, in the Introduction, Lakoff and Johnson list the 'three major findings' of cognitive science: 'the mind is inherently embodied', 'thought is mostly unconscious', and 'abstract concepts are largely metaphorical'.[30] They are confident the evidence from their research into the cognitive basis of language brings to an end the a priori philosophical speculation of the last 2500 years.

For Lakoff and Johnson 'our most basic philosophic beliefs are tied inextricably to our view or reason'.[30] As their findings are at odds with 'central parts of Western philosophy', they predict that philosophy will never be the same again. They suggest their new understanding of the reasoning process as inherently tied to bodily functions will provide a shock for traditional philosophy.[31]

Then they list the differences between the new and the old views of reason. Contrary to philosophical tradition cognitive science has shown that reason is embodied, evolutionary, not universally transcendent, mostly unconscious, largely metaphorical, and emotionally engaged. Looking at the history of philosophy their findings overturn Cartesian dualism, Kantian autonomy and universal morality, utilitarian economic rationalism, phenomenological introspection, the poststructuralist decentred subject, Fregean objective meaning, mind as computer theories, and Chomskyan genetic syntax.[32]

For Lakoff and Johnson, past 'philosophical questioning' or 'philosophical reflection' has not discovered the fundamental facts about the mind revealed by their scientific investigation. Their programme in *Philosophy in the Flesh* is to give an overview of 'what philosophy can become' by using the 'methods of cognitive science and cognitive linguistics'.[33] Then in Part 2, they analyse the basic concepts 'that philosophy must address such as time, events, causation, the mind, the self, and morality' and begin the study of 'philosophy itself' by examining the history of philosophy in Part 3. Significantly, they do not address Wittgenstein's 'philosophy' in the review.

Central to the task of understanding traditional subjects such as metaphysics, morality, and the self by the new methods of cognitive science is the appreciation that most cognition is carried on below the level of consciousness. Here 'cognitive' refers not just to the conscious conceptual or propositional structure of language but to 'any kind of mental operation that can be studied in precise terms'.[34]

Then, seemingly paradoxically, Lakoff and Johnson assert that even though 'we have no direct conscious awareness of what goes on in our minds' they are confident that 'cognitive unconscious' is accessible to cognitive science through its theories.[35] They maintain that 'unless we know our cognitive unconscious fully and intimately'[36] we cannot understand the traditional subjects of philosophy.

Beginning with a chapter on the 'embodied mind', Lakoff and Johnson review the findings of cognitive scientists about 'primary metaphor and subjective experience', 'the anatomy of complex metaphor', 'embodied realism', 'realism and truth', and 'metaphor and truth'. In the final paragraph of chapter 8, they concede that 'the metaphoric character of philosophy is not unique to philosophic thought. It is true of all abstract thought, especially science'.[37] They acknowledge that even their cognitive scientific understanding is available only through 'conceptual metaphor'. They are confident that the apparent difficulty, though, should not obscure their finding that 'conceptual metaphor is one of the greatest of our intellectual gifts'.[37]

When Lakoff and Johnson turn to analyse basic philosophical ideas in Part 2, they suggest their approach is 'opposite' to the common procedure of applying a 'purely philosophic methodology'. Instead of the 'philosophy of time', for instance, they provide a 'cognitive science of time'.[38] First they acknowledge that 'each idea has an underspecified nonmetaphorical conceptual skeleton' which is 'fleshed out by conceptual metaphor'. But then they say they will argue that each of the ideas is 'not purely literal, but fundamentally and inescapably metaphorical'.[38] Again their programme seems somewhat paradoxical.

In Part 3, where Lakoff and Johnson examine the history of philosophy from the perspective of cognitive science, they approach philosophy as a 'form of conceptual activity'.[39] When 'philosophers construct their theories of being, knowledge, mind, and morality, they employ the very same conceptual resources and the same basic conceptual system shared by ordinary people in their culture'. Cognitive science 'offers' a conceptual analysis of the 'strange questions' about such things as 'being', 'truth' and 'good'. It provides a critical assessment of theories with 'constructive philosophical theorising' about self understanding and how to act in the world.[40] They end the Introduction by asserting that 'all philosophic theories are necessarily metaphoric in nature'.[41]

After reviewing the history of philosophy from the pre-Socratics to Chomsky, Lakoff and Johnson conclude their book with an 'empirically responsible' look at 'person', 'evolution', and 'spirituality'.[42] Contrary to the traditional western conception of the person, which is influenced by the claim for God's universality, they say that a person is embodied and has a pluralistic morality. Turning to evolution, they recognise that it does not entail 'survival of the best competitor'[43] because it could equally entail the 'survival of the best nurtured'. They say 'nothing of this sort is part of literal evolutionary theory'. And the idea of the disembodied soul central to the biblical tradition is a fiction only explicable through understanding how humans perceive and think in their bodies through metaphor.

Lakoff and Johnson propose an 'embodied spirituality' because without 'sex and art and music and dance and the taste of food' spirituality is 'bland'. Their 'philosophy in the flesh' shows how our physical being with its 'flesh, blood, and sinew, hormone, cell, and synapse' makes us 'who we are'.[44]

From Lakoff and Johnson to Shakespeare

The weight of empirical evidence Lakoff and Johnson muster in support of the priority of the body over the mind lends overwhelming scientific support to the natural logic Shakespeare articulates in his *Sonnets*. Their investigation of the significance of metaphor for cognitive processes shows that much of human thinking is based in unconsciously stored bodily metaphors that determine how the world is viewed. Their findings support the attitude evident in Shakespeare's drama, Duchamp's art and Mallarmé's poetry, which are self-critical toward the imagery they use to convey meaning.

Yet despite the overwhelming support for natural logic from Lakoff and Johnson's empirical work, a number of times throughout their book they equivocate over the relation between the literal and the metaphorical. While sometimes recognising the presence of the literal, within a paragraph or so they assert that all understanding is metaphorical. It is as if their intensive research into metaphors continually forces out any consideration of the significance of literal expression. They devote no space to explaining the relation between the literal and metaphorical.

The essay will now consider the example of Darwin, Wittgenstein, Duchamp, and then Shakespeare to show why philosophy involves the clear understanding of the difference between the literal and the metaphorical.

Charles Darwin

Lakoff and Johnson's demonstration that the body is prior to the mind through their scientific analysis of cognitive processes is in complete agreement with Darwin's argument in *The Descent of Man* that the mind is derived through evolutionary processes. In Darwin's discussion of 'mental powers' and 'moral sense' he shows that the mind exhibits no features not explicable through evolutionary processes and that there is no support for a belief in the separation of mind and body.

But while Lakoff and Johnson and Darwin arrive at the same conclusions about the relation of the body and mind, their conceptions of the role of philosophy are quite different. Whereas Lakoff and Johnson view philosophy as just another area of understanding subject to scientific investigation, Darwin uses his philosophic understanding to structure his investigations and present his findings.

In the *Origin of Species* Darwin employs a philosophic approach advocated by the philosopher William Whewell (1794-1866). To give the mass of evidence he had accumulated in support of evolution a sound basis he adhered strictly to the principle of *vera causa*. By first presenting evidence for empirically observable phenomena he was able to make logical claims about events not directly observable. Darwin organised *Origin of Species* so that his work on artificial variation in domestic species became the basis for his generalisations about natural variation over evolutionary time.

Darwin's standing in the scientific community is a direct consequence of his lifelong adherence to the principle of *vera causa*. His work has an integrity and veracity unmatched by other writers whose findings involve both direct observation and reasoned speculation. In terms of the difference between the literal and the metaphorical established by Lakoff and Johnson, Darwin first laid out his groundwork of literal observations before embarking on his metaphorical suggestions for the prehistory of evolution. For him philosophy was not a subject for empirical examination as it provided the foundation on which everything else rested.

Darwin's philosophy was not susceptible to theoretical revision. The consistency of his life's work rested on a secure philosophic foundation that enabled him to explain successfully the evolution of 'mental powers' and 'moral sense'. The opposite is the case for Lakoff and Johnson. Even though the results of their empirical research are in accord with natural logic, their equivocation about whether the literal is literal or unavoidably metaphorical epitomises their confusion over the status and role of philosophy.

The consequence of Lakoff and Johnson's subjection of philosophy to empirical review is their conflation of the literal and metaphorical. They were unwilling to appreciate that philosophy identifies the logical conditions for understanding on which metaphorical cognitions are constructed. The literal basis of language is the precondition for metaphorical development. Darwin's genius lies in never confusing his philosophic method with his empirical investigations. The significance of Darwin's appreciation that philosophy provides the logical groundwork for any scientific investigation (after all Lakoff and Johnson said that their scientific analysis was couched in metaphor) will become apparent when Wittgenstein's attitude to philosophy is considered.

The other constant in Darwin's philosophic approach is his awareness of the sexual as the logical basis for the erotic logic of the human mind. Darwin's focus on the sexual in both the *Origin of Species* and in *The Descent of Man and Selection in Relation to Sex* recognises that the sexual is the logically prior condition for human persistence. In *The Descent of Man* Darwin first considers the logic of human descent from mammalian forbears and then spends two thirds of the volume considering secondary sexual characteristics. From the literal status of the sexual evolves all the secondary sexual characteristics including the erotic logic of the mind.

For Darwin, the sexual is the prototypical human activity in the logic of evolution. The erotic dynamic of the mind follows from its prototypical status. Yet in Lakoff and Johnson's books on cognitive metaphor, the sexual and the erotic barely rate a mention, and are not analysed systematically as are traditional metaphysical concepts such as 'being', 'cause' and 'time' and other theoretical concepts of academic philosophy. Lakoff and Johnson's unwillingness to investigate the pervasiveness of the sexual and sexual metaphor across cultures shows an ignorance of Darwinian scientific principles and blindness to his appreciation of the function of philosophy.

Ironically, in a book titled *Philosophy in the Flesh* Lakoff and Johnson do not consider the sexual connotations of the word 'flesh'. Nor do they consider the role of metaphor in the highest form of metaphorical expression, the mythological, where, for instance, the Son of God is called the 'Word made Flesh'. Even though they say they want to provide an 'empirically responsible philosophy' that critiques the 'objectivist myth' and 'subjectivist myth' of the last 2500 years, their use of the word myth to characterise philosophical theories reveals an ignorance of the logical conditions for mythic expression.

Ludwig Wittgenstein: the grounding of philosophy

The work of Ludwig Wittgenstein, who some consider the most profound of the twentieth-century philosophers, offers a way to understand better the relation between the literal and the metaphorical. While Lakoff and Johnson acknowledge Wittgenstein's contribution to removing 'mistaken views about conceptualisation and reasoning' with his notion of 'family resemblances', for them his work comes before the 'age of cognitive science'.[45] They do not investigate his views on the function of philosophy or on the status of 'philosophical theories'.

The absence of an extended discussion of Wittgenstein in Part 3 of *Philosophy in the Flesh*, which considers a number of lesser philosophers, is intriguing. The neglect is most likely because Wittgenstein's understanding of the function of philosophy is quite different from that expounded by Lakoff and Johnson. Whereas they see philosophy as an ongoing procedure similar to their investigations as cognitive scientists, and hence subject to the critique of science, Wittgenstein understood philosophy as a way of seeing the logical conditions for life as clearly as possible, and a way of critiquing views that were at odds with the logical conditions for life.

So when Wittgenstein philosophised he accepted as a grounding those things in life it makes no sense to question. Among these were the state of 'nature', 'parents', 'family', 'forebears', and the everyday objects and events that form the basis of certainty. Wittgenstein is the first philosopher not to use philosophical argument to justify a religious or otherwise metaphorical understanding of the world. In Lakoff and Johnson's terms, he first clarified those things that are literal and then used them as a basis for evaluating the logic of metaphorical speculations.

Wittgenstein progressed only gradually toward the clarity of his later thought expressed in *On Certainty* but his attitude to the function of philosophy remained constant throughout his life. In the *Tractatus* he hoped to demonstrate the logic of the relation between the world and language but failed because he was using the inappropriate atomism of Russell and Frege. The world of discreet atoms and molecules did not have the correct logical multiplicity to capture the complexity of language. His failure in the *Tractatus* indirectly revealed the conceit in traditional metaphorical theorising and led to his appreciation of the groundedness of understanding in nature. He developed an approach based on life or nature, drawing on natural metaphors to capture more exactly the logic of language.

In Wittgenstein's second period of writing he determined that language was subject like games to conventions or rules, but as with the infinite variety of games there seemed to be no single set of criteria to apply to all language games. Instead, language games were forms of life analogous to biological relationships such as family resemblances. As language is logically a social construct and not a private monologue, its rules could be examined to gauge how words are used in everyday language. Wittgenstein argued that, compared with the inconsistencies found in traditional metaphysical speculation, everyday speech was logically sound. So an analysis of ordinary language was more likely to reveal the structure and criteria for human cognition and expression.

Contrary to Lakoff and Johnson, for Wittgenstein philosophy did not entail proposing philosophical theories that were subject to scientific analysis. Philosophy was the logical means to evaluate any form of expression whether scientific or artistic for the consistency between its literal and metaphorical statements. Even though Wittgenstein had difficulty accepting all the implications of Darwinian evolution for the nature of the human mind, he used the same approach as Darwin for maintaining a philosophic poise throughout his life.

Lakoff and Johnson's equivocation over the role of the literal has been noted. As they are driven by their cognitive scientific discoveries in the realm of metaphorical expression they could not accommodate the literal and so cannot accommodate Wittgenstein's challenge to 2500 years of philosophical theorising to which they tied their project. Because they cannot appreciate the logic of the literal then their assertions about the significance of metaphor is awry, and their characterisation of 'theories' as 'myths' is symptomatic of their unphilosophic approach to science. By claiming that philosophy is based in theory they remain within the ambit of the academic philosophy they critique in Part 3 of *Philosophy in the Flesh*.

Some of Wittgenstein's last writings were on the philosophy of psychology. He investigated rather simple optical illusions to better understand the relation between 'seeing' literally and 'seeing as' metaphorically. But despite his clarity about the function of philosophy Wittgenstein was unable to develop a systematic expression of the relation between literal and metaphorical languages. If Wittgenstein sensed a gap in his understanding of language, Lakoff and Johnson seem not to be aware of the illogicality in mistaking psychology for philosophy.

Marcel Duchamp: the sexual and the erotic

Philosophy in the Flesh, for reasons known to the authors, did not analyse the metaphorical status of myth or examine the implications of its erotic logic. Despite the metaphorical richness of their title they restricted themselves to more prosaic metaphors and image schemas. In their final chapter Lakoff and Johnson do consider the implications of the embodied mind for 'persons', 'evolution', and 'spirituality', where they discuss the idea of an embodied God, but they end by advocating a panentheism in which the divine is seen in all things[45]. They are unable to identify the logical conditions for mythologies much less the mythological basis of John's Gospel, which talks of the 'word made flesh'.

Yet, if the history of metaphorical language is to be fairly scrutinised, mythologies, as the most significant expression in the language, should surely be subjected to the same investigative processes as bodily dispositions and the history of 'objectivist philosophy'. And if the sexual process is the logical dynamic for the perpetuation of humankind then the erotic logic of language should be the foremost in an analysis of the history of metaphor.

Lakoff and Johnson's reluctance to make the sexual/erotic central in their challenge to the objectivist tradition arises in part from the general ignorance of the erotic logic of all mythologies. As long as mythologies were believed to be literal stories where a male God creates the world and makes the male then the female and then returns through a virgin to be reincarnated as his own son, to die on a cross and be resurrected, then the eroticism central to such stories was proscribed to the extent that no philosopher, even those as secular or sceptical as Kant and Hume and Wittgenstein, has examined the implications of eroticism in myth.

Only the work of Stephane Mallarmé and Marcel Duchamp begins to grasp the deep illogicality of taking biblical mythology literally. Mallarmé was able to work past the illogicalities of his Christian upbringing to create poetry of deep eroticism with an awareness that eroticism derives logically from the sexual. His deeply symbolic poetry shows how to write with consistency at a proto-mythic level.

Duchamp then took the process a step further. Learning from Mallarmé's achievement, his major work, *The Bride Stripped Bare by Her Bachelors, Even* or the *Large Glass*, sets down the logical conditions for any mythic expression. He purposely represents the female above the male to establish the correct priority of female over male and shows how their unconsummated relationship is basic to the erotic logic of artistic expression. He first accepts the logic of the literal as a precondition and then gives it metaphorical expression. In the *Large Glass* he takes that expression to its mythical limit without losing the consistency of his original insight into the literal relations in life.

Lakoff and Johnson's lack of awareness of Mallarmé and of Duchamp's achievement is not surprising, as Duchamp's *Large Glass* has not received the philosophic attention it warrants and only a critic like Octavio Paz has shown an awareness of its critique of traditional mythologies. Without the tools for mythic analysis critics end up speculating about Duchamp's sexual predilections, or turn hopefully to biblical or other mythologies.

Duchamp's achievement is similar to Darwin's in that both recognise the need to reject the priority of the male-God prejudices of traditional beliefs to arrive at consistent understanding. Their appreciation of the logic of art and biology respectively inverts the literal belief in the biblical myths. Only then can Darwin's empirical research conform to his logical expectations.

And Duchamp first establishes the logical conditions for any artistic expression before he makes readymade items of extraordinary simplicity but with mythic impact.

Despite Lakoff and Johnson's suggestion of a panentheism to replace the illogicality of biblical priorities, they insist that only through empirical evidence can the case against objectivism be won. Yet while Darwin's case was virtually undeniable through the preponderance of evidence alone, he stands apart from all other evolutionary thinkers and the volumes of facts disclosed in support of evolution by his logical exactness and rigour.

So there seems to be a co-relation between Lakoff and Johnson's determination to depend on the empirical and their unwillingness to provide evidence if not argument for the role of the sexual/erotic in language. In a personal comment Johnson said he was aware of the omission from *Philosophy in the Flesh* and wanted to address the issues but Lakoff and he 'agreed that there was not sufficient empirical evidence from their researches to provide an adequate analysis'. But Darwin shows that no amount of facts and figures can make up for an absence of logical insight in the challenge to the illogicalities in traditional apologetics.

William Shakespeare

Shakespeare lived in the period when the methods of science were being redefined by thinkers such as Francis Bacon. He was a contemporary of Galileo and would have been aware of the astronomical theories of Copernicus. There were also considerable advances in other sciences in the Renaissance, particularly when compared with the relatively anti-scientific attitude of the Medieval period.

Shakespeare's interest in a philosophy grounded in natural observations is evident in his regard for Aristotle, who challenged Plato's otherworldly idealism with a nature-based metaphysics and ethics. But Aristotle was still conditioned by Platonic ideas about the place of man in nature and the roles of men and women.

When the logic of Shakespeare's *Sonnet* philosophy is considered it should not surprise that his arguments are firmly based in observations of nature. What could seem surprising to theory-based expectations of thinkers like Lakoff and Johnson is that Shakespeare's logic anticipates the discoveries of Darwin, the language philosophy of Wittgenstein, the mythic logic of Duchamp, and their own appreciation of the cognitive structure of language.

If it is possible to understand the world aright without waiting for the results of scientific enquiry, then Shakespeare's *Sonnet* logic seems to do just that. It is both evidential and predictive in a way that Lakoff and Johnson's programme is not. A scientific approach using the theoretical tools of cognitive science could not reveal the logic of mythic expression available in the *Sonnets*.

When Shakespeare's *Sonnet* logic is laid alongside Darwin's logic, it seems that 300 years previously he had accepted the logical priority of the body over the mind. His argument that increase in Nature from female and male progenitors is prior to the possibility of truth and beauty not only correctly places the body before the mind, it establishes the correct relationship between aesthetics and ethics, something Lakoff and Johnson fail to derive from their scientific analysis of language.

When the *Sonnet* logic is compared with the two periods of philosophy of Wittgenstein, it provides a critique of the atomic model Wittgenstein employed in the *Tractatus* by insisting that the human dynamic of male and female in Nature is the required model for the correct logical multiplicity between language and the world. It anticipates Wittgenstein's rejection of the atomic model and his move toward a model based in Nature and the family dynamic.

The similarity between Shakespeare's philosophy that lays down the logical conditions for life and Wittgenstein's attempt to do the same in his second period counters Lakoff and Johnson's claim that only science can resolve philosophical problems. In fact the *Sonnet* philosophy encompasses Wittgenstein's two periods of philosophising. It is more consistently systematic than the *Tractatus* hoped to be, and more true to life than *Philosophical Investigations* was able to be.

The poetry of Stephane Mallarmé, with its densely metaphorical symbolism, should be explicable by the scientific techniques of Lakoff and Johnson. But if they are unprepared to investigate biblical expressions such as 'word made flesh', then they are not in a position to appreciate Mallarmé's recognition that language as a product of the mind is logically erotic. Mallarmé held Shakespeare in high regard and emulated his writing, giving his own poetry a similar density of metaphorical allusion, though he lacked Shakespeare's mythic sensibility.

It is Marcel Duchamp who provides the logical connection between Mallarmé and Shakespeare, even though Duchamp did not know of Shakespeare's comprehensive articulation of the mythic dynamic. Shakespeare bridges the gap between Duchamp's largely pictorial and barely annotated appreciation of the mythic logic of art and Lakoff and Johnson's demonstrations of the corporeal logic of words in language. In his *Sonnets* he more completely and precisely sets down the logical conditions for mythic expression, and in his 36 plays and four longer poems he shows how to write at a mythic level by using the sexual/erotic resources of language.

Shakespeare's use of imagery, because it is based in the natural logic of language that acknowledges the priority of the body over the mind, conforms to Lakoff and Johnson's critique of the objectivist tradition 400 years before their research laid bare the body schematic logic of language. Shakespeare's hierarchy of images conforms to Lakoff and Johnson's determination that categories of thought or objects are classified in language as 'super ordinate, basic level, and subordinate'.[46] An analysis of Shakespeare's images by Caroline Spurgeon in *Shakespeare's Imagery*[47] reveals a preference for the prototypical as against the generic or the specific. He uses the generic and specific in the speech of characters who are either pompous or foolish.

The organisation of the *Sonnets* is precise in its recognition of the priority of the female over the male and the body over the mind or the sexual over the erotic. The two sequences devoted to female and male and the 14 increase sonnets establish the physical basis for truth and beauty or the dynamic of understanding.

But because the physical is archetypically sexual Shakespeare takes the logical step avoided by Lakoff and Johnson to characterise the process of thought and language as archetypically erotic. If Lakoff and Johnson had carried out even a cursory examination of myths they would have recognised the ubiquity of the erotic in all mythologies.

Conclusion

The erotic logic at the heart of all mythologies provides a reflexive acknowledgement of the priority of the body over the mind. As works of literature at the highest level, mythologies express the logical conditions for their effectiveness as myth. Their erotic logic acknowledges the priority of the sexual dynamic over the dynamic of the mind. The history of religious belief and theology, though, has illogically concluded that the erotic basis of myth points to a world beyond sexual contingency.

The logical mistake is at the crux of the problem Lakoff and Johnson investigate empirically as cognitive scientists with their critique of the 'objectivist' tradition. But empirical evidence is not needed for an appreciation of the logic of myth. Ironically the required logic is hinted at in their title *Philosophy in the Flesh*.

Lakoff and Johnson's engagement with the history of thought brings with it an awareness not just of the body as the logical basis for language but of the 'flesh' as the living vehicle for communication. But while their analysis of traditional image schemas examines many aspects of human expression they stop short of questioning the succinct expression of the word and flesh in the mythic logic of the Bible.

By confining their challenge to the last 2500 years of the objectivist tradition Lakoff and Johnson are unable to consider the origins of male dominance and male God religions to see why philosophy became a matter of justifying the status of the male God rather than articulating the logic of life. If they expanded their perspective beyond the 4000 years since the male usurpation of female priority and considered the evidence from the artifacts of the last 30,000 years, they would see more clearly the reasons behind their inability to appreciate the logic of life.

Lakoff and Johnson's unwillingness to address the relationship between literal language and embodied metaphor is symptomatic of the unwillingness of the objectivist tradition to accept the primacy of nature and the priority of the female over the male. The logic of life does not need the sanction of scientific theories.

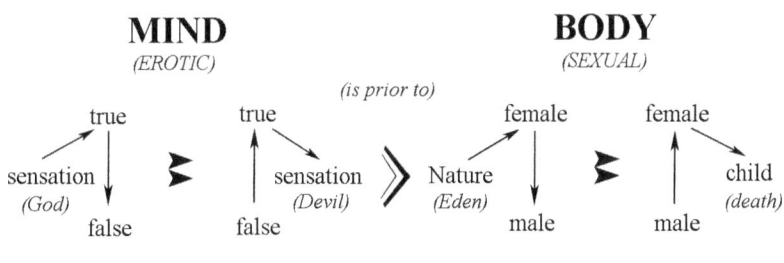

God template

Lakoff and Johnson's attack on the objectivist tradition using the tools of cognitive science is an attempt to rectify the illogical consequences of the *God template* derived in these volumes from Shakespeare's *Sonnets*. Because the objectivist tradition idealises the function of the mind, and seeks to categorise ideas about the world into tidy sets, Lakoff and Johnson recognise the need to invert the traditional views of the world.

But their challenge does not question the whole of the illogical *God template*, and instead focuses on the relation of false and true and true and false in the first part of the template. Because the dynamic of true and false is the province of science, it becomes immediately clear why they equivocate over the literal and the metaphorical, why they still talk of understanding 'truth', and why they are not drawn to critique ideas at the level of the mythic.

Shakespeare shows in his *Sonnets* that the only way to correct 4000 years of male-based illogicality is to completely turn about the mythological template behind traditional thought to re-establish the priority of nature and the female so that the logic of language is not compromised. He is then able in his plays to generate a mythic level of expression with consistency.

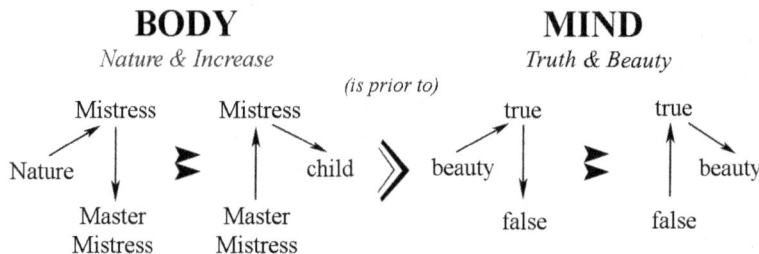

Nature template (Sonnets)

The tendency for scientists to believe they can provide answers to the unanswerable questions about human life in the universe, simply because they can answer questions about observable phenomena, leads Lakoff and Johnson to subject philosophical questions to their scientific programme. But Darwin, at the highest level of empirical integrity, has shown that the role of science is proscribed by the logic of life. And as Duchamp has shown, the logic of myth can be expressed without an empirical programme, and he also shows in the hilarious mechanisms of the *Large Glass* how the pretences of science can be mocked in a work with mythic integrity.

Shakespeare's *Sonnets* are exemplary in their combination of both empirical observation of human behaviour and language and in their expression of the logical conditions for any mythic possibility. They seem to be the only text available that seamlessly combines an understanding of the potentialities of the scientific and the possibilities of the mythic.

9
Thomas Jefferson

Thomas Jefferson's reference to the 'Laws of Nature' and to 'Nature's God' in the first few lines of the *Declaration of Independence* (1776) and his insistence on the religious and political freedoms guaranteed by the First Amendment to the *American Constitution* (1791) ensured that pluralism became the founding credo of the United States. Yet, despite the widespread recognition of Jefferson as the spiritual father of the United States, the philosophic basis of his framework for tolerance has not advanced much beyond its original enigmatic expression.

These notes will suggest that the philosophy of Shakespeare's *Sonnets* of 1609 not only provides a sound logical base for Jefferson's pluralism, but that Shakespeare's application of the philosophy in the social/political dynamic of his 36 1623 *Folio* plays and four longer poems provides an opportunity to enrich the pluralistic dynamic. The notes will concentrate on correspondences between the *Sonnet* philosophy and the *Declaration of Independence* and the *Constitution*. As Thomas Jefferson was responsible for the wording of the *Declaration*, it will discuss his understanding of the relation of nature and God and his campaign to separate Church and State.

So the logical structure of the *Sonnets* will be compared with the political structure heralded in the *Declaration* and legitimated in the *Constitution*. Then the mythic logic of the *Sonnets* will be used to identify elements in the *Declaration* that could elevate it from being an abstract framework, with little other than legislative definition in the *American Constitution*, to a wellspring for an inclusive mythic logic based in nature.

Shakespeare's natural philosophy of 1609

These four volumes demonstrate that in the period in which the New World was discovered and colonised Shakespeare was formulating a philosophy in his *Sonnets* of 1609 that set out to critique and correct the traditional attitude toward biblical mythology. In particular he restores the logical priority of nature over mythology and the priority of the female over the male. And in each of his plays and longer poems he demonstrates how to generate a mythic expression consistent with the natural logic articulated in the *Sonnets*.

Although the four volumes are the first in 400 years of scholarship to present the *Sonnet* philosophy, many students of Shakespeare have recognised that his plays and poems are based primarily in nature, rather than in biblical mythology. Ironically, though, while commentators admit that Shakespeare's plays show no evidence of an adherence to traditional beliefs, many feel duty bound to suggest he was at least a closet believer (if only in support of his status as England's national poet).

But both Shakespeare in his *Sonnet* philophy and Jefferson in the *Declaration* and *Constitution* wanted to move beyond the biblical politics of a pre-global Euro-centric world. The plurality of the *Sonnet* philosophy, which derives the logic of mythic expression from the dynamic of the natural world, anticipated the advance toward plural global politics heralded in the *Declaration* and guaranteed by the *Constitution*. This is despite the fact that Jefferson, even though he would have been aware of the general regard for nature in the works of Shakespeare, was ignorant of the precisely formulated philosophy of the *Sonnets*.

In Jefferson's day the biblical paradigm was fast collapsing as a credible world-view under the philosophical critique of thinkers such as Spinoza, Locke, and Hume. Added to the logical attack was the theoretical critique by social/political/scientific thinkers of the seventeenth and eighteenth centuries. Their concern for the consequences of allowing a religion to be instrumental in the politics of a state inspired a new attitude of secularisation when the American colonies asserted independence from their European forbears. The memory of Christian intolerance and even atrocities in Britain, Europe and the Americas in the sixteenth and seventeenth centuries, and the awareness, by those who wrote the *Declaration* and *Constitution*, of a new political order emerging in eighteenth century France created an opportunity to institute a less irrational society.

The philosophy in the *Sonnets*

As this is one of a series of short essays to be incorporated in the four volumes that detail Shakespeare's philosophy, no more than an outline of the basic elements of his natural logic will be given. It is sufficient to remember that the *Sonnet* philosophy acknowledges the priority of nature over the sexual dynamic, and that the sexual dynamic entails the logical requirement for humans to increase if they wish perpetuate themselves. Then, once the logic of the increase dynamic within nature is acknowledged, it follows that the possibility of increase is prior to the dynamic of understanding or truth and beauty.

The relationships of the major elements of the *Sonnet* philosophy are represented diagrammatically in the *Nature template*.

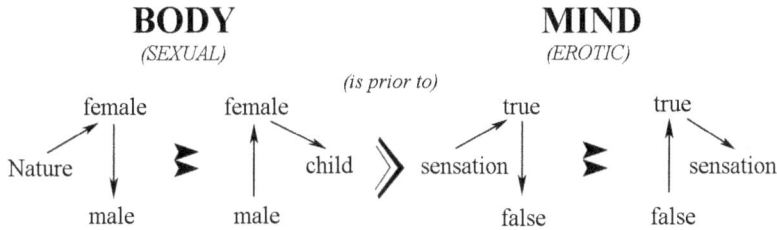

The Nature template

The linear arrangement of the elements captures the logical entailment beginning with nature as the given, through to the sexual dynamic and the dynamic of sensations and language. The word 'beauty' on the right represents all sensations in the mind including idealised thoughts such the absolute as God. In the *Sonnet* logic, nature is the possibility that encompasses all else, while the ideal as God is consequential on the development of the human mind in nature.

The *Sonnets* are unique in the way they reflexively lay out the natural logic of life. As well as articulating natural logic they simultaneously acknowledge their dependence as an expression on the priority of the body over the mind. Shakespeare's plays and longer poems have an unmatched veracity and felicity because they are based in a philosophy that recognises the sexual dynamic of human increase out of nature is prior to the erotic dynamic of the desires of the mind. Writing that expresses the logic of the priority of nature and the sexual dynamic over the inherent eroticism of human understanding is potentially mythic.

The inverted logic of the Bible

Genesis, as a book begun around the time of the transition from oral to scribal culture, seems, in the eroticism of the relations between God and mankind, to acknowledge the logical limitations of the written word. Genesis recognises the erotic logic of the act of writing in that writing is logically distinct from the biology of the sexual act. While the complete inversion of the natural order in the mythology of Genesis suggests it was originally written to acknowledge the priority of life over art or the sexual over the erotic, at some point in the history of the Hebrew culture the erotic mythology of Genesis was given priority over the sexual relationships in nature.

The reduction of the anti-nature male-based dynamic in Genesis to a religious dogma, enforced as fact by Hebrew and Christian culture, inverts for social, political and personal expediency, the natural priorities of life and art. Because the myth of Genesis is so erotic in its complete inversion of sexual logic, the doctrinaire belief in Genesis as fact has meant the religions based on the priority of the male God have become bastions of their own irredeemable irony.

When the order of events dictated by religious prerogatives is substituted in the template for natural logic, the result is riddled with inconsistencies and contradictions (as noted by the philosophers of the Enlightenment).

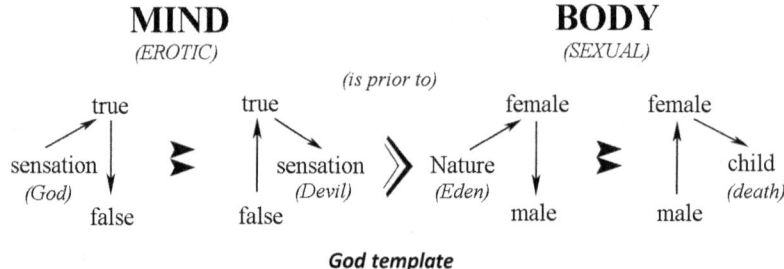

God template

Whereas in the template for natural logic the priorities follow consistently from left to right, it is not possible to represent the biblical priorities consistently. The *God template* can only attempt to indicate the consequences of inverting natural logic because the dogmas of faith can be represented only crudely. Some of the familiar inconsistencies are the priority given to the erotic God of the mind over nature, the unnatural priority of male over female, the confounding of false and true so that evil supplants good, and the life-defying connection of procreation or birth with the finality of death.

The book of Genesis expresses the mythological awareness of the Hebrew peoples, and provides the mythological basis for the other books of the Hebrew Bible. It is not until the New Testament that the erotic logic of myth is again asserted. The Christian Bible both acknowledges the mythological dynamic of Genesis but, as the founding myth for a new religion, expresses the eroticism of Genesis in terms of Jesus Christ. The eroticism of such doctrines as the Immaculate Conception, the virgin birth, Christ's death and resurrection without offspring, and the promise of a non-sexual heaven, are key indicators that a new religious myth has been invented. And as with the myth of Genesis, believers in the New Testament accepted the erotic logic of the myth as fact, so perpetuating the inversion of the sexual and the erotic in their minds.

Biblical myths, old and new, commit the logical sin of accepting as fact their own erotic desires. The lack of irony or any form of humour in the Bible, compared with the pervasive irony and humour in Shakespeare, is a sure indication of the intent to deceive. Shakespeare demonstrates in all his plays that the illusions created through language are useful fictions that need the irony of awareness to ensure they remain useful fictions.

Shakespeare shows in his 154 sonnets, 36 plays and four longer poems, how to create a multiplicity of expressive possibilities with the correct logical consistency at the mythic level from the basic elements of natural logic. Because his philosophy is consistent and coherent, his critique in the *Sonnets* of over-idealised expectations and his critique in the plays of the tyranny of the ideal provide the appropriate methodologies for operating in a society with pluralistic expectations.

The Declaration of Independence

When the relevant statements of the *Declaration of Independence* and the *American Constitution* are compared with the logic of the *Sonnets*, there is a correspondence that might be expected if the *Declaration* was a rejection of the social/political dynamic of the old world. Thomas Jefferson in particular was determined to institute a society in which religious dogma could not play a part in the politics of the State. For Jefferson, the idea of a religion having a role in government was a violation of the intent of 'Nature's God'. As a deist he believed that God the creator was immanent in nature so all one had to do was to act in conformity with the Laws of Nature.

In the first few lines of the *Declaration*, the rejection of the theistic belief in a God who actively intervenes in the world in favour of a deistic God who creates the natural world and whose intent is evident in natural law is given precise expression. Jefferson reflects the shift in sensibility by mentioning the word 'Nature' twice before he mentions 'God'. To emphasise his belief that the creator's work is evident in nature, the phrase 'Laws of Nature' precedes 'Nature's God' (just as the word 'Nature' precedes 'God'). For deists it is not possible to know God or the creator of the world otherwise.

> When in the course of human events, it becomes necessary for one people to dissolve the political bands which have connected them with another, and to assume among the powers of the earth, the separate and equal station to which the Laws of Nature and of **Nature's God** entitle them, a decent respect to the opinions of mankind requires that they should declare the causes which impel them to the separation. We hold these **truths to be self-evident**, that **all men are created equal**, that they are **endowed by their Creator with certain unalienable Rights**, that among these are **Life, Liberty, and the pursuit of Happiness**.[1]

Deists like Jefferson believed that once God created the world he did not intervene in its progress and destiny. All 'men' were created equal and endowed with 'unalienable Rights'. Even though, like most of his contemporaries, Jefferson understood the world in pre-Darwinian terms (he believed in the immutability of species, even hoping to find living examples of old world fossils in the American West or elsewhere) he intuitively grasped the Darwinian logic that mind-based rights were derived from nature.

Jefferson (and his colleagues) were determined to reject a society based on a belief in a theistic God, who could be petitioned for favours and who made his intentions known through personal revelation. Their experience was that the theistic basis of Judeo/Christian belief led inevitably to a proliferation of feuding sects and to the persecution of atheism, its logical counterpart.

Because the attributes of theism and atheism are psychological attributes from within the human mind, like gnosticism and agnosticism, they are perpetually opposed. The pluralistic advantage of Jefferson's adherence to deist logic is apparent in the illogic of coining words like adeistic or anature. The soundness of his philosophic insight into the distinction between the natural logic of deism and the psychology of theism provides the logical precondition for a pluralistic society.

The formulators of the *Declaration* wished to remove themselves from all they considered iniquitous and injurious in the English unification of Church, Crown and parliament. Because the sectarian injustice and violence in the old world was seen as a direct consequence of the Church as an arm of the State, Jefferson and his colleagues wished to subscribe directly to the laws of the natural world, which lack the absolute evil of Christian schism and retribution. So in their desire to emphasise the implications of their insight into natural logic, the *Declaration* appealed to 'Nature's God'.

So it is not surprising that the First Amendment to the *Constitution* reinforces the *Declaration's* emphasis on nature by forbidding Church involvement in the running of the State. The appeal to the Laws of Nature has a logical significance for the establishment of the State. The pluralism inherent in Jefferson's deism through nature meant that logically he was one step away from demoting God the creator to his correct place in natural logic.

Unbeknown to Jefferson the move had been made by Shakespeare 200 years earlier in the natural logic of the *Sonnets*. The first few lines of the *Declaration*, which prioritise nature over God in human affairs, point in the direction of the *Sonnet* logic. The significance of nature in the plays and poems of Shakespeare finds a resonance in a New World that wished to put behind it the worst effects of unbridled idealism, as they showed themselves in the Reformation and Puritan excesses in England and Europe.

The intent of the *Declaration*, though, (as in the works of Shakespeare) was not to deny the importance of the psychology of belief for individual citizens. Hence, in keeping with the relationship of nature and God, the writers of the *Declaration* talk of the 'Creator' providing for individual human hopes and aspirations by guaranteeing 'certain unalienable Rights, that among these are Life, Liberty, and the pursuit of Happiness'. And the First Amendment of the *Constitution* was enacted in part to protect those who resorted to the psychology of theistic belief.

The reference to 'Nature's God' is the one mention of God by name in the *Declaration*. The only other allusion to a deity in the lives of 'men' is at the conclusion where 'the Supreme Judge of the World' is invoked to ensure the 'rectitude of our intentions'. Again the Supreme Judge is evident through Natural Laws and Rights. Significantly, against Jefferson's vehement objection, Congress then added the words 'with a firm reliance on the protection of divine Providence' to the *Declaration*. Jefferson retained his own version, which he would show in protest.

Jefferson and his colleagues quarantined the iniquities in religious dogma by subjecting the beliefs based in the God of the Bible to the Laws of Nature. The plurality of the young American nation was guaranteed by relocating the male Gods of idealistic theisms within the laws of Mother Nature. Jefferson had correctly identified the removal of the male Gods of the Bible to their appropriate place in nature's logic as the primary logical requirement for a nation to exist in harmony and justice. (The wording in the *Declaration* recalls Shakespeare's critique of the idealising Master Mistress in the *Sonnets*. The male as Master Mistress, who is second to the female as Mistress, is governed by Nature as the sovereign mistress.)

The *Constitution* and the First Amendment

The *Declaration's* determination to remove the theistic God from political power is given direct expression in the *Constitution*. No mention is made of the idea of God in the seven Articles of the *Constitution* or the ten Amendments of the Bill of Rights. Instead, in the First Amendment in the Bill of Rights, the logical divide between the State and the Church is stipulated. The express intention is to forbid any one religion from becoming the religion of the nation. As with the *Declaration*, though, the right for any individual to exercise their psychological right to believe what they will is defended, on condition that their religion is second to the logic of the State based in nature.

Amendment 1

Freedom of religion, speech, and the press; rights of assembly and petition

Congress shall make no law respecting an establishment of religion, or prohibiting the free exercise thereof; or abridging the freedom of speech, or of the press; or the right of the people peaceably to assemble, and to petition the government for redress of grievances.

A comment is added in the World Book from which the above text was taken.

Many countries have made one religion the established (official) church and supported it with government funds. This amendment **forbids Congress to set up or in any way provide for an established** church. It has been interpreted to **forbid government endorsement of, or aid to, religious doctrines**. Congress **may not pass any laws limiting worship**, speech, or the press, or preventing people from meeting peacefully.[1]

The *Declaration of Independence* and the Articles and Amendments of the *American Constitution* create a nation in which no religion can become the established power of the State but in which all religions have freedom of expression and assembly. The obvious intention and effect is that if any religion (all the major religions prioritise the male God over the female) were to assume control, the consequence would be a return to intolerance and so to sectarian bloodletting.

Of immediate interest then is the logical status of the structure or framework provided for by the *Constitution*, which has successfully contained the sectarian tendencies of the multitude of religious denominations active in the United States of America. The issue is a profound one for a country whose citizens frequently voice their belief in a male God, even when the belief leads to bizarre expressions of self-interest. It is not uncommon for Americans to thank their God for small miracles but excuse him the responsibility of overwhelming disasters, natural or man-made. And, despite the injunction of the First Amendment, theistic practices, such as prayers in schools and in Congress, have accrued political sanction in American public life.

What, then, is the logic of the structure of the *Constitution* that guarantees a peaceful co-existence in a veritable Babel of beliefs. If the intent of Jefferson and others was to base their nation in the Laws of Nature, a philosophy is required to articulate the natural logic of their hopes at the mythic level.

Beyond singular mythologies to Shakespeare's mythic logic

Other than for the philosophy of Shakespeare's *Sonnets*, there is no philosophic system based in nature with the appropriate logical structure that fulfils the pluralistic expectations of the *Constitution*. All other philosophies in some measure explicitly or tacitly conform to the idealistic programme of the Judeo/Christian paradigm or, having rejected the illogicality of such beliefs, espouse if not scepticism then at least pragmatism.

The *Constitution* as it stands is a very pragmatic document that outlines the role of Congress, the Executive and the Judiciary. Other than for the *Declaration of Independence*, and the First Amendment, it creates a bare framework under which the various belief systems and moral attitudes of the nation are then constrained to co-exist.

Somewhat ironically, the *Declaration* and *Constitution* are enshrined in Philadelphia and Washington, effectively superseding the biblical Commandments or the dogmas of the Churches. And Jefferson is regarded as the political, poetic and spiritual father of the nation. Americans look to the founding documents as if they were more than abstract principles even though they might wish their own religious beliefs had priority.

If the acknowledgement of the logical relation of nature and God was integral to the establishment of the nation, then the current level of religious belief across the nation seems retrograde. But because the *Declaration* and the *Constitution* do not elaborate on the pan-mythic intent to establish a nation under the 'Laws of Nature', is not surprising that the populace seeks psychological consolation in the old mythologies.

The continued belief by many Americans in the illogicality of biblical transcendence has coincided with the absence of an expressive elaboration of a logico/mythic basis for the *Constitution*. And the absence of a philosophic paradigm capable of doing justice to the intent of the founding documents and providing for the mythic needs of citizens has created a vacuum in which constant public avowal in the old beliefs is required.

Compared with the retrograde persistence of biblical dogma within the American culture, the interest in Shakespeare's plays is growing exponentially. Whereas once only a select few plays were acted irregularly, there is now a virtual competition to stage or film every play, even those plays once considered traditionally obscure or offensive to the old beliefs.

The growing recognition that the works of Shakespeare have a mythic resonance for the modern spirit, suggests his works contain an understanding that might develop the abstract guarantees of the *Constitution* into a consistent expression of mythic logic. When it is realised that Shakespeare's *Sonnets* articulate the philosophy behind all his plays and longer poems, and that the philosophy articulates the logical conditions for any mythic possibility, the significance of the philosophy for the contemporary pluralistic American society should be evident.

The mythic depth of Shakespeare's plays has been acknowledged by a number of commentators. The plays have frequently been compared with the Bible for their profundity of insight into the psychology of the human condition. Many commentators prefer the works of Shakespeare because they lack the self-serving dogma of the male-based Bible. They are aware that Shakespeare's works, with their true to life characterisations, faithfully represent the dynamic of life and art.

Until the discovery and elaboration of his *Sonnet* philosophy in these four volumes, the relationship between the works of Shakespeare and the *Declaration of Independence* and the *Constitution* has been restricted to the allusions made to him or his works by thinkers such as Jefferson, Emerson, and Thoreau. It is not surprising, though, that the efforts of the thinkers of the American revolution created a framework that expressed a more consistent attitude toward humankind's place in nature, and simultaneously enacted Articles and Amendments that forbade any religion, and particularly the male-God based religions, from any association with the State. Since the late 1700s, however, there has been no development of their insights into the logic of life and the illogicality of male-based beliefs.

The tendency in American philosophy to look to nature for succour, especially in the natural philosophy of Emerson or Thoreau, has been overly romantic in its rejection of idealism. Shakespeare's logic in contrast shows precisely how to contextualise the romantic and idealist temperaments within the mythic logic of life. But because commentators have gravitated to either an idealist or romantic approach to myth, Shakespeare's articulation of the logical conditions for all human thought out of nature has remained insuperably difficult for them to understand.

A pluralistic society in a pluralistic world

Jefferson gave physical expression to the disestablishment of theism when he designed the University of Virginia. By insisting the University be funded by the State, and by putting its library instead of a chapel at the centre of the campus, he created the world's first secular university.

And 200 years previously, Shakespeare and his colleagues had staged plays across the Thames to escape religious intolerance. In all his plays Shakespeare argues against the injustices that arise when the idealising tendency in humankind overreaches the logic evident in nature. Each play begins with a situation of gross psychological posturing and ends with the restoration of philosophic balance. To demonstrate the applicability of his logic to a complete social dynamic his characters range from kings and cardinals to lovers and beggars, any of who is capable of destructive self-delusion.

Because Shakespeare's plays and poems express a consistent mythic philosophy, which specifically addresses the negative consequences for individuals and societies that exhibit excessive religious idealism, they seem purpose made for a society in which the intentions of the founding documents are so often subsumed in an excessive faith in religious transcendence. The *Sonnet* philosophy, and its practical exercise in 36 plays and four longer poems, provides a natural antidote to the psychological excesses of male-based faith. As the most profound and extensive set of deliberations on the logic of myth out of nature ever written, the plays give detail and colour to Jefferson's bare intention to ensure Church and State are separated for the good of the State.

The present legislative status of the *Constitution* proscribes religious hegemony so that the logical inconsistencies behind the mythological beliefs of the Hebrews, the Christians, the Muslims, and others, are controlled to ensure their peaceful co-existence within the State. But, because of the headstrong tendency of theism to place itself above the *Constitution*, the advantage of having a comprehensive mythic philosophy that provides an overview of all mythic possibilities should be obvious.

The works of Shakespeare not only foreshadow the framework of the *Constitution* as an abstract of the natural logic of life but, by recovering the status of nature as logically female and the priority of the female over the male, and by generating a consistent understanding of aesthetics and ethics, they give added legitimacy to the *Constitution*, and enhance its philosophic potential as a mythic recourse that can mitigate the psychological differences in a society that accommodates competing beliefs.

Epilogue

The global world has not yet caught up with the pluralistic philosophy of Shakespeare. But neither has it appreciated the mythic logic in the art of Marcel Duchamp. Duchamp, a naturalised American of the twentieth century, is the only other artist to create work at the mythic level and note the logical conditions of its operation. Duchamp's pervasive influence on American and world cultures is considered elsewhere in this volume.

10

Riane Eisler

This essay on Riane Eisler concludes Volume 4 because she seems to understand better than most how human biology impacts on the constitution of the human mind. And as an accomplished lawyer and advocate she also takes the logic of human life and applies it steadfastly to the logic of the social and political dynamic at the heart of the *American Constitution*.

In her seminal books *The Chalice and the Blade* (1987) and *Sacred Pleasure: Sex, Spirituality and the Politics of the Body* (1996), Eisler uses a range of scientific and historical evidence and argument to support her understanding of human rights. She envisions a society where the promulgation of human rights does not require a compensatory set of rights for women and children. Under her 'cultural transformation theory' a society would be based on what she calls a partnership model rather than the dominator model of the last 5000 years.

Eisler draws evidence from historical, biological, mythological, archaeological, and psychological sources to distinguish between dominator and partnership societies. In dominator societies either male or female assume power over the other, whereas in partnership societies the natural priority of the female is respected without 'justifying the inference' that 'women here dominate men'.[1]

As a female conscious of her logical status, Eisler's understanding accords with the critique of the recent history of male dominated cultures by Duchamp, Darwin and Shakespeare. As males they take responsibility for the iniquities that follow so readily on the presumption of male priority. Together with Eisler they make a compelling case for female/male partnership.

The primacy of female culture

Eisler draws on the work of the archaeologist Marija Gimbutas who, with others, has gathered overwhelming evidence that societies and civilizations for over 30,000 years were respectful of female priority. The evidence from sites throughout Old Europe shows that the primary focus of cultural practices was the female. The great majority of artifacts found in dwellings and gathering areas represented females or female body parts. Statuettes of which the *Venus of Willendorf* is the most famous celebrate the sexual logic of human life as do the many representations of vulvae and breasts. As Gimbutas says, 'the symbolic significance of the vulva remained universal throughout Europe for some thirty thousand years'.[2]

Notable in the artifacts and artworks, such as cave drawings or petrographs, throughout the whole of Old Europe is the absence of the depiction of interpersonal violence or scenes of warfare. Eisler's conclusion is that the societies that accepted the priority of the female and acknowledged the rightful worth of the male sustained a state of natural balance in which violence was needed only infrequently to resolve conflict. And because the natural priority of the female was respected, such societies did not have repressive attitudes toward sexual activity. They were at ease with the give and take of sexual pleasure.

In what can be surmised of the mythologies of the female-based societies of Old Europe, the mother Goddess (or Goddesses) of fertility predominated as a natural consequence of biological imperatives. In any particular culture a number of Goddesses were named as were a number of subsidiary male Gods. The relation of Goddesses and Gods in the mythologies reflected the natural logic of everyday life.

At issue is not the existence of Goddess cultures in the pre-historic era, but the acceptance across the whole of Old Europe of the primacy of the female for a period of more than 30,000 years. Although the oral mythologies of the ancient European culture were recorded only after the invention of writing, the general pattern of female priority emerges primarily from a study of the archaeological evidence. But it has also been possible to extrapolate back from the remnants of Goddess mythologies in biblical and other texts.

The rise of male-based religions

According to Riane Eisler, then, the evidence suggests that for 30,000 years, from Spain in the west to Mesopotamia in the east, societies in Old Europe acknowledged the natural priority of the female and integrated the role of the male without apparent conflict. Yet around 5000 years ago male power and violence usurped the priority of the female-based societies.

Eisler notes the connection between male God religions of the Hebrew Bible and other male-based religions such as the Christian and the Muslim that have held political sway for the last few millennia. She is particularly critical of the way male-based religions instituted a male God as creator of the world and relegated womanhood to a secondary status and frequently to servitude and denigration through cultures of fear and pain.

The evidence suggests the inversion of natural priorities began when the masculine prowess that sustained nomadic cultures encountered and subverted female-based agrarian cultures. Eisler's case for the ascendancy of male power over female priority 5000 years ago draws on Marija Gimbutas' understanding of nomadic cultures. Gimbutas theorises that the nomadic tribes of Northern Europe or Africa survived in inhospitable climates of tundra or desert by virtue of male strength. But the continual reliance on masculine virtues led to a society in which women's rights were gradually subsumed. Then when the nomadic tribes invaded the pastoral/agricultural societies, in which the priority of the female was still respected, they enforced male superiority.

The female basis of shared social responsibility was superseded by a culture of male-based hierarchical power required to suppress and denigrate the natural rights of women. Eisler considers the development of male dominant religions that regard the female's life-perpetuating sexuality as inherently evil and symptomatic of a death wish in a set of beliefs that values death over life. For her its modern consequence is the threat by weapons of mass destruction to most forms of life on the planet.

While Eisler recognises there have been attempts to mitigate some of the negative consequences of male God priority for womankind by individuals such as Christ and Luther, they were unwilling or unable to correct the illogicality of male God priority. Even attempts to assert that the Godhead was gender neutral fail to recover the natural priority of the female and hence the natural balance in a culture.

The persistence of male-dominated societies has coincided with the rise in male God religions with their blatant contradiction of the natural order.

But even when the conditions for a culture's survival no longer require the pre-emptory exercise of male power, as might have been the case many times over the last 5000 years, the persistence of male-based institutions has ensured the natural priority of the female has not been allowed to reassert itself.

The factor most responsible for institutionalisation of male power was the invention of writing. The advent of the written word at a time when male-based cultures were establishing dominance ensured their 'commandments' were inscribed as the unquestioned 'word' of the male God. The power attributed to the infallible word of God in proclamations such as the first three commandments of Moses enforced the usurped superiority of male over the natural priority of female and prevented a return to partnership cultures.

Riane Eisler shows her awareness of the relation of enforced male dominance and the invention of writing around 3000 BC when she acknowledges that 'most of written history carries the dominator stamp'[3] and when she talks of 'recorded or dominator history'[4]. In *Sacred Pleasure* she suggests that women particularly should 'rebuild myth'[5] to recover the priority of the female and give expression to the values of partnership. How this is possible will be discussed later in the essay.

Recovering the natural order

In her writings Eisler records the history of male-based iniquities toward women, and even toward men, to demonstrate the need for a cultural transformation. To advance the process of cultural transformation she uses biological and logical arguments to show that the priority of the female is not a social construct but a living reality. Ironically, the illogicality of imposing male superiority has led to the compensatory post-modern claim that all cultural agendas are social constructs.

But biologically the human female is the primary entity and the male the secondary entity. The female has the greater number of shared features with an originary asexual life form. The male by contrast has fewer features in common with the asexual form and those features are clearly derived from female precursors.

Although the emergence of the male as a logical entity is essential for the evolutionary shift to sexual differentiation, the male's status at the head of the evolutionary process does not imply superior rights. The opposite is the case. The male's evolutionary advantage is conditional on his ability to recognise and accept his dependency on the female priority. If the male demands priority and by abuse of his usurped power threatens through nuclear annihilation the existence of humankind, the consequence is not the survival of the male but a return to the state of nature that predates the rise of sexual species. The male is both biologically derived from the female and is dependent on her for his persistence.

Eisler appreciates that logically the female is prior to the male. But because the human female and male are co-dependent, the logical relationship of female and male is one of partnership rather than dominance. As she says, 'looked at from a strictly analytical or logical viewpoint, the primacy of the Goddess – and with this the centrality of the values symbolised by the nurturing and regenerating powers incarnated in the female body – does not justify the inference that women here dominated men'.[6]

To claim male priority by asserting the existence of the male God of the Jews and the Christians and Muslims, has been shown to be illogical by philosophers such as Hume. So any claim for male dominance is wrong both biologically and logically. Eisler corrects the biological and the logical imbalance in the traditional understanding of the female/male dynamic.

Sexual dominance

The usurpation of priority over female-based cultures by the male God religions had illogical consequences for the status of sexuality. To maintain their sense of priority male-based cultures have not only dominated through violence and fear, they denied the logic of sexual persistence basic to the priority of the female.

Riane Eisler is in no doubt that the institutionalisation of male dominance led to the repressive attitude to sexuality that is typical of Hebrew, Christian and Muslim social systems. 'Males are ranked over females; violence and abuse are systemic and institutionalised; the social structure is hierarchic and authoritarian; and coercion is a major element in sexuality. And it's all supposed to be just human nature'.[7] In male-based religions where the female is not accorded human status, fifty percent of the population is relegated to powerlessness and servitude.

The natural attitude to sexuality over 25,000 years of female based cultures, which is expressed in their mythological pantheon of Goddesses and Gods as represented in their artifacts, was denigrated in the over-written male-based mythologies as unnatural and evil. Eisler discusses in detail the history of repression over the last 5000 years, a repression still practised today.

As she says, 'a very misleading and pathological image about sexuality exists in our culture'.[8]

Symptomatic of the repressive attitude is the refusal of Marija Gimbutas' publisher to accept the title of her seminal book *Goddesses and Gods of Old Europe*.[9] They insisted the title read *Gods and Goddesses of Old Europe* and it was not until the second edition, when Gimbutas' reputation was secure, that the original title was sanctioned.

Eisler deplores the corruption of natural values particularly in periods of fundamentalist religious fervour. She notes with irony that although the Christian mythology is written in erotic terms, the faithful were 'flagellating their bodies…And the Mediaeval Church, instead of offering these people therapy, canonised them'.[10]

As mythologies express a particular culture's vision of origin and persistence Eisler argues that the forceful annexation of the priority of the female by the male leads not only to an inversion of values but also to a denigration of sexuality. And once sexuality is demonised then any form of physical pleasure is readily proscribed as evil.

Sacred pleasure

In the process of considering the female/male relationship from the vantage of the various disciplines Eisler emphasises the logical connection from sexuality to spirituality. She affirms the natural logic that 'sexual pleasure and spiritual pleasure come from the same source'.[10] She acknowledges Darwin's insight that the mind is derived from bodily characteristics through evolution. The spirituality of the Goddess religions of Old Europe is an 'embodied spirituality'.[11]

The archaeological evidence from the religious observances of Goddess worshipping cultures of Old Europe supports the primacy of sexual priorities and energies. Even the male-based dominator misogynist religions, by their denigration of sexuality and prohibitions on its expression and women's freedom, acknowledge the primacy of the sexual. Their programme of life denial and lust for death speaks of a psychological fear of life that they alleviate by taking retribution on the female.

Eisler is precise when she distinguishes between the sexual or the logic of reproduction and the erotic or the pleasures or desires associated with secondary sexual characteristics. While there is a logical requirement for humankind to persist through sexual means there is not a universal requirement for everyone to do so, or for anyone to devote themselves entirely to the increase process. Rather Eisler reasons that the body, both female and male, is specifically designed for the experience of pleasure separate from the act of coitus. Masturbation, particularly for the female, is a form of pleasuring unrelated to intercourse. The female orgasm as a clitoral event establishes the independence of the erotic for the female.

Because the sexual dynamic provides the logical connection to posterity, it is not surprising that expressions of the eternal relationship between human nature and nature should be characterised by the sexual. Eisler is able to show that the Goddess religions of Old Europe and the logic of human life naturally express the sexual logic of persistence. She records and applauds the logic of sexual metaphors in religious expression.

Ironically, even those religions that seek to deny sexual logic adhere to the logic of sexual persistence by casting their mythologies in the erotic. As the erotic is the logical expression of the sexual dynamic within the dynamic of the mind, then the erotic elements in all mythologies acknowledge the primacy of the sexual dynamic whether they intend to or not.

The priority of the body over the mind

So far this essay has followed Eisler's programme for the recovery of the natural priority of the female and the logic of female/male partnership. Her recognition of the primacy of the female, the significance of the sexual dynamic, the relation of the erotic to the sexual, and the illogicality of traditional male God priority are consistent with the natural logic of Darwin and Shakespeare. Her philosophic mind avoids the illogicalities that affect even Marija Gimbutas.

For instance, in *Sacred Pleasure* Eisler counters Gimbutas' fanciful claim that 'there is no evidence that in Neolithic times mankind understood biological conception'.[12] She points to evidence from a 8000-year-old plaque 'demonstrating that our Neolithic ancestors understood the connection between sexual intercourse and birth'[13] and makes the observation that if women and men understood how animals and plant procreated, then it is sensible to expect that they knew the biology of conception. Gimbutas' erroneous understanding reflects an inability to uncover the logic behind God or Goddess beliefs. Her desire for a return to Goddesses religions of the past blinds her to the logic of human persistence, from out of which Eisler develops a more exacting appreciation of human desires.

Eisler's willingness to consider the logical relation between the body and mind is a reflection of her more philosophic disposition and her acceptance of the findings of Darwinian science. Characteristically she says 'the way a society structures the most fundamental human relations – the relations between the female and male halves of humanity, without which our species could not survive – has major implications for the *totality* of a social system. It clearly affects the individual roles and life choices of both women and men. Equally important, though until now rarely noted, is that it also profoundly affects all our values and social institutions'.[14]

Throughout her writings Eisler is conscious of the logical relation between nature at large, the sexual dynamic of the body, and their implications for the effective operations of the mind. She does not consider human sexuality a 'baser instinct' or a 'lower drive' but as 'part of what we might call a higher drive – an indispensable part of what makes our species human'[15]. If the logic of nature is adhered to as it was in the female cultures for 25,000 years, a society and its understanding of the world shows greater consistency and peacefulness. But if a society does not adhere to the logic of nature the consequence is a corruption of the function of aesthetics and ethics resulting in an inability to control and predict conflict and dissent.

While Eisler does not present an exacting analysis of the aesthetic and the ethical dynamic, she appreciates that the 'polarisation into absolute good and absolute evil' in dominator societies leads to the 'idealisation and institutionalisation of cruelty, violence, and insensitivity'.[16] She is also aware that 'cynicism has long been the refuge of disillusioned idealists'.[17] Her consistency of understanding enables her to advocate in social and political forums with insight and incisiveness.

The mythic dynamic

Besides critiquing male-based cultures and institutions using archaeology and biology, Eisler also considers the status of mythologies in the last 5000 years of recorded history. She shows that the mythologies of female-based cultures gave priority to the female and incorporate the male in a partnership while recognising his logical dependence on the female. With the shift to male-based cultures, where the male Gods usurp the role of the female, the expressive relationship becomes one of dominance and denigration.

If myth was previously transmitted orally in the cultures of Old Europe, then not only could it vary in the telling, it could not be inscribed as the unvarying myth of a culture. Before the advent of the written word, religious expression had the non-exclusive status that Jefferson recovered by writing tolerance into the *American Constitution*. Any form of religious expression, be it of the Goddess or of the Gods, was secondary to the natural conditions of existence and the natural exercise of power in a particular culture.

If male-based cultures of violence and misogyny did arise and were the cause of the overthrow of Goddess cultures around the time that the written word became the primary means of codifying behaviour in laws and mythologies, then the shift to male dominance expressed in the mythologies became enshrined because males had assumed control of the new technology. The culture of scribes and priests ensured male dominance and female subservience was written into laws.

The evidence of Genesis points to just such a scenario. The creation of the world by a male God, the formation of Adam prior to Eve, the control of the 'knowledge of good and evil' by the male God, the denigration of the female as sinful and sex as evil, and the confusion of languages in Babel, which retrospectively pillories the many languages already in existence in favour of the written word of the Hebrew Bible, show the usurpation in progress.

So the Bible bears witness to the inversion of natural logic by the assertion of male priority for which Gimbutas and Eisler find evidence in the archaeology and in the altered mythologies in the period around 3000-1000 BC. The use of the written word to secure male dominance is still evident in the appeals to the male-God based edicts of the Bible and Koran and the inevitable violent disagreements over interpretation.

Understanding the logic of myth

The final chapter of *Sacred Pleasure* is given over to the status of the mythic and Eisler's hope that creative minds will rewrite mythic texts to express the equality of female and male in nature. Yet it is in her proposals for a new mythic awareness that Eisler's arguments are least incisive and reveal an ignorance of the artistic dynamic required to write at a mythic level. This is evident in her earlier wondering whether Greek mythmakers 'had a sense of tragicomic irony or whether, like some artists of today, they were just "telling it like it is".[18]

While Eisler is aware that to 'change our realities we also have to change our myths',[19] in myth the ideas must not only encapsulate the natural logic of life but must be written by a poet capable of giving expression to the required depth of insight. It is not by accident that only the first few chapters in Genesis and in three of the Gospels are written at a mythic level, and that most cultures have a single mythology around which other legends and tales are centred.

Oddly, while Eisler should realise she is one of the few capable of writing books such as *The Chalice and the Blade* and *Sacred Pleasure*, she falls for the common misunderstanding that anyone can create a work of art even at the mythic level. Her suggestion that traditional 'fairy tales' be transformed mythically to recognise the priority of the female in a partnership relationship is misguided in that fairy tales do not sublimate the full erotic logic essential to mythic expression. While Eisler is aware of the distinction between the sexual and the erotic, she abandons her awareness when she encourages all artists to be mythic.

Eisler's and Gimbutas' difficulties arise at the beginning of their account of the shift from female partnership cultures to male dominator cultures. While the rise of male dominant cultures in nomadic tribes would have contributed to the destruction of female-based cultures Eisler mentions only in passing the other vehicle of male dominance. She talks of 'recorded or dominator history', correctly recognising that the dominator religions out of the Middle East coincide with the advent of the written word.

As long as there is a tendency to look for a religious or 'spiritual' counter to male God priority by re-instituting Goddess worship the consequence of the effects of the written word will not be addressed. If the primary cause of the demise of the Goddess religions is the social and political usurpation of power by the male then the cyclical nature of female/male dominance and the reasons for the overwhelming male dominance around 3000BC remains speculative. But if the effect of 'recorded or dominator history' is recognised, both historic and contemporary misogyny can be addressed.

As long as Eisler's argument is based in archaeology and comparative mythology, the logic of myth will escape her. And the final chapter in *Sacred Pleasure* points to the heart of the problem. Her analysis of artistic practice fails to take account of those artists such as Marcel Duchamp who are capable of giving ideas mythic expression. It is not sufficient to encourage all artists to create their own revisions of the dominator biblical or other mythologies.

Eisler is coy in failing to acknowledge her own special talent to argue coherently for women's rights, something she does more coherently than other women's rights advocates. She is also coy to expect artists who work literally or even symbolically to operate at the mythic level. In any culture only a few individuals achieve mythic depth in their work.

Duchamp and Shakespeare

These essays, and the four volumes as a whole, acknowledge the type of talent required to operate at the mythic level and identify two practitioners who not only work at such a level but articulate the logical conditions for operating at the mythic level. Both Marcel Duchamp and William Shakespeare created specific works that show how they recover the priority of the female over the male and formulate the distinction between the sexual and the erotic as fundamental to mythic expression.

Marcel Duchamp's ubiquitous role in twentieth-century culture is a silent witness to his unique achievement of giving mythic expression to the deepest aspirations of the culture. But twentieth-century critiques of his work have failed to note his articulation of the logical conditions for any mythic expression in art.

But it is Shakespeare who most comprehensively confronts the inconsistencies of the written word when it is engineered to give validity to a male-dominant culture. Compared with Duchamp's primarily pictorial and plastic presentation of the inconsistencies, Shakespeare's use of words directly confronts the inconsistencies of biblical and other male-based mythologies by formulating a consistent mythic expression.

Shakespeare's *Sonnets* are based in nature, they recognise the priority of the female over the male and the logic of increase, they acknowledge the priority of the body over the mind, and they correctly account for the logic of aesthetics and ethics, and in doing so they articulate the logical conditions for any mythic possibility. In *Sexual Pleasure* Eisler does show an awareness of the logic behind the increase argument of the first 14 sonnets when she says 'there is little question that the human need for love stems from a biological fact: that without love…we humans do not survive'.[20] At the level of Darwinian science she is clear about the natural logic of life. But unlike Shakespeare she does not know how to connect the biology of the body systematically to the mythic expression of the relationship of body and mind.

Eisler's level of insight into the natural logic of body and mind and the significance of a mythology to a particular culture is evident in her comments on two of Shakespeare's plays. Inevitably she shows no appreciation that the

Sonnet philosophy articulates the mythic logic behind all his plays. As she is unaware of Shakespeare's achievement at a level of insight which gives him an overview of the mythic possibility, she misrepresents the role of Kate in the *Taming of the Shrew*.[21] And although she lauds the role of Portia in the *Merchant of* Venice[22] her ignorance of the *Sonnet* logic leads her to suggest that Shakespeare's Kate expresses a negative attitude to women.

She thinks that classics like Shakespeare's *Taming of the Shrew* exhibit the 'eroticisation of brutality and violence' that 'serves to maintain the domination of one half of humanity by the other'.[23] She cites Portia from the *Merchant of Venice* as a rare instance of a 'heroine modeling spunk and independent action' to counter the tales where the heroine uses 'her body as currency to pay for her deliverance by a powerful male'.[22]

Because the *Sonnet* philosophy is the philosophy behind all his poems and plays, then the issue being addressed in the *Taming of the Shrew* is the over masculinised personality of the shrewish Kate, who is brought back into balance with natural logic by the already naturally achieved male Petruchio. Eisler falls into the trap of reading the *Taming of the Shrew* out of the context of the arrangement of the 36 plays in the 1623 *Folio* and without the advantage of knowing the 1609 *Sonnet* philosophy.

Church and State

In the essay on Thomas Jefferson it was suggested that the influence of Shakespeare can be felt in the determination in the eighteenth-century America to separate Church and State. There is a consistent argument throughout Shakespeare's plays for limitations on the role of the Church and the recovery of the natural logic of mythic expression. The religious turmoil in the Europe of his day led eventually to the ring fencing of the Catholic Church in Italy within the Vatican City, to making the Anglican monarchy in England apolitical, and to the complete separation of Church and State in France.

If Shakespeare's analysis of myth is added to Eisler's evidence for female priority, then her advocacy for the separation of Church and State (as guaranteed by the *American Constitution*) and for women's equality before the law receives a logical sanction of unprecedented precision and comprehensiveness only hinted at in her statements accepting the priority of the female over the male and in her prescription for a revival of female-based myth and story.

For Eisler the 'two basic human types are male and female. The way the relationship between women and men is structured is thus a basic model for human relations'.[24] If male dominance prevails then 'the force-backed ranking of man over woman, man over man, race over race, and nation over nation that can only be maintained by inflicting or threatening pain'.[11]

If the *American Constitution* prevents the possibility of any religion assuming power then it also prevents Goddess religions from taking priority. Duchamp and Shakespeare, and Eisler as far as she goes, set out the logical conditions for social and political consistency at the level of statehood. They do not argue for a new religion to replace the male-based religions currently attempting to undermine the natural logic of the *Constitution*. They advocate, as Jefferson did in the *Declaration of Independence*, a society that conforms to the Laws of Nature.

The priority of the female

Throughout her writing Eisler vehemently denounces the influence of male-based dominator religions such as Christian, Hebrew, and Islam with their denigration and enslavement of women, who constitute one half of the world's population. She recognises that it is in the mythologies of those religions that the illogical male superiority is expressed and promulgated. Even the Ten Commandments begin with three laws that relate solely to male dominance. Above all other iniquities inflicted on half of humankind, the abuse of myth to enforce rigid male dominance is the focus of her condemnation.

Eisler's response to the iniquities is to be an activist in both personal and public domains for a woman's right to be equal and valued. At the constitutional level she advocates the incorporation of women's (and children's) rights into a single statute of human rights. She argues they should not be separate and so conditional on male-based rights. She has established the Partnership Institute to promote the natural justice of equal treatment for female and male in personal relations, in the home, school and society.

The USA already has a Statute or Amendment to the *Constitution* forbidding any religion from becoming the State religion. To complete the logical pattern, an amendment that guaranteed equality of female and male because female is prior to male and the male is dependant on the female would remove another cause of iniquity and division resulting from male domination. If France and America can set the standard for natural government by suppressing the tendency of male-based religions to assert dominance, an amendment that constitutionalises female priority as an example to the Jewish, Muslim and fundamentalist Christian world would proscribe a male-based injustice and give societies a chance to concentrate on issues that arise in the natural course of events.

Conclusion

These four volumes of *Shakespeare's Sonnet Philosophy* have presented evidence and argument for a profound philosophy in the *Sonnets* of great consistency and comprehensiveness as the basis for all Shakespeare's poems and plays. The first three volumes suggested Shakespeare was in part responding to the religious atrocities of his day and in part to the logical inconsistencies in biblical mythologies. From those concerns he was able to articulate a philosophy based in nature that recognised the priority of the female over the male for a coherent understanding of truth and beauty.

The volumes, and particularly Volume 4, have considered other thinkers who have dismissed the illogicalities of biblical faiths. Darwin, Duchamp, Mallarmé, Lakoff and Johnson, Nietzsche, Jefferson, Freud, and Joyce, have in varying degrees argued for the natural basis of understanding.

It is only in this last essay, though, that a thinker has been considered who lifts her sights out of the male-God dominated period of recorded history to present a case for the period of 25,000 years in which female cultures thrived in relative harmony. From that vantage it is then possible to see that the period of recorded history has been usurped by male-driven prerogatives that have led to societies that have been in perpetual war over issues of belief prejudiced by excessive religious idealism.

Riane Eisler is not alone in noting the short period of time in which male dominance has perverted the natural logic of life. Other thinkers such as Marija Gimbutas, David Loye, Merlin Stone, Ashley Montagu, Elinor Gadon, and Buffy Johnson, to name a few, have in different ways argued for a return to a society based on partnership and natural values. But unlike some who would see a Goddess-based religion replace the male-God religions of the Bible, Eisler is able to acknowledge the need for a spiritual dimension to life without losing sight of the basic logic of human life within nature in which the female is logically prior to the male.

Eisler's understanding of life seems to accord with the *Nature template* derived from Shakespeare's *Sonnets*. She lacks only the mythic overview that

Shakespeare so precisely laid out in the *Sonnets* as the basis for all his poems and plays.

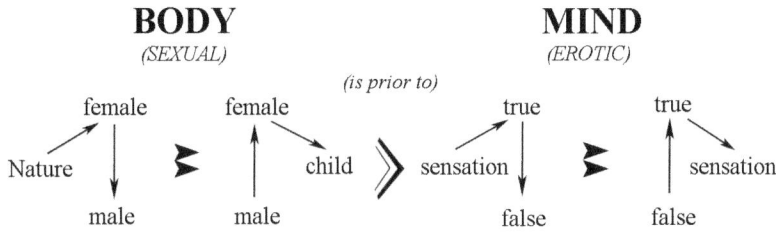

Nature template

Eisler's more philosophic approach is consistent with her strident advocacy of the separation of Church and State and of the promulgation of comprehensive human rights. Her Cultural Transformation Theory expresses her desire to reconcile personal experiences and values with cultural justice. She senses that the time is ripe for the recovery of natural values on a globe threatened by 5000 years of religious paranoia.

If Aristotle heralded a return to nature after the heady idealism of Plato, he also exemplified the male-based prejudice of the last 5000 years. Eisler records that, 'As Aristotle explicitly stated…just as slaves are naturally meant to be ruled by free men, women are meant to be ruled by men'. She comments that 'the same philosophical premises have also been integral to the other major tradition that has shaped Western civilization: our Judeo-Christian heritage'.[25]

Four hundred years ago Shakespeare, who mentioned Aristotle twice, had already formulated the philosophy needed to correct the anti-nature beliefs of excessive male-God idealism and to institute a philosophy based in nature and the priority of the female over the male to enable a consistency in truth and beauty.

References

Part 1

Introduction and Chapter 1

1. Thierry de Duve, *Pictorial Nominalism: On Marcel Duchamp's Passage from Painting to the Readymade*, University of Minnesota Press, 1991, p. 8.
2. Ibid., p. 175.
3. Ibid., p. 176.
4. James Johnson Sweeney, *The Bulletin of the Museum of Modern Art*, Vol. XIII, no. 4-5, 1946, pp. 19-20.
5. Pierre Cabanne, *Dialogues with Marcel Duchamp*, New York, Da Capo Press, 1979, p. 43.
6. Robert Lebel, *Marcel Duchamp*, New York, Paragraphic Books, 1959, p. 15.
7. Richard Hamilton, BBC's Monitor Programme, September 27, 1961, in Pontus Hulten, *Marcel Duchamp*, London, Thames and Hudson, 1993.
8. Interview with George Heard Hamilton, January 19, 1959, in *The Art Newspaper*, London. Vol. III, no. 15, February 1992, p. 13.
9. James Johnson Sweeney, 'A conservation with Marcel Duchamp', in Michel Sanouillet and Elmer Peterson, *Salt Seller*, London, Thames and Hudson, 1975, p. 133-4.
10. Ibid., p. 133.
11. Ibid., p. 134
12. Jerry Tallmer, 'A Toothbrush in a Lead Box; Would it be a Masterpiece', *Village Voice* (N.Y.), vol. IV, no. 24, 8 April 1959.
13. Pierre Cabanne, p. 67.
14. Lou Spence, *Time* (N.Y.), Vol. 54, no. 18, October 31, 1949, p. 42.
15. Jerry Tallmer.
16. Otto Hahn, 'Passport no. G255300, Interview with Marcel Duchamp', trans. Andrew Rabeneck, *Art and Artists*, N.Y., Vol. 1, no. 4, July 1966, pp. 6-11.
17. Interview with Georges Charbonnier, January 13, 1961, in Pontus Hulten, *Marcel Duchamp*, London, Thames and Hudson, 1993.
18. Ibid.
19. Marcel Duchamp, *The Creative Act*, in Robert Lebel, *Marcel Duchamp*, New York, Paragraphic Books, 1967, p. 77.
20. Interview with Otto Hahn, *L'Express*, July 23, 1964, in Pontus Hulten, *Marcel Duchamp*, London, Thames and Hudson, 1993.

21. Interview with Georges Charbonnier, December 9, 1960, in Pontus Hulten, *Marcel Duchamp*, London, Thames and Hudson, 1993.
22. Arturo Schwarz, *The Complete Works of Marcel Duchamp*, New York, Abrams, 1969, p. 140.
23. Ibid., p. 143.
24. Jerry Tallmer.
25. Rosalind Constable, 'New York's avant-garde and how it got there', *New York Herald Tribune*, N.Y., May 17, 1964, pp. 7-10.
26. Thierry de Duve, *Kant after Duchamp*, Cambridge Massachusetts, MIT, p. 29.
27. Alain Jouffroy, 'Une revolution du regard', Conversation with Marcel Duchamp, in Octavio Paz, *Appearance Stripped Bare*, trans. Rachel Phillips and Donald Gardiner, New York, Viking, 1978, pp. 73-4.
28. James Johnson Sweeney.
29. Pierre Cabanne, p. 43.
30. Interview with Philippe Collin, June 21, 1967, in *Marcel Duchamp*, Basel, Hatje Cantz Publishers, 2002, pp. 37-8.
31. Arthur Miller, *Los Angeles Times*, August 16, 1936.
32. Marcel Duchamp, Speech delivered at Hofstra College, May 13, 1960, in Pontus Hulten, *Marcel Duchamp*, London, Thames and Hudson, 1993.
33. Letter to Andre Breton, Oct 4 1954, *Affect^t/Marcel, The Selected Correspondence of Marcel Duchamp*, ed. Francis M Naumann and Hector Obalk, Trans. Jill Taylor, London, Thames and Hudson, 2000, p. 342.
34. Octavio Paz, *Marcel Duchamp or The Castle of Purity*, Trans. Donald Gardner, London, Cape Goliard, 1970, p. 20.
35. James Johnson Sweeney.
36. Octavio Paz, p. 34.
37. Leo Bersani, *The Death of Stephane Mallarmé*, Cambridge University Press, 1982, p. ix.
38. Gordan Millan, *A Throw of the Dice: The Life of Stephane Mallarmé*, New York, Farrar, Straus, Giroux, 1994, p. 154.
39. Marcel Duchamp, *Notes and Projects for the Large Glass*, Selected, ordered, and with an introduction by Arturo Schwarz, New York, Abrams, 1969, p. 202.
40. Interview with Alain Jouffroy, 1964, in Arturo Schwarz, *The Complete Works of Marcel Duchamp*, New York, Abrams, 1969, p. 197.
41. Interview with Richard Hamilton, in Arturo Schwarz, *The Complete Works of Marcel Duchamp*, New York, Abrams, 1969, p. 80.
42. Pierre Cabanne, p. 88.
43. Ibid., p. 88.
44. Arturo Schwarz, p. 115.
45. Robert Lebel, p. 67.
46. Octavio Paz, pp. 28-9.
47. Letter to Michel Carrouges, Feb 6, 1950, in *Affect^t/Marcel, The Selected Correspondence of Marcel Duchamp*, ed. Francis M. Naumann and Hector Obalk, Trans. Jill Taylor, London, Thames and Hudson, 2000, p. 288.

48. Interview with Katherine Kuh, in Rudolf E. Kneuzli, Francis M. Naumann, *Marcel Duchamp, Artist of the Century*, Cambridge, MIT Press, 1989, p. 93, note 63.
49. Marcel Duchamp, *The Creative Act*, p. 78.
50. Lawrence Steefel, in *Marcel Duchamp in Perspective*, ed. Joseph Masheck, New York, Da Capo Press, 1975, p. 101, note 27.
51. Letter to Serge Stauffer, May 26, 1961, Epigraph in *Marcel Duchamp*, Richard Hamilton and Ecke Bonk, Paris, the typosophic society, 1999.
52. Letter to Andre Breton.
53. Arturo Schwarz, p. 36, n. 4.
54. Ibid.
55. Craig Adcock, *Marcel Duchamp's Notes from the Large Glass: An N-Dimensional Analysis*, Umi Research Press, 1983, p. 386, n. 65.
56. Letter to Serge Stauffer, August 19, 1959, in Pontus Hulten, *Marcel Duchamp*, London, Thames and Hudson, 1993.
57. John Russell, "Exile at Large. Interview', *Sunday Times*, London, June 9, 1968, p. 54.
58. Arturo Schwarz, p. 115.
59. Marcel Duchamp, pp. 26, 30, 112, 114, 146.
60. Pierre Cabanne, p. 100.
61. Letter to Michel Carrouges.
62. Letter to Hans Richter, November 11, 1962, in *Marcel Duchamp in Perspective*, ed. Joseph Masheck, Werner Hofmann 'Marcel Duchamp and Emblematic Realism', New Jersey, Prentice Hall, 1975, p. 65.
63. Interview with Philippe Collin.
64. Interview with Alain Jouffroy, December 8, 1961, in Pontus Hulten, *Marcel Duchamp*, London, Thames and Hudson, 1993.
65. Ibid.
66. Western Round Table on Modern Art, 'Modern Art Argument', *Look*, Vol. 13, no. 23, November 8, 1949.
67. Ibid.
68. Marcel Duchamp, *The Creative Act*, p. 77.
69. Letter to Jean Mayoux, 8 March 56, in Ecke Bonk, *The Portable Museum*, p. 252.
70. Ibid.
71. Ibid.
72. Interview with Otto Hahn.
73. William Seitz, 'What's Happened to Art?', An Interview with Marcel Duchamp on Present Consequences of New York's 1913 Armory Show, *Vogue*, (N.Y.), no. 4, February 15, 1963.
74. Interview with George Charbonnier, December 23, 1960, in Pontus Hulten, *Marcel Duchamp*, London, Thames and Hudson, 1993.
75. Marcel Duchamp, p 70, n. 31.
76. Ibid.
77. Arturo Schwarz, p. 174.
78. Otto Hahn.

79. Interview with George Heard Hamilton.
80. Arturo Schwarz, p. 88, n. 52.
81. Walter Hopps, foreword, *Marcel Duchamp, Fountain*, Houston, 1989, p. 98.
82. Pierre Cabanne, p. 43.
83. Interview with Don Morrison, '2 Cents' Worth', *The Minneapolis Star*, October 19, 1965.

Chapters 2 to 4
1. Ludwig Wittgenstein, *Tractatus Logico-Philosophicus*, trans. D. F. Pears and B. F. McGuiness, London, Routledge and Kegan Paul, 1961, proposition. 6.54.
2. Ludwig Wittgenstein, *Culture and Value*, ed. G. H. von Wright, trans. Peter Winch, Chicago, University of Chicago, 1980, p. 18.
3. Ludwig Wittgenstein, *Philosophical Investigations*, trans. G. E. M. Anscombe, Oxford, Basil Blackwell, 1968, no. 67.
4. Ludwig Wittgenstein, *On Certainty*, ed. G. E. M. Anscombe and G. H. von Wright, trans. Denis Paul and G. E. M. Anscombe, Oxford, Basil Blackwell, 1974, no. 211.
5. Ibid., no. 282.
6. Ibid., no. 335.
7. Ibid., no. 358.
8. Ibid., no. 359.
9. Ludwig, Wittgenstein, *Culture and Value*, no. 48.
10. Ibid., no. 49.
11. Ibid., no. 84.
12. Ibid., no. 86.
13. M. O'C. Drury, 'Conversations with Wittgenstein', in *Ludwig Wittgenstein, Personal Recollections*, ed R. Rhees, New York, Rowman and Littlefield, 1981, p. 160.
14. Ibid.
15. Emmanuel Kant, *Kritik der reinen Vernunft*, 1787, in William. H. Calvin, *How Brains Think*, London, Weidenfeld and Nicholson, 1996, p. 113.
16. Stephen J. Gould, *Dinosaur in a Haystack*, London, Jonathan Cape, 1996, pp. 159, 176.
17. Daniel Dennett, *Darwin's Dangerous Idea*, New York, Simon and Schuster, 1995, p. 398.
18. Ibid., p. 188.
19. Ibid., p. 188.
20. Robert J. Richards, *Darwin and the Emergence of Evolutionary Theories of Mind and Behaviour*, Chicago, University of Chicago Press, 1987.
21. *The Oxford Companion to Philosophy*, ed. Ted Honderich, Oxford University Press, 1995, p. 256.
22. Charles Darwin, *The Descent of Man and Selection in Relation to Sex*, London, John Murray, 1909, p. 148.
23. Ibid., p. 149, n. 5.

24. Antonio R. Damasio, *Descartes' Error, Emotion, Reason, and the Human Brain*, New York, Grosset/Putnam, 1994.
25. William Hazlitt, in *Shakespeare, the sonnets: a casebook*, ed. Peter Jones, London, Macmillan, 1977.
26. T. S. Eliot, Introduction, G. Wilson Knight, *The Wheel of Fire*, London, Methuen, 1965, p. xv.
27. Ibid., p. xix.
28. Ibid., p. xix.
29. Ibid., p. xx.
30. W. H. Auden, Introduction, *The Sonnets, and Narrative Poems*, ed. Sylvan Barnet, New York, Signet, 1964, p. xxiii.
31. Benedetto Croce, in *Shakespeare, the sonnets: a casebook*, ed. Peter Jones, London, Macmillan, 1977.
32. Garry O'Connor, *The Life of William Shakespeare*, pp. 283-4.
33. Ibid., p. 284.
34. James Johnson Sweeney, p. 137.
35. Lawrence D. Steefel, in John Golding, *Marcel Duchamp, The Bride Stripped Bare by Her Bachelors, Even*, Penguin 1973, p. 22.
36. Ted Hughes, *Shakespeare and the Goddess of Complete Being*, London, Faber and Faber, 1994, p. 58.
37. John Kerrigan, *Shakespeare's Sonnets and A Lover's Complaint*, London, Penguin, 1987, p. 26.

Part 2

1. Marcel Duchamp

1. Calvin Tomkins, *Marcel Duchamp*, New York, Owl Books, 1998, p. 465.
2. Octavio Paz, *Marcel Duchamp or The Castle of Purity*, Trans. Donald Gardner, London, Cape Goliard, 1970, pp. 28-9.
3. Calvin Tomkins, *Ahead of the Game: Four versions of the avant-garde*, Penguin, 1968.

2. Stephane Mallarmé

1. Anthony Hartley, *Mallarmé*, London, Penguin, 1965, p. ix.
2. Ibid., p. 17.
3. Ibid., p. 51.
4. Gordon Millan, p. 156.
5. Ibid., p. 154.
6. Mary Ann Caws, *Stephane Mallarmé, Selected Poetry and Prose*, Trans. Bradford Cook, New York, New Directions, 1982, p. 89.
7. Ludwig Wittgenstein, *On Certainty*, no. 559.
8. Gordon Millan, p. 159.
9. Anthony Hartley, p. 66.

10. Ibid., p. 14.
11. Octavio Paz, p. 34.
12. Marcel Duchamp, p. 22.
13. Anthony Hartley, p. 14.
14. Mary Ann Caws, pp. 91-101
15. Leo Bersani.

3. Sigmund Freud and Karl Jung

1. Sigmund Freud, *The Interpretation of Dreams*, ed. James Strachey and Alan Tyson, London Penguin, 1991.
2. Carl Jung, *The Psychology of the Unconscious*, New York, Dodd, Mead, 1965.
3. Carl Jung, *Man and his Symbols*, London, Anchor, 1964.

4. James Joyce and T. S. Eliot

1. T. S. Eliot, *Notes Toward the Definition of Culture*, London, Faber and Faber, 1948, p. 122.
2. Ibid., p. 33.
3. Ibid., p. 30.
4. Ibid., p. 34.
5. T. S. Eliot, Introduction, G. Wilson Knight, *The Wheel of Fire*, London, Methuen, 1965, p. xx.
6. Ibid., p. xix.
7. S. L. Goldberg, *Joyce*, London, Oliver and Boyd, 1962, p. 10.
8. Ibid., p.106.

5. Germaine Greer

1. Germaine Greer, *The Whole Women*, London, Doubleday, 1999, p. 1.
2. Germaine Greer, *Shakespeare*, Oxford, Oxford University Press, p. 99.
3. Ibid., p. 58.
4. Ibid., p. 11.
5. William. H. Matchett, *The Phoenix and the Turtle: Shakespeare's Poem and Chester's 'Love's Martyr'*, The Hague, Mouton, 1965.
6. Germaine Greer, *Shakespeare*, p. 12.
7. Ibid., p. 12.
8. Ibid., p. 107.
9. A. C. Bradley, *Shakespearean Tragedy*, Cleveland, Meridian Books, 1963, p. 30.
10. J. B. Leishman, *Themes and Variations in Shakespeare's Sonnets*, London, Hutchison, 1968, p. 177.
11. Germaine Greer, *Shakespeare*, p. 96.
12. Ibid., p. 88.
13. Ibid., p. 91.
14. Ibid., p. 92.
15. Ibid., p. 95.

16. Ibid., p. 94.
17. Ibid., p. 96.
18. Ibid., p. 98.
19. Ibid., p. 99.
20. Ibid., p. 103.
21. Ibid., p. 112.
22. Ibid., p. 113.
23. Ibid., p. 114.
24. Ibid., p. 40.
25. Ibid., p. 13.
26. Ibid., p. 14.
27. Ibid., p. 125.
28. Ibid., p. 17.
29. Ibid., p. 59.
30. Ibid., p. 67.
31. Ibid., p. 84.
32. Ibid., p. 118.
33. Ibid., p. 119.
34. Ibid., p. 120.
35. Ibid., p. 121.
36. Ibid., p. 123.
37. Germaine Greer, *The Female Eunuch*, London, Paladin, 1970, p. 224.

6. Stephen Booth and Helen Vendler

1. Stephen Booth, *Shakespeare's Sonnets*, New Haven, Yale University Press, 2000.
2. Helen Vendler, *The Art of Shakespeare's Sonnets*, Harvard University Press, 1997.
3. Stephen Booth, p. ix.
4. Ibid., p. x.
5. Ibid., p. 501.
6. Robert Graves, 'A study in Original Punctuation and Spelling', *The Common Asphodel*, London, 1949.
7. Stephen Booth, p. 511.
8. Ibid., p. 512.
9. Ibid., p. 514.
10. Ibid., p. 515.
11. Ibid., p. 516.
12. Helen Vendler, pp. 13, 24.
13. Ibid., p. 25.
14. Ibid., p. 13.
15. Ibid., p. 3.
16. Ibid., p. 17.
17. Ibid., p. 34.
18. Ibid., p. 32.

19. Ibid., p. 26.
20. Ibid., p. 36
21. Ibid., p. 33.
22. Ibid., p. xv.
23. Ibid., p. xvi.
24. Ibid., p. 37.
25. MacDonald P. Jackson, 'Aspects of Organisation in Shakespeare's Sonnets', *Parergon*, 17.1, July 1999, pp. 109-34.

7. Friedrich Nietzsche and Ludwig Wittgenstein

1. Robert Wicks, *Nietzsche*, Oxford, One World, 2002, p. 80.
2. Ibid., p. 38.
3. Ibid., p. 31.
4. Ibid., p. 92.
5. Ibid., p. 114.
6. Ibid., p. 78.
7. Ludwig Wittgenstein, *Tractatus*, prop. 6.421.
8. Ludwig Wittgenstein, *Lectures and Conversations on Aesthetics, Psychology and Religious Belief*,. Berkeley, University of California Press, 1967.
9. Ludwig, Wittgenstein, *Culture and Value*, no. 48.
10. Ibid., no. 49.
11. Ibid., no. 84.
12. Ibid., no. 86.
13. Friedrich Nietzsche, *Daybreak*, ed. M. Clark, B. Leiter, trans R. J. Hollingdale, p. 140, section 240.
14. Alfred von Weber Ebenhof, *Bacon (Shakespeare) and Friedrich Nietzsche*, www.sirbacon.org/nietzsche.htm, accessed 22.06.04.
15. Ibid.
16. Ibid.
17. Ibid.
18. Ibid.
19. Friedrich Nietzsche, *Daybreak*, ed. Charles Taylor, trans. R. J. Hollingdale, CUP 1982, Book 1, note 76.

8. George Lakoff and Mark Johnson

1. Mark Johnson, *The Body in the Mind*, Chicago, University of Chicago Press, 1987.
2. George Lakoff, *Women, Fire, and Dangerous Things*, Chicago, Chicago of University Press, 1987.
3. George Lakoff and Mark Johnson, *Metaphors We Live By*, Chicago, Chicago University Press, 1980.
4. George Lakoff and Mark Johnson, *Philosophy in the Flesh*, New York, Basic Books, 1999.
5. Ibid., p. xi.
6. George Lakoff and Mark Johnson, *Metaphors We Live By*, p. 146.

7. Ibid., p. 10.
8. Ibid., p. 58.
9. Ibid., p. 180.
10. Ibid., pp. 186-8.
11. Ibid., pp. 189-90.
12. Ibid., p. 229.
13. Ibid., p. 230.
14. George Lakoff, *Women, Fire, and Dangerous Things*, p. 92.
15. Ibid., pp. xv-xvi.
16. Ibid., p. 13.
17. Mark Johnson, *The Body in the Mind*, p. ix.
18. Ibid., p. x.
19. Ibid., p. xi.
20. Ibid., p. xiii.
21. Ibid., p. xiv.
22. Ibid., p. xvi.
23. Ibid., p. xx.
24. Ibid., p. xxi.
25. Ibid., p. xxxvi.
26. Ibid., p. xxxvii.
27. Ibid., p. 212.
28. Ibid., p. 213.
29. George Lakoff and Mark Johnson, *Philosophy in the Flesh*, p. xi.
30. Ibid., p. 3
31. Ibid., p. 4.
32. Ibid., p. 6.
33. Ibid., p. 8.
34. Ibid., p. 11.
35. Ibid., p. 12.
36. Ibid., p. 15.
37. Ibid., p. 129.
38. Ibid., p. 134.
39. Ibid., p. 338.
40. Ibid., p. 342.
41. Ibid., p. 345.
42. Ibid., p. 552.
43. Ibid., p. 561.
44. Ibid., p. 568.
45. Ibid., p. 567.
46. George Lakoff, *Women, Fire, and Dangerous Things*, p.46.
47. Caroline Spurgeon, *Shakespeare's Imagery: and what it tells us*, Cambridge University Press, 1971.

9. Thomas Jefferson

1. See 'Constitution of the United States', *World Book Encyclopedia*, Chicago, World Book Inc., pp. 996-1016.

10. Riane Eisler

1. Riane Eisler, *The Chalice and the Blade*, San Francisco, Harper Row, 1987, p. 27.
2. Marija Gimbutas, 'The "Monstrous Venus" of Prehistory, in *In all her names, exploration of the feminine in divinity*, ed. Charles Muses, Harper San Francisco, p. 30.
3. Riane Eisler, Interview with Jerry Snider, *Magical Blend*, January 1996, www.partnershipway.org/html/subpages/articles/sacredpleasure.htm, 22.06.04
4. Riane Eisler, *Sacred Pleasure, Spirituality and the Politics of the Body*, Harper San Francisco, 1996, p. 361.
5. Ibid., p. 378.
6. Riane Eisler, *The Chalice and the Blade*, p. 27.
7. Riane Eisler, Interview with Mark Harris, *Conscious Choice*, February 1999, www.partnershipway.org/html/subpages/articles/sexspirtevol.htm, 22.06.04.
8. Ibid.
9. Marija Gimbutas, *The Goddesses and Gods of Old Europe, 6500-3500 BC*, Berkeley, University of California Press, 1982.
10. Riane Eisler, Interview with Jerry Snider.
11. Riane Eisler, from *Tikkun*, January 1999, www.partnershipway.org/html/subpages/articles/spiritual.htm, 22.06.04
12. Marija Gimbutas, *The Goddesses and Gods of Old Europe*, p. 137.
13. Riane Eisler, *Sacred Pleasure*, p. 63.
14. Riane Eisler, 'The Goddess of Nature and Spirituality, An Ecomanifesto', in *In all her names, exploration of the feminine in divinity*, ed. Charles Muses, Harper San Francisco, 1991, p. 10.
15. Riane Eisler, *Sacred Pleasure*, p. 49.
16. Ibid., p. 135.
17. Ibid., p. 304.
18. Ibid., p. 85.
19. Ibid., p. 126.
20. Ibid., p. 173.
21. Riane Eisler, *The Chalice and the Blade*, p. 142.
22. Riane Eisler, *Sacred Pleasure*, p. 271.
23. Ibid., p. 223.
24. Riane Eisler, *The Chalice and the Blade*, p. 168.
25. Ibid., p. 118.

Index

References to figures and diagrams in the text are italicised as are references to individual sonnet quotations.

Entries for authors associated with one of the principal contributors who feature in this volume are listed in a separate entry under that contributor.

Art movements and individual artists are listed under 'art' and 'artists'.

aesthetics, 2, 4, 5–7, 10, 13, 14, 15, 24, 25, 32, 45–9, 53, 61, 79, 83, 103, 107–11, 117–9, 125, 135, 143, 150, 211: as absolute, 57; beauty as, 8, 57, 107, 151, 153; and judgment, 6, 24, 46–7, 86; logic of, 15, 16, 29, 47, 59, 61, 105, 142; and science, 5, 6–7, 84. *See also* sensations
alchemy, 9, 30, 39, 43, 146, 163, 164: sonnet 14, 99
Alien Poet, 97: rhyme and, 97; sonnets 78 to 86, 97, 187, 201
American Constitution, 241–4, 245, 248–9, 251, 261, 264
Apollinaire, Guillaume, 30
apologetics, 6, 15, 39, 63, 64–5, 69, 72, 73, 75, 80, 81, 82, 85, 89, 90, 126, 186, 220: Christian, 15, 47, 66, 142, 169, 174
Aristotle, 180, 223, 236, 267
art, 4, 7, 8, 9, 12, 14, 18–19, 23, 25, 45, 48, 50, 58, 63, 145, 147, 150, 163, 164, 167: abstract, 17, 57, 87, 124, 142, 167; avant-garde, 5, 11, 21, 33, 40, 131, 134–5; beauty in, 57; conceptual, 11, 120, 124; content of, 18–19; Cubism, 11, 17, 87, 142, 145, 153; as erotic, 31, 39, 100, 115, 235; formalist, 4, 9, 12, 18, 20, 22–3, 27, 28, 30, 40, 56, 57, 87, 124–5; Futurism, 17, 153; history of, 9, 14, 23, 26, 29, 30, 40, 56, 86, 131; and life, 134, 164, 244, 251; as masturbation, 53; Modernism, 9, 27, 30; Neo-Dada, 46; painting, 13, 20–2, 27, 50, 56; as pictorial, 35; as retinal, 11, 27–8, 40, 45, 120; Succession, 11; Surrealists, 28, 163; works of, 22–3, 25, 29, 30, 31, 39, 40, 60, 131
artists: Gustave Courbet, 28; Paul Cezanne, 10, 11, 33; Wassily Kandinsky, 13, 56; Joseph Kosuth, 5, 22, 124; Edouard Manet, 33; Henri Matisse, 133; Francis Picabia, 132; Pablo Picasso, 33, 133; Raymond Roussel, 32, 33, 145

beauty, 4, 5, 107–9, 171, 187: as aesthetics, 8, 107, 153; as indifference, 49–52; and seeing, 8, 107–10; as sensations, 50, 107, 243; Rose as, 104; template, 110, *110*, *153*; and truth, 108, 135, 150
Bible, 125, 149, 159, 180, 189, 194, 196, 210, 222, 244–5, 261: belief in, 136, 154, 248; mythology of, 39, 80, 116, 134, 155 157, 239, 242, 245
biology, 4, 7, 10, 16, 36, 38, 40, 44–5, 52–3, 63, 71, 76, 100, 107, 141, 144, 160, 177, 253, 259: evolutionary, 39, 75
body, 18, 35, 38, 61, 63, 64, 79, 81–4, 111–3, 145, 163, 175: priority over mind, 35, 39, 63, 64, 65, 73, 80, 83–5, 101, 140, 161, 221, 230, 237–8, 243, 259–60; as sexual, 39, 61, 84, 101, 142; template, 111, *111*, 113, 152, *152*, 161, *161*
body/mind, 34, 60, 75, 82, 86
Booth, Stephen, 194–8, 201–6: and Bible, 196–7; Christianity and, 196–8, 202; multitude of meanings, 195–8; *Shakespeare's Sonnets*, 194

Christianity, 78–9, 82, 90, 91, 118, 123, 136, 138, 166–7, 180–1, 188, 191–2, 196–205, 207, 211, 242, 245, 255, 257, 265–6: Adam and Eve, 32, 141, 146, 261; and apologetics, 15, 47, 66, 142, 169, 174; erotics in, 118, 244; judgment, 201; male God in, 10, 47, 118, 133, 182, 184–5, 206, 207, 255, 257; mythology of, 31, 36, 59,

167, 197, 205, 258; theology, 64, 156, 238; virgin birth, 32, 118, 141, 178, 245
Church, 179, 184, 186, 189, 241, 252
Coleridge, Samuel Taylor, 91, 187
common sense, 175, 196
content, 4, 12, 13, 14, 21, 23, 27, 28, 29, 30, 32, 52, 54, 57, 87, 97, 132, 143, 145, 201, 205, 218
contradiction, 46, 59, 105, 154
Croce, Benedetto, 91, 187

Dante Alighieri, 90, 167, 174, 194: *The Divine Comedy*, 96, 168
Darwin, Charles, 4, 9, 16, 39, 60–1, 62, 63, 64, 71, 72, 74, 75–86, 121–2, 125–7, 135, 153, 211, 230–2, 235–6, 240, 246, 258–60, 263, 266: evolution, 60, 61, 63, 67, 84–5, 87, 88, 124, 148, 230, 234, 253; evolutionary ethics, 76; *The Descent of Man*, 7, 61, 64, 77–8, 86, 121–2, 148, 152, 230, 231; mental powers, 7, 60, 78–9, 81, 88, 122, 230–1; moral sense, 7, 60, 64, 78–9, 81, 88, 122, 230–1; natural selection, 77, 221; *The Origin of Species*, 77–8, 121, 230, 231; secondary sexual characteristics, 8, 78, 122, 232; vera causa, 79, 231
Darwin, Charles, literature: Antonio Damasio, 60, 82; Daniel Dennett, 76–7: automata, 76; Stephen Gould, 76; Anthony Flew, 75–6; Robert J. Richards, 77
death, 79, 137, 244, 255
De Duve, Thierry, 2–6, 8, 9, 12, 14, 22, 26, 39, 55, 56, 61, 86, 87, 92, 124–5, 127, 146: blank canvas, 23, 27, 56–7, 124; formalism of, 11, 12, 13, 22, 26, 62, 87, 124–5; *Kant after Duchamp*, 3, 4, 6, 8, 14, 22–3, 27, 39, 46, 55, 57, 59, 61, 86, 87; and nominalism, 11–12, 14, 26, 27, 49, 56, 86; *Pictorial Nominalism*, 8, 10, 12, 14, 19, 20, 21, 22–3, 59, 61, 86, 87; art as a proper name, 55; and psychology, 8–10; 'This is Art', 12, 14, 15, 19, 20, 21, 22–3, 56, 59, 124; 'tube of paint', 12, 56–7, 124; Urinal, 15, 24, 26
Descartes, Rene, 64–5, 85, 140, 142, 154, 222, 228
desire, 16, 34, 35, 41, 142, 146, 157
Duchamp, Marcel, 2, 4, 7, 8–9, 23, 26, 39, 45, 51, 63, 75, 86, 91, 93, 98, 113, 118–20, 121, 125–7, 131–5, 144–7, 163, 165, 173, 219, 230, 235, 252, 253, 263, 266: 4th dimension, 8, 31, 39–45, 52, 88, 100, 133; 3rd dimension, 8, 31, 40–45, 52, 88, 100; as aesthete, 16, 120, 133, 146; and aesthetics, 2, 6, 15, 23, 25, 28, 32, 33, 57–8, 64, 66, 68, 86, 87, 91, 95, 100, 119, 146, 163; and aesthetic echo, 48, 147, 152; algebraic comparison a/b, 14; art co-efficient, 30, 95; as artist, 98, 105, 113; Bachelors, 16, 35, 43, 51, 52–3, 81, 94–5, 98, 113–5, 146, 164; beauty of indifference, 49–52, 147; Bride, 16, 35, 36, 37, 52–3, 81, 94–5, 98, 114–5, 146, 164; chance, 145–6; choice, 46, 58; colour, 10, 11; and eroticism, 3, 13, 14, 16, 18, 35–7, 56, 87–8, 100, 145–6, 154; esotericism, 33; and ethics, 16, 33, 87, 95, 115, 119; and family, 18; humour, 16, 36, 50; and ideas, 54; indifference, 16, 46, 64, 98, 110, 147; individual and, 16, 55; infra-thin, 5, 54; ironism of affirmation, 39, 52–3, 147; and irony, 13, 16, 19, 36, 145; and language, 49, 50, 146; Munich, 29; mythic expression of, 6, 13, 14, 32, 87, 91, 115, 118, 121, 124, 263, 236–8, 240; pictorial nominalism of, 10, 11, 35, 86, 124; puns, 36, 50; and retinal, 27–8, 40, 57, 87, 120; sexual and, 44; and spectator, 19, 20, 22, 25, 55; and taste, 19, 20, 22, 24, 45, 47–8, 54, 147
Duchamp, Marcel, interviews and literature: Craig Adcock, 42; Andre Breton, 29, 107, 163; Pierre Cabanne, 17, 18, 21, 28, 36, 44, 57; Michel Carrouges, 39, 41; Georges Charbonnier, 24, 25, 50; Philippe Collin, 28, 46; Rosalind Constable, 26; Denis de Rougemont, 21; John Golding. 8, 9, 27, 132; Otto Hahn, 25, 49, 54; George Heard Hamilton, 19, 54; Richard Hamilton, 132; Walter Hopps, 54; Alain Jouffroy, 27–8, 46; Katherine Kuh, 39; Robert Lebel, 18, 38, 40, 42; Jehan Mayoux, 49; Arthur Miller, 29; Don Morrison, 58; John Russell, 43; William Seitz, 50; Lou Spence, 21; Serge Stauffer, 41–2; Lawrence Steefel, 40–2, 94; James Johnson Sweeney, 17–18, 20, 28; Jerry Tallmer, 21, 26; Calvin Tomkins, 132, 134
Duchamp, Marcel, works and writings, 59: *Bicycle Wheel*, 22, 29; *The Blind Man*, 15, 24, 51; *Bottle Rack*, 56; *Box of 1914*, 7; *Box in a Valise*, 12, 15, 24, 40; *Coffee Mill*, 17; *The Creative Act*, 25, 30, 48; *Dulcinea*, 17; *Etant donnes*, 4, 5, 14, 16, 22, 93, 131, 132, 163; *Fountain*, 14, 15, 24, 51; *Green Box*, 7, 54, 107; *King and Queen Surrounded by Swift Nudes*, 18; *Large Glass*, 2–6, 8, 12–13, 16–18, 23–4, 26–30, 31, 32, 35, 40, 43, 51–5, 61, 68, 81, 86, 87, 90, 92, 93–101, 107, 118–9,

continued

Duchamp, Marcel, works and writings *continued*
124, 131–4, 145–6, 163–4, 205, 235, 240;
Notes, 11, 16, 22, 35, 40, 42, 44, 50–1, 54, 87,
100; *Nude Descending a Staircase*, 17, 29, 149;
Opposition and Sister Squares Reconciled, 51;
Passage from the Virgin to the Bride, 12–14, 23,
26, 27; *Pharmacy*, 29; readymades, 2, 5, 11, 12,
13–14, 16, 17, 18, 19, 23–4, 26–30, 31, 39, 40,
46, 52–3, 55, 56–7, 61, 87, 90, 92, 93, 119,
124–6, 131–5, 145–6, 163; *Rrose Selavy*, 14,
50, 98, 113, 115; *Standard Stoppages*, 94; *White Box*, 7, 19
Duchamp, Teeny, 43, 93

Eisler, Riane, 126, 192, 253: body and mind,
258, 260, 263; *The Chalice and the Blade*,
253, 262; Church and State, 264–5, 267;
cultural transformation, 253, 256, 267;
erotic and, 258; female priority, 254–6,
259–60, 263, 265–6; human/women's
rights, 253, 262, 265; male dominance,
253, 255–7, 260, 262, 265–6; male God,
255–6; Marija Gimbutas, 254, 255, 258,
261, 266; and myth, 253, 256, 260–2;
partnership, 253, 256–7, 259, 260, 262,
265; *Sacred Pleasure*, 253, 256, 259, 261–2;
sacred pleasure, 258–9; writing, 255
Eliot, T. S., 166–8, 171–6, 187: as Christian,
166–8, 173, 174; and Dante, 167–8, 173,
174; and erotics, 175; *Four Quartets*, 172;
and Pound, 166, 176; ragbag
philosophy, 90, 168; and time, 172, 174;
The Wasteland, 166
emendations, 89, 95, 196, 197, 199, 201,
202–3: compositors, 199, 202; Edmund
Malone, 197
eroticism, 2, 3, 8, 13, 15, 31, 34–45, 52–3,
60, 63, 99, 104, 117–8, 122, 138, 140–4,
154, 194, 203, 214–5, 219, 235: 3rd
dimension, 36; as desire, 41, 115, 141, 175;
Duchamp's, 14, 16, 18, 36, 87, 98, 100,
154; as mind, 34, 38, 39, 142, 145;
mythic as, 115, 218; as mythology, 14, 36,
118, , 157, 177–8, 259; as non-sexual, 32,
115; sexual as prior to, 35, 38, 39,
45, 59, 60, 88, 100, 103, 105, 107, 135, 141,
162, 263; truth and beauty, 106, 153
ethics, 2, 4, 5–7, 8, 15, 58, 61, 64, 79, 81,
83, 105, 107–11, 117–9, 135, 143, 188,
211: as difference, 16; as ideas, 6, 16, 49,
58, 69, 107, 123; language as, 6, 47, 66,
117, 135, 146, 147; as moral, 80–1, 84, 91;
science as, 7; as truth, 151–3
evolution, 72, 77–8, 80, 81, 98, 174, 236
eyes, 50, 109, 148: sexual eye, 148; as stars, 109

family 18, 40, 71: child, 52, 82, 102, 111,
141; father, 39, 71, 102; mother, 39, 71, 102
female, 4, 45, 52, 82, 102, 111, 114–7, 123,
141, 171, 211, 217: *Large Glass* as, 133;
priority over male, 6, 80, 81, 85, 94,
107–8, 114, 116, 122, 133, 135, 141, 164,
176, 177, 179, 182, 192, 208, 210, 215,
218–9, 235, 238, 242, 252, 254–6, 263,
266–7
Freud, Sigmund, 9, 10, 43, 156–65, 216,
266: dreams, 158; *Interpretation of dreams*,
159; and myth, 159; Oedipus, 156;
psychotherapy, 9; sexual and, 156–8,
161–2, 164, 165

gender, 178, 219: feminine, 179, 210, 218;
masculine, 178, 179, 192, 210, 218
Genesis, 82, 133, 141, 146, 169, 175, 244–5,
261
God, 34, 47, 49, 65, 67, 85, 139, 141, 146,
169, 183–4, 189, 227, 247: atheism, 49,
210, 246; as male, 6, 45, 80, 100, 118, 133,
154, 156, 157, 171, 172, 174, 177–9, 182,
189, 192, 206, 207, 209–11, 222, 235,
239, 244, 249, 251, 255–7, 266; as ideal,
110, 151, 185, 243; template, 123, 154,
154, *161*, 175, *175*, 192–3, *193*, *206*,
219–20, *219*, *239*, 240, 244, *244*
Greenberg, Clement, 5, 22, 23, 27, 56, 57, 124
Greer, Germaine, 179: and Christianity,
182–8, 191–2; *The Female Eunuch*, 180;
feminism, 179, 191; and God, 183–4, 189;
and idolatry, 185, 191–3; *King Lear*, 183–5,
191; marriage, 189–91; and nature, 184–5;
and scepticism, 184, 192; Shakespeare,
180–5, 183; *The Whole Woman*, 180;
women's rights, 179, 188, 192–3

Hegel, Georg, 80–1, 83, 137
homosexuality, 116–7
Hughes, Ted, 91, 92, 101
Hume, David, 64, 67, 80, 85, 156, 157, 192,
235, 242, 257: is and ought, 83; scepticism,
85
ideal, 80, 81, 106, 137, 149, 165: as absolute,
35, 80, 143, 149, 151, 245; as beauty, 45; as
God, 110, 151, 185, 243; sensation of the
mind, 34, 48, 151, 219
idealism, 30, 39, 59, 65, 69, 73, 84, 110,
115, 148, 171, 180, 185, 188, 190, 236,
247, 260: male-based, 137, 176, 178, 206,
266–7; priority of mind, 136; scientific, 69;
youthful, 168
ideas, 9, 21, 28, 48, 60, 65, 82, 84, 107, 125, 145,
150: as ethics, 6, 16, 49, 58, 69, 107, 123

immortality, 38, 68, 93: verse as, 149
increase, 4, 93, 100–1, 122, 135, 178, 187, 218, 243: argument, 101, 105, 108, 111, 117, 175, 183, 189, 201, 204, 218, 263; priority of, 101, 108, 149, 176; sonnets 1 to 14, 8, 101, 105, 108, 117, 187, 190, 238, 263; as store, 108; template, 102, 110, 117

Jefferson, Thomas, 179, 185, 261, 264: *American Constitution*, 241–2, 245, 248–9, 251, 261, 264; Bill of Rights, 185, 248; Church and State, 241–2, 247, 252, 264–5; *Declaration of Independence*, 241–2, 245–9, 251, 265; a deist, 245–7; First Amendment, 241, 247, 248–9; Laws of Nature, 241, 245–7, 249, 250, 265; Nature's God, 241, 246–7; pluralism; 241–2, 245–7, 249, 250–2

Johnson, Mark, 60, 71, 82, 221–4, 225–40, 266: body and mind, 221, 223, 226–8, 230; *The Body in the Mind*, 71, 221, 225–7; cognitive and, 228–9; empirical and, 230–1, 236, 238–40; image schemas, 226, 238; imagination, 225–7; language, 221; *Metaphors We Live By*, 71, 221, 223–4; and objectivists, 221, 223, 226, 235, 236, 238–9; panentheism, 234, 236; philosophy and, 221–2, 225–8, 231–4, 236–7, 240; *Philosophy in the Flesh*; 71, 221–2, 227–9, 232, 234, 236, 238; and science, 222, 226–32, 233–4, 236–40

Joyce, James, 168–76: Molly Bloom, 170–1, 176; eroticism in, 175; *Finnegan's Wake*, 168–70, 176; and Hamlet, 169; and history, 169, 172; *King Lear*, 169; monomyth, 168–9; all myths, 172, 176; *Portrait of the Artist as a Young Man*, 168; *Ulysses*, 168–70, 173; and Vico, 169, 172

Judeo/Christian, 32, 133–4, 156, 160, 166, 171, 173, 175, 199, 209, 213, 246, 249, 267: mythology of, 157–8, 169

judgment, 24, 46–8, 83, 201: sonnet 14, 109

Jung, Carl, 10, 156–65, 266: and ideal, 160, 163; and mythology, 156, 165; *Psychology of the Unconscious*, 159; symbols and, 156–8, 164, 165

Kant, Emmanuel, 5, 8, 13, 14, 26, 57–61, 64, 68, 74, 79, 81, 83, 124–7, 157, 211, 222, 228, 235: aesthetic judgment, 6, 15, 46–7, 57, 59; apologetics, 6, 10, 14, 47, 60–1, 64, 67–8, 80, 85; the beautiful, 14, 57; the disgusting, 15, 57; and God, 47, 68, 81; moral maxim, 61

Kerrigan, John, 101, 105

Lakoff, George, 60, 71, 82, 221–2, 224–5, 227–40, 266: body and mind, 221, 223–4, 228, 230; categories, 225, 239; cognitive and, 225, 228; empirical and, 230–1, 236, 238–40; language, 221; *Metaphors We Live By*, 71, 221, 223–4; and objectivists, 221, 223, 235, 236, 238–9; panentheism, 234, 236; philosophy and, 221–2, 225–8, 231–4, 236–7, 240; *Philosophy in the Flesh*; 71, 221–2, 227–9, 232, 234, 236, 238; and science, 222, 226–31, 233–4, 236–40; *Women Fire and Dangerous Things*, 71, 221, 224–5

language, 6, 16, 34, 49, 58, 82, 107, 117, 135, 201, 208, 214: as difference, 49, 52, 84, 146; as ethics, 6, 47, 66, 117, 135, 146–7; Wittgenstein, 56, 63, 69, 220; as words, 50

life, 36, 45, 65, 70, 73, 80, 83, 85, 92–3, 99, 119, 125, 135, 144, 210–11, 233, 239; and art, 134, 164, 244, 251

logical multiplicity, 80, 85, 245: of body/mind, 109, 111, 125, 154; in Ludwig Wittgenstein, 7, 88, 123

Mallarmé, Stephane, 3, 8, 16, 32–5, 39, 45, 88, 121, 126, 135, 136–155, 222, 230, 235, 266: the abyss, 34, 136, 140, 144; aesthetics, 146–7; *The Afternoon of the Faun*, 32, 53, 139, *139*, 143; *The Clown Punished*, 148, *148*; and effects, 137, 139, 140, 142, 143, 148, 149; eroticism, 33, 35, 138, 140–3, 149, 154, 237; esotericism, 33, 146; and Hamlet, 148–9; *Herodiade*, 32, 35, 143; *Igitur*, 149–50; poetry and, 136, 139, 141, 143, 149; sexual and, 139–41, 140, 143–4; symbolism in, 33, 136, 146, 149–50, 237; and things, 136–7, 140, 142, 143, 149; *Un coup de dés*, 33, 143–4, *143*; *The Virginal, Living and beautiful Day*, 138; *The Windows*, 137, *137*; writing and, 136, 143–4, 148

Mallarmé, Stephane, literature: Leo Bersani, 8, 154; Henri Cazalis, 136, 140, 153; Gordon Millan, 34

male, 4, 45, 52, 82, 102, 111, 114–7, 123, 171, 211, 217: priority of female, 6, 80, 81, 85, 94, 107–8, 114, 116, 122, 133, 135, 141, 164, 176–7, 179, 182, 192, 208, 210, 215, 218–9, 235, 238, 242, 252, 254–6, 263, 266–7

Master Mistress, 98, 159, 178, 206, 248: 126 sonnets to, 96, 100, 116; female priority, 96, 98, 108, 177; as male, 100; as number 9, 97; and Poet, 110; truth and beauty, 108

mind, 6, 10, 28, 35, 64, 75, 79, 81–4, 111–3,

continued

mind, *continued*
137, 140, 145, 158, 168, 210, 214, 219, 253: beauty and truth in, 152; desire, 16, 141; as erotic, 36, 39, 44, 88, 101, 115, 137, 231–2; intuition, 25, 58, 188;
sensations in, 171; sexual/body as prior, 35, 39, 63, 64, 65, 73, 80, 83–5, 101, 140, 221, 230, 237–8, 243, 259–60; template, 112, *112*, 113, 151, *151*, 153, 162, *162*
Mistress, 98, 160, 171, 248: 28 sonnets to, 96, 100; beauty and truth, 108, 151; as female, 100; priority over male, 96, 98, 108, 177; as a unity, 98
mythic, 2, 3, 4, 8, 13, 14, 18, 23, 30, 32, 40, 59, 105, 114–8, 125, 145, 155, 176, 192, 250: critique, 14; as erotic, 115, 218; in *Large Glass*, 12, 31, 52, 53, 54, 87, 93, 100, 114–5, 133, 145, 205; logic of, 2, 11, 29, 31, 40 52–3, 62, 100, 118, 134–5, 146, 159, 173, 211, 214, 237, 240, 241, 250, 262–3; Poet, 114; Shakespeare, 55, 122, 205
mythology, 14, 18, 29, 30, 31, 40, 78, 92, 115, 118, 146, 180, 208, 253: biblical, 82, 132, 133, 136, 155, 168, 174, 184, 211, 213, 222, 235, 242, 261–3, 266; as erotic, 14, 36, 118, 157, 177–8, 234, 238, 259; female-based 261; male-based, 59, 133, 178, 257, 263; nature as prior, 160; traditional, 37, 52, 59, 105, 114, 132–4, 142, 158, 164, 171, 177, 214, 250, 252

naming, 21, 26, 27, 39, 62, 116, 146
natural logic, 16, 67, 82, 86, 87, 88, 122, 134, 135, 144, 145, 149, 154, 162, 164, 174, 177, 183–6, 192, 205, 206, 207, 220, 221, 230, 238, 245, 252, 264
Nature, 4, 8, 58, 61, 65, 67, 81, 85, 93, 98, 99, 105, 111, 115, 122–3, 135, 158, 163, 165, 168, 171, 180–2, 203, 208, 214, 217, 246, 251, 266–7: prior to God, 133, 179, 185, 188, 209–11, 247; as number 154, 96, 100, 114; audit by, 106; as female, 116, 177, 252; not Goddess, 116, 185; *Large Glass* as, 133; and Poet, 114; priority of, 6, 83, 85, 94, 102, 135, 149, 150, 152, 172, 176, 178, 242–3; sovereign mistress, 96, 116, 177, 248; template, *100* 110; as a unity, 98. *See also* sovereign mistress
Nature template, 16, 87, 113, *113*, 151, *151*, 154, 160–1, *160*, 174, *174*, 193, *193*, *204*, 205, 218, *218*, 220, 243, *243*, 266, *267*, 240
Neo-Platonism, 91, 181
Nietzsche, Friedrich, 208–15, 266: Apollo and Dionysus, 209–10; Francis Bacon, 209, 217; *Birth of Tragedy*, 208, 210; and

Christianity, 208–9, 217; eternal recurrence, 212, 218; and female, 210; *Gay Science*, 209; genealogy of morals, 212; God is dead, 209–11, 218–9; good and evil, 208, 212, 219; *Julius Caesar*, 209, 215–6; and life, 208–10, 212; *Macbeth*, 216; and males, 210; and nature, 208, 210; superhuman, 81, 210, 216, 219; will to power, 209, 219, Zarathustra, 210–1, 217
nominalism, 37, 49, 57, 86, 124
numbers: **1**, 94, 100; **2**, 106; **9**, 94, 97, 100, 106; **11**, 106; **14**, 105–7, 119; **28**, 96–7, 100, 106; **126**, 96–7; **145**, 97; **154**, 96–7, 100, 106
numerology, 95–6, 99, 116, 125, 187

Paz, Octavio, 2, 4, 8, 30, 31–2, 39, 92, 125, 127, 132–4, 146, 235: *Appearance Stripped Bare*, 3; *The Castle of Purity*, 3, 52; criticism of myth, 31, 52
persistence, 78, 101, 110, 154, 163, 178, 208, 259
Philadelphia Museum of Art, 15, 24, 40, 131
philosophy, 2, 5, 8, 36, 63–5, 81, 113, 186, 221, 225, 221–2, 225–8, 231–4, 236–7, 240: and Duchamp, 11, 28; Shakespeare's, 2, 3, 8, 62, 74, 86, 89, 90, 92, 113, 121, 135, 162, 163, 179, 183, 186–9, 203, 215, 241
Platonism, 11, 12, 30, 31, 39, 149, 180–2, 191, 267
Poet, 98, 103, 105, 109, 118, 119: and argument, 109; as I me and my, 114; and Master Mistress, 97, 113–4, 110; and Mistress, 97, 113–4, 171; as number 145, 97, 114, 119; as a unity, 57, 114
poetry, 35, 141, 147, 149, 150, 196: and increase sonnets, 103–5, 109, 114, 187, 201, 204, 218
psychology, 8–10, 27, 31, 34, 39, 43, 50, 58, 64, 75, 145–6, 156–8, 234, 253; of belief, 10, 136, 137, 139, 143, 157, 167, 173, 183, 227, 247–9

reason, 58, 59, 60–1, 64, 65, 81, 82, 227–8
religion, 24, 25, 28, 29, 31, 36, 47, 48, 71, 93, 135, 143, 148, 156, 167, 185, 190, 211, 227, 242, 248: Catholic, 37; and eroticism, 38, 115; male-based, 239, 254–7, 265–6
Renaissance, 9, 28, 92, 132, 195
Romanticism, 37, 42, 44, 47, 120

scepticism, 64–5, 68, 85,134, 220, 249, 235
Schopenhauer, Arthur, 64–5, 80; and Will, 81, 83, 208

Schwarz, Arturo, 8–9, 10, 26, 27, 38–9, 41–3, 51, 92, 132, 146: and incest, 10, 43
science, 5–7, 68, 69, 70, 71, 73, 93, 115, 222, 226–32, 233–4, 236–40: and aesthetics, 5, 84; as amoral, 69, 84; as ethics, 7, 84
sensations, 6, 48, 59, 60, 82, 84: all senses, 47, 109, 152; as aesthetics, 5, 8, 16, 45, 47–8, 52, 57, 63, 68–9, 83, 115, 123, 151; beauty as, 8, 50, 107 243; of the mind, 152, 174, 243; perceptions, 5, 60
sexual, 2, 3, 8, 15, 16, 31, 37–45, 52–3, 59, 63, 99, 117–9, 122, 140–4, 154, 158, 177, 194, 203, 214–5, 235, 257–8: as 4th dimension, 36, 87; consummation, 35, 36, 41, 44, 105, 115, 133–4, 139, 146; dynamic, 8, 64, 72, 77, 82, 105, 122–3, 152, 203, 208, 243, 259; masturbation, 44, 146, 175; as prior to erotic, 35, 38, 39, 45, 58, 60, 88, 100, 103, 105, 107, 135, 162, 263
Shakespeare, William, 16, 39, 63, 69, 72, 85, 112, 119, 120, 127, 135, 148–54, 159–60, 165, 166, 214–5, 222, 230, 253, 259: aesthetic and ethics, 59, 66; authorship, 95, 122; Anne Hathaway, 170, 189; mythic expression of, 6, 56, 113, 116, 118, 119, 150, 163, 169, 173, 214
Shakespeare's plays, 2, 18, 30, 66, 89, 93, 113, 117, 118, 119, 125, 126, 148, 159, 167, 169, 174, 176, 177, 181, 187, 238, 240, 241, 245, 250, 251 264, 267: *Comedy of Errors*, 186; *Julius Caesar*, 159, 209, 216; *King Lear*, 169, 183; *Love's Labour's Lost*, 186, 188; *Macbeth*, 216; *Measure for Measure*, 186, 189, 191; *Merchant of Venice*, 77, 264; *Much Ado About Nothing*, 190; *Romeo and Juliet*, 186; *Troilus and Cressida*, 185; *Taming of the Shrew*, 264; *Twelfth Night*, 186, 189, 191
Shakespeare's poems, 30, 66, 89, 93, 113, 117, 118, 148, 159, 167, 169, 177, 238, 241, 250, 267: *A Lover's Complaint*, 93, 186; *The Phoenix and the Turtle*, 180–2, 187; *Venus and Adonis*, 184–5
Shakespeare's sonnets, 18, 30, 45, 47, 51, 53, 62, 66–7, 70, 81, 86, 88, 92, 93–120, 124, 177, 205, 239, 240: 1609 edition, 194–5, 203, 241; argument in, 187; Mr. W. H., 170; philosophy of, 89, 125, 157, 159, 162, 179, 186–9, 201, 222, 236, 242–3, 266; sonnet 3, 101; sonnet 9, 102, 200; sonnet 10, 114; sonnet 11, 77, 102, 108; sonnet 13, 102; sonnet 14, 99, *99*, 105–7, *107*, 108–9, *108*, 117, 119, 164, 200; sonnet 15, 109; sonnet 16, 117; sonnet 17, 103, 114; sonnet 18, 103, *103*, 200; sonnet 19, 103; sonnet 20, 103–4, *104*, 109, 185, 218; sonnet 21, 218; sonnet 55, 201; sonnet 79, *104*; sonnet 105, 184; sonnet 111, 202; sonnet 116, 91, *104*, 196, 200; sonnet 126, 96, *96*, 116, 172, 200; sonnet 127, 109; sonnet 128, 109; sonnet 129, 91, 196–7, 200; sonnet 130, 109; sonnet 135, 109; sonnet 136, 109; sonnet 137, 109; sonnet 138, 109; sonnet 145, 196, 200; sonnet 146, 196–8, 200; sonnet 152, 109, 203; sonnet 153, *104*, 109; sonnet 154, 109, 200
society, 20, 46, 167, 251–2, 260
State, 179, 186, 251
subject matter, 17–18, 30, 32
Symbolism, 3, 33, 37, 139, 140

taste, 5, 14, 20, 24, 45, 47, 54, 57, 147
templates: Beauty and truth, 110, 112, 117, *153*; Body, 111, *111*, 113, 152, *152*, 154, 161, *161*; God, 123, 154, *154*, *161*, 175, *175*, 192–3, *193*, *206*, 219–20, *219*, *239*, 240, 244, *244*; Increase, 102, 110, 117; Mind, 112, *112*, 113, 151, *151*, 153, 162, *162*; Nature, 16, 87, 113, *113*, 151, *151*, 160–1, *160*, 174, *174*, 193, *193*, *204*, 205, 218, *218*, 220, *240*, 243, *243*, 266, *267*; Nature female/male, *100*, 110, 117; Truth and beauty, 111, *111*, 112, 117, 153
thought, 5, 65: and language, 58, 82
truth, 4, 50, 68, 107–10, 171, 187: and beauty, 99, 101, 105, 107, 109, 122–3, 150, 175, 179, 181, 187, 203–4, 237–8, 243, 266–7; as ethics, 151–3; and increase, 107, 176, 243; as saying, 8, 69, 107–10; and sexual, 153; swearing as, 109; template, 111, *111*, 117, *153*

unity: of 154 sonnets, 96; of 28 sonnets, 96; of *Large Glass*, 94; of number 100, 96; of number 145, 97; of nature, 96; Master Mistress not a unity, 96; of Mistress, 96, 98; Poet, 57, 114

Vendler, Helen, 194–5, 201–6: *Art of Shakespeare's Sonnets*, 195; couplet ties, 200–1; figures of speech, 201, 205; key words, 200–1; lyrical and, 195, 198–9; ur-language, 199, 201; words, 198
Wicks, Robert, 209, 210
Wittgenstein, Ludwig, 4, 6, 7, 16, 62, 63–74, 75, 81, 122–3, 124, 126–7, 147, 153, 135, 141, 186, 207–15, 232–4: *continued*

Wittgenstein, Ludwig *continued*,
  atomic model, 66, 69–70, 73, 88, 122, 207, 220, 233, 237; biological metaphors, 7, 73, 80, 87, 88, 123; Catholicism, 208, 211; and certainty, 71, 141, 233; ethics and aesthetics, 66–9, 73, 80, 85, 88, 123, 147, 152, 208, 212; and Darwin, 66–7, 88; family resemblances, 7, 70–1, 141, 207, 232–3; forms of life, 7, 65, 70–1, 73, 123, 141, 207; and language, 7, 56, 63, 65, 66, 70, 73, 88, 113, 121–3, 141, 147, 207, 209, 212, 220, 236; language games, 7, 66–7, 70–1; logical multiplicity, 7, 67, 69–70, 73, 80, 88, 113, 123, 207, 233, 237; the mystical, 67, 69; *On Certainty*, 65, 233; parents and, 70–1, 233; *Philosophical Investigations*, 65, 70, 207–8, 237; private language, 65; and psychology, 234; *Tractatus*, 65, 66, 67, 70, 73, 147, 207–8, 212, 220, 233, 237
Wittgenstein, Ludwig, literature: Ferdinand de Saussure, 49; Maurice Drury, 72; G. E. Moore: naturalistic fallacy 83
world, 140: and language, 65, 69, 70, 73, 75, 88, 111, 113, 123, 139, 146, 237; and mind, 6, 7, 10, 187

www.ingramcontent.com/pod-product-compliance
Lightning Source LLC
Chambersburg PA
CBHW071347290426
44108CB00014B/1461